American Architecture Now

American Architecture Now

Barbaralee Diamonstein

with

I. M. PEI
HUGH HARDY
CESAR PELLI
RICHARD MEIER
JOHN PORTMAN
FRANK O. GEHRY
CHARLES MOORE
MICHAEL GRAVES
RICHARD WEINSTEIN
JONATHAN BARNETT
ROBERT A. M. STERN
CHARLES GWATHMEY
JAMES STEWART POLSHEK
EDWARD LARRABEE BARNES

Introduction by Paul Goldberger

RIZZOLI
NEW YORK

The book *American Architecture Now* is a series
of interviews edited and conducted by Barbaralee Diamonstein
at The New School for Social Research/
Parsons School of Design in New York

for my father
and for Tim,
my models of
strength and grace

CONTENTS

PREFACE

Architecture, on the verge of the 1980s, is in the midst of an identity crisis, as the profession struggles to redefine itself, its relationship to the other arts, and to the general public. Since many critics and historians are at a loss to describe what is happening in architecture today, it seemed sensible to go directly to the source—the architects themselves—to broaden the discussion and make it accessible to a wider public.

American Architecture Now, a series of videotaped conversations that examine the evolving careers and opinions of fourteen distinguished American architects, was held during the spring of 1980 at New York's New School/Parsons School of Design. They are presented here in edited form, and comprise a record of one of the most vibrant periods in the history of American architecture; one marked by a shift in values; artistic, social and practical in nature. This movement has engendered a vigorous and multisided debate on the future of the profession among architects, and the increasingly interested public.

For me, *American Architecture Now* developed almost inevitably, from my involvement with architectural preservation, through *Buildings Reborn: New Uses, Old Places,* a book and still-traveling museum exhibition on adaptive reuse; and as a member of the New York City Landmarks Preservation Commission, and the boards of the Landmarks Conservancy, and the Municipal Art Society. But most important was the realization during the course of my work as the curator and project director of the Architectural League Centennial Exhibition, that the historic gap between architecture, and the public it is meant to serve, was beginning to narrow. So it seemed a good time to broaden the audience for architecture as a form of cultural expression, and to clarify the meanings of contemporary architecture for the general public, through a series of informal discussions conducted before a live audience.

It was David Levy, the managerially-minded aesthetician, the protean dean of the Parsons School of Design, who suggested the project be the first of the Van Day Truex Memorial Lecture Series. Truex, the well-known designer, was the devoted former president of Parsons. The series is meant as testimony to his concern for the role of art and design in daily life. Consequently, Dean Levy and I agreed to make the course available to the widest possible audience at the lowest possible admission fee, and without any charge to students of architecture and urban design. As in the case of the interviews for *Inside New York's Art World* (conversations with leading artists, museum directors and gallery owners), these, too, were audio- and videotaped as a permanent record available to students and a larger public, and have been donated to the Columbia University Oral History Archives. The videotapes were made possible by a grant from The Rockefeller Foundation, through its vice-president, Dr. Joel Colton. For their generous support, and the enlightened manner in which they gave it, I am especially grateful.

The recent surge of interest in architecture hardly needs comment. It is clear that ever more people are concerned and intrigued with the role of architecture as it forms the quality and character of their lives, especially as it embraces its dual role as an historical art as well as a profession. As a result of these combined forces, this project evolved.

To my delight (and dismay), more than 700 arrived for the first session, necessitating a move to larger quarters. In spite of the lack of intimacy in the larger auditorium, the architects themselves maintained an easy tenor and presented a remarkably generous and candid picture of their work, its impact, and its origins. Architects, unlike other artists, are trained to defend their proposals and articulate their opinions to the public, and those participating in this series will not disappoint the general reader. Here are many views not merely voiced, but explained with clarity, conviction, patience, and of course, with the personal flair and vigor that comes across only in informal conversations. To each of them, for sharing ideas so freely, from aesthetic inspiration to budgetary or zoning constraints, my appreciation. And to Adrianne Benton, my ebullient and efficient assistant, for her help in making the project a reality, my special thanks as well.

In transition from oral to written form, the transcripts have necessarily been condensed and edited for clarity. But the spirit, if not each letter, of the individual conversations has been respected. I hope you will agree, that taken together, the honesty and vitality of these words, though greatly varying in meaning, help to document a lively and controversial period in architectural history.

Barbaralee Diamonstein
22 June 1980

INTRODUCTION

In the early decades of the twentieth century, as modernism began its long process of evolution, it was not uncommon for architects in both Europe and the United States to present their views in the form of long treatises, book-length discussions of their work and the philosophy behind it. Louis Sullivan, Frank Lloyd Wright, and Le Corbusier, among others, left significant written work, created, one supposes, on the premise that if the pen was not mightier than the T-square, it at least could guarantee a wider audience than certain built works of architecture were likely to have.

The word for these architects never substituted for the art of building, but it did serve that art in a crucial way—books like Sullivan's *Autobiography of an Idea* or Le Corbusier's *Vers une Architecture* became essential weapons in the arsenal of the modern movement. There are no real equivalents to such works today; they seem not to suit the current mood of pluralism. Indeed, perhaps the only book of recent years to achieve a status equal to that of the architectural treatises of the early part of the century, Robert Venturi's *Complexity and Contradiction in Architecture,* was written as much as an answer to these modernist treatises as it was a new theory in itself.

The fact of the matter is that we are less accustomed to thinking of architects in terms of their own words today—we are not used to reading their own explanations of their work or of their theoretical preferences. For all of the verbal activity of the nation's academic architectural salons of the last decade, places like the Institute for Architecture and Urban Studies in New York, surprisingly little in the way of architects' speaking on their own has filtered through to the public.

This is where this book of interviews is able to fill a crucial need: though the architects herein are not continuing directly in the tradition of architectural treatises, they are restoring to us some sense of the significance of verbal communication in the making of architecture. Here are words, all of them the architects' own, and there is not a single one of them that does not offer some sort of insight, however minor, into the workings of an architectural mind.

What astonished me as I read these interviews was how little of a sense of polemic there was to them. These are architects talking, not preaching, and the difference is refreshing indeed. The fourteen architects included here represent fourteen different kinds of work and, it is fair to say, fourteen different views of what buildings should be, and yet they all seem to accept their differences—not one of these designers lectures us about how he has the one true way, the only path to the kingdom of architectural heaven.

And the architects are not only pleasingly free of dogma, they are surprisingly articulate. Much of the credit for this must go to Barbaralee Diamonstein, who, as all good interviewers do, is able to make herself almost disappear; we remember the answers and not the questions, which is just as it should be. This is not the abrasive style of interviewing that was so popular on television a few years back; Barbaralee Diamonstein has done her research well. She is thorough and intelligent—her goal is to make these people talk, and many of them do so better here then ever before.

If there are no strong polemics here—no use of this platform to hammer out a rigid architectural gospel—that does not mean that there is no conviction, or sense of principle. These interviews make it clear that each of these architects has firm ideas indeed, and that their ideas are frequently in conflict. We see each of them as he *is* here—they all come through strongly as personalities; their words are as revealing of their natures as is anything about their architecture.

Charles Moore, for example, seems at first rather self-mocking, but is gradually revealed to take himself as seriously as, say, Michael Graves—who takes himself *very* seriously and talks long and awkwardly about architecture in general, but then, when pressed with questions about his own projects, becomes organized, articulate, and even witty. James Stewart Polshek lets us know, though he never says so directly, that what fascinates him most is the *process* of making architecture—he speaks of people and politics, not of form; I.M. Pei's remarks mix a sense of deep conviction with a streak of pragmatism, just as his architectural practice does; Charles Gwathmey comes off as absolutely rigorous and organized and clean, seemingly as self-assured as any of his buildings.

Richard Meier is rather more easygoing than one might expect, but then again, Meier's architecture is, for all its discipline, a bit more romantic than Gwathmey's. Frank Gehry, on the other hand, is more cantankerous than he might be expected to be; perhaps this was his uneasiness at being the only Californian in the midst of an East Coast group of architects. Whatever the reason, it results in a lively exchange, full of energy. John Portman is intelligent but rather lacking in irony—he speaks more earnestly than many of his colleagues in this series, jaded as they are by their exposure to the more academic architectural scene of the East and West coasts. Portman's huge practice is more financially successful than that of any of the other architects here, but it is in Atlanta, and that continues to shape his outlook.

Portman's is a view of architectural practice totally opposite from that of Hugh Hardy, who, on the subject of his New York firm, Hardy Holzman Pfeiffer Associates, says, "We rejected everything. We rejected the A.I.A., we rejected midtown, we rejected contractors, we rejected working drawings, we rejected design. We rejected everything but clients." It is a wonderful bit of self-mockery—but it is the mocking of one who is quite certain of his own value, and has no fears that his remarks will be taken literally.

Robert Stern absolutely sparkles—he defends his work with clarity and with wit. It is no surprise that he is a writer, for he is at ease with words, and yet he also seems at ease with his architecture—his brand of historical allusionism is defended with less nervousness and more conviction than ever before.

But all of these architects speak with a certain assurance, and perhaps that is the most surprising thing of all here. They all tell stories well—they all turn out to be closet raconteurs, as it were, ready to tell tales of their own projects at the most casual suggestion. The interviews with Edward Larrabee Barnes and Cesar Pelli particularly come alive in this fashion. The best moments in almost all of these interviews involve specific stories about specific buildings—it is here that these architects seem most comfortable, most certain that there is no substitute for their own words.

In the end, then, these interviews exist at a considerable distance from the tradition of architectural polemics. We have the architects' own words, but they are for the most part words of description, not words of analysis. But they tell us a great deal—more, perhaps, than much critical analysis of the last decade has done. Taken together, these interviews give us the sense of a profession unrestrained by narrow dogma, but one that is committed to an architecture that balances aesthetic concerns with social, economic and political ones; a profession that is committed to innovation, but not to irrationality; a profession that seems to want to accommodate to forces of history and culture and also to make pure form and space. If one gets the impression here of a profession that is thoughtful more than purely intellectual, one also senses a group of practitioners that is alert, fresh and lively. There is a sense of energy to all of these conversations, as if the talking could go on and on with greater pleasure.

Paul Goldberger

EDWARD LARRABEE BARNES

Alexandra Conway

Edward Larrabee Barnes
Born Chicago, Ill., 1915
B.S. Harvard University, 1938
M. Arch. Harvard University, 1942

Diamonstein Edward Larrabee Barnes is appreciated as much for his flexible, adaptable approach to design, as he is for his practicality as an engineer. His best-known buildings range from the Walker Art Center in Minneapolis, hailed as the best space in the country for exhibiting contemporary art, to the Haystack Mountain School, on the Maine sea coast, which influenced a number of younger architects, and helped fuel the shingle-style revival, to a Richardsonian polychrome church, recently completed in Burlington, Vermont. Until this year, Mr. Barnes had never designed a building for Manhattan. He has certainly caught up in a hurry, because he has three projects underway: the IBM office building, the Asia House, and the Klein Building.

Ed, the world of art concerns you almost as much as the world of architecture. That has manifested itself in such diverse places as your designs for the Walker Art Center in Minneapolis, the Scaife Gallery, which is an addition to the Carnegie Institute in Pittsburgh, the Marlborough Gallery in New York, the Wichita Art Museum in Kansas, the American Indian Arts Museum in Santa Fe, the Fort Lauderdale Museum of the Arts in Florida, and the Dallas Museum of Fine Arts in Texas. There will be a gallery in the new IBM Building, and of course, in Asia House as well.

Hardly anyone has designed more spaces and places to exhibit works of art. Perhaps you could tell us how it all began.

Barnes The first museum we worked on was the Walker Art Center. I don't think they would have picked me at that time, since I hadn't done any museums. But the job was a small one. We were simply adding a little bit to their existing building. I see that Justin Lamb is here this evening; he worked on Walker, and he will remember that after we'd designed for about a year, we advised them to tear the existing building down. Then the job got to be a big job. We not only had the wing, but a building. It turned out that the original building was sitting on bad soil and was slumping. It was impossible to add on to it, and stop it from sinking. So to their surprise, the Walker Art Center found themselves working with an architect who had never done a museum before. And I must say, it was a very, very happy experience. Martin Friedman, the museum's director, is a wild man. The museum has a tiny permanent collection and his policy is to have very exciting visiting shows, very experimental shows—farther out, I would say, than anything you would see typically at New York's Museum of Modern Art. It has to be on the fringe of what's going on. But Friedman was open to all kinds of architectural ideas. Working on that building for four or five years was an absolute honeymoon.

Diamonstein What was your chief consideration in designing that space?

Barnes The problem in museum design, I feel, is to focus on the art, and on the way people go through the museum, and not on making an architectural monument. The problem with many museums is that the architecture upstages the art. I was dedicated to the idea of anonymous white spaces, which is exactly what Martin Friedman wanted. The question was how to arrange these spaces so that the galleries themselves could become a procession. Usually you think of museums like the Metropolitan, with an enormous Grand Central Station hall, with no art in it—a sort of stage for pomp and circumstance—and then galleries beyond it. At the Walker, you are immediately caught up in a succession of white rooms which go up like a spiral staircase to the top of the building, where there is a sculpture garden. The idea is to get people involved immediately with whatever the museum has that day, what they're showing. No fooling around. Once in the building, you're immediately caught up in it, and are thinking of the art.

Diamonstein Most artists are not accustomed to an anonymous space, where the architecture takes a back seat, so to speak, to the art. How did artists respond to that museum?

Barnes I'll come back to the question of taking a back seat. The artists liked it. They really were very, very nice about it after the opening and since then, I have had a lot of nice letters. I think the question is: can a building of that kind be strong architecture, positive architecture? I feel very definitely that the rooms themselves have to represent calm, well-proportioned spaces. The sequence and the sense of flow must work, and the way you move through it must be graceful. I think it's a very difficult thing to explain how you can do architecture with a strong central idea, with just as self-centered an idea as any building, and at the same time have that idea opt for this function of bringing out these various shows which go through it. It's not just an anonymous building, I think that's what I want to say.

Diamonstein You referred both to the processional space, and to the sequence. I presume you mean both the passage through the architectural space, and chronologically through the exhibits. Do the layouts of your various museums and of the galleries have anything in common structurally? The museums obviously are all different, but is there any unifying principle?

Barnes Let me describe another museum to show you what's different and what's the same. The Indian Museum that we're working on in Santa Fe also involves flow; the way you move through the exhibits; the sense of transitional space just like Walker. But it doesn't look a bit like Walker. This Indian Museum is for Pueblo and Navaho art, and I had Alfonso Ortiz—an Indian activist and scholarly anthropologist—to advise me. He explained to me that the Pueblos are a peaceful, introverted people—stable agrarians who have stayed in the same place for centuries. The Navahos are nomadic—a people who have moved from New Mexico to Mexico and back—who have suffered oppression and survived—whose styles in art have reflected the periods of peace and exile in their transient lives. So the design concept was to have a round inward-looking Kiva-like room in the center with cases containing pots and Kachina dolls arranged on circular ramps—this was the Pueblo collection. We wrapped around this room an angular space with a series of galleries sometimes limited and sometimes expansive showing the history of Navaho art in chronological order. Thus, the Pueblo space was centripetal, and the Navaho space centrifugal, suggesting the static and dynamic nature of the two societies. You see, this museum, like Walker, is designed for flow, but, in addition, the spaces have symbolic meaning: they reflect the character of the subject matter.

Diamonstein Natural light is of considerable concern to you in museums. Is this the best light for art? How do you accomplish it?

Barnes The use of material light is a controversial question in the museum world. Today conservationists say that you have to show prints and drawings and watercolors in no more than 10 foot candles, whereas with oil paintings, 50 foot candles is acceptable. So if you are putting on a show where you want to show different media together—such as a Paul Klee show—there is a problem of how to handle the fluctuating light demands. All museums have to operate at night, so there must be a basic underlying electric light system. And daylight is an added option which many conservationists oppose because of the vulnerability of the art. But it is an option which every layman wants. People want to see art in daylight, the way it was painted—even in changing light, sometimes warm, sometimes cool.

In the Dallas Museum we are using sky light directed at the walls as we did in Pittsburgh, and in addition we are designing the galleries around courtyards. You will see art *with* nature. For example the Monet paintings may be seen next to a courtyard with water lilies and willows and wisteria. We hope the association with certain kinds of flickering elusive light will be clear. However, to accomplish this we must satisfy the conservationists that no sun or ultraviolet light will ever touch the art. This will be difficult, but if we pull it off it will be beautiful—light from the top, light from the side, continual change with the time of day.

Diamonstein While we are on the subject of art museums, why don't we talk about the relationship between art and architecture today. How do you see that relationship currently, and what do you think should be the future of that collaboration?

Barnes That's an awfully interesting question, because when you ask historians about it, they immediately think of the Middle Ages or Greece—a range of thought from the architectural space to the sculptural detail, where there seems to be no clashing of gears or conflicting points of view. We are living in a period of protest, not in the Middle Ages. While some art today is complacent, much of it is—if you think about it—a commentary on the transient quality of society, on the absurdities of society, on the existential quality of society, and therefore, it doesn't add up in purpose. It often happens that when an architect is asked to work with a sensitive sculptor, he will feel his mission is to cut across the grain rather than to reinforce it. The best example I have of this is a wonderful sculptured deck on top of the Walker Art Gallery. It has a view of Minneapolis and a special promontory where we wanted the best piece of sculpture. Martin Friedman said that Richard Serra, the sculptor, would come and do a major piece. Serra is a very powerful sculptor and I was delighted. And so we had a meeting in our office, and discussed the promontory where the art was to go. Serra went away, came back in two weeks, and he said, "I've got it, I know what I'm going to do." Then he began to get tense, and his lip began to twist, and his teeth came down, it seemed to me, and he said, "I'm going to have a forty-foot-long bullet of steel, eight feet high, and eight inches thick, rusty, shipped to Minneapolis. And we will have a crane standing next to this bullet, and we will swing it for two hours. Then we will smash it into the elevator tower, and the bricks will fall out, and the sheetrock will fall out, and the concrete blocks will fall out, and my sculpture will stick into the building. And that's my sculpture." Martin Friedman said, "Well, Ed, I think that's a good idea, what do you think?"

Diamonstein And how did you reply?

Barnes Well, I knew him well enough not to die, but we decided not to do it quite that way. But for the new IBM I'm working now with Larry Bell. The IBM Building is, I suppose, if you simplified it, a simple prismatic form, a little bit like Donald Judd sculpture. Essentially, I like Bell very much because he has these simple volumetric glass forms. They're often glass cubes, and the glass is tinted and changes; it's sometimes slightly mirrored. While the form itself is extremely simple and prime, the actual surfaces are never quite where you think they are. In this case, I think that his work will be sympathetic to the building, not a protest. He's working on a glass and water fountain, which I think would reinforce the idea of the building.

Diamonstein Do you actively seek collaboration in your buildings?

Barnes Yes. But I haven't had enough of that experience, I think there is going to be more. With the current trend in architecture, I think you're going to see more and more experimentation. Too much of the fifties was spent simply doing a plaza, and putting Henry Moore in just the right place in the plaza, which is a little bit like putting a monogram on a shirt. It really isn't what I call involvement between the sculptor and the architect. I mean to have the sculptor and the architect really involved with each other, you either have to have the facade of a cathedral, or you have the Serra thing sticking into a building. But you have to get together. I think that the kind of sanitary relationship which we went through in the fifties and sixties is over. In the profession there's all kinds of talk about illusionistic effects, using paintings mixed with architecture. I think the eighties are going to be a very exciting decade in that regard.

Diamonstein You once said that in your education, you viewed architecture as some sort of sculpture. Do you still hold that view?

Barnes Yes, I think that some of architecture is sculpture. There are things that architecture is, that sculpture isn't. It is a social instrument, connected with history and society, and structure and technology. There are many things about architecture that are rooted in society and technology, that you don't see in sculpture. But there's a side of architecture which is absolutely pure sculpture. It should be.

Diamonstein Gyorgy Kepes was quoted last week as having said that much of the public art sprinkling the countryside resembles knickknacks on a Victorian mantelpiece. Is that a view you share?

Barnes Yes, there is a lot of public art which is just junk. But in fairness, most of the backgrounds are dismal. Think of the young artist who got the commission to do a clay sculpture or something for the main square. Look at the main square—it is not St. Mark's, it is usually a parking lot of some sort, or a scene against no-parking signs. The city setting is almost impossible for so many of these pieces. It's unfair to blame it all on the sculpture.

Diamonstein Before we talk specifically about the three buildings that you are building in New York City, perhaps we should comment on the state of building in New York these days. Can one architect really have much effect on the cityscape?

Barnes Well, I think it's difficult. Chicago, where I came from, has much more personality than New York, in terms of architectural character. The fact

that many Germans settled there, that the steel frame was just develop-
ing, and that Sullivan had a tremendous influence. But he's only one
person. There was Richardson—he did some buildings out there, but he
isn't dominant either.

In New York the question is, does one architect dominate or should
one architect? In New York, there is no common spirit and clean structure, the way there was in Chicago. What there is in New York are the
New York zoning laws, which are designing a lot of buildings. I think we
all know what has come in waves, the setback building, the building that
goes straight up, the building back of the plaza. The educated eye can
spot zoning ordinances more easily than architects.

Diamonstein How much of a building is designed by zoning laws, and how much is
designed by architects?

Barnes An awful lot is designed by zoning. For example on the Klein Building—
George Klein is the commercial developer—we spent our first month com-
puting every inch of rentable space that we're allowed to put on the lot.
And what bonuses to give the city in terms of parks, and what amenities
to give the city in order to be allowed to build more floors. The setback,
the exact relation to the street, and all of these things, are so tightly
controlled. Producing a building with good proportion, and a sense of
form, is very, very difficult.

Diamonstein What do you see now as the major aesthetic challenges to building in
New York City?

Barnes Building-to-building relationships, it seems to me, is where it's at. There
was a time when an architect felt, I'll make a plaza, or investigate if I can
make a plaza, or put a building in the middle of it, and see if it really
makes any difference what's next to it. Particularly in New York City,
because of this compaction of buildings, the awareness of what's next to
what is so terrific, it happens to be what's going on in the schools. When I
was in architectural school, we were often given ideal problems to design,
isolated problems, a satellite town on farmland, or a single building, or a
house on top of a hill. Now, almost all the problems at the Harvard
Architectural School, when I went around and looked at them, were what
are now called contextual problems. In architectural schools, they're giving students building sites between a Gothic church and a gas station, or
crowded in between other buildings, or mixed into a transportation network or something. And that of course is already going on in the profession. People like myself weren't educated that way, but found out that it
was important. When this new wave of architects comes out of the
schools, with a sense of caring about context, it seems to me that the cities
are going to have the concerns that you see in a place like Florence. There
it's perfectly clear that one palazzo knew what the next palazzo was
doing, and that there was some sense of continuity, even with changing
styles. So I see tremendous hope for the city. It won't look like a number
of disparate things—isolated, lonely—but will be well-knit.

Diamonstein You once said that the most exciting thing about New York is its wonderful gridiron of streets. It gives everything form, and permits privacy and
variety. You went on to call it a graph paper against which all goods are
displayed. As a foil that saves New York, the street lines must be reinforced. Tell us how the IBM Building relates to the gridiron of the city.

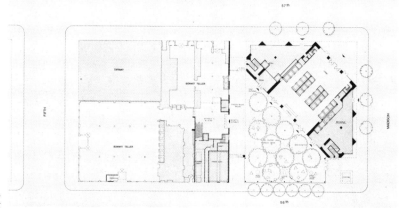

IBM Building, plaza level,
New York, N.Y., drawing

Asia Society, New York, N.Y.,
model
Picture credit: Alexandra Conway

IBM Building, New York, N.Y.,
model
Picture credit: Louis Checkman

Barnes The IBM Building is being built now—on the corner of Fifty-seventh and Madison, it's half the block. Building by zoning, we had to leave sixty percent of that block open. We could build on the other forty percent. Only forty percent could have a tower. The rest had to be low, no more than 65 or 70 feet high. We had a choice about where to put the tower, and where to put the open space. As I think many of you know, the Seagram Building set a pattern which was imitated up and down Sixth Avenue, of setting the building back, not on the street line. The Seagram is an exception on Park Avenue so that its plaza is a lovely space, framed by other buildings set forward. That same pattern of setting the building back 75 or 80 or 100 feet from the street, is what you see along Sixth Avenue. And after that had been built, the architects and the right thinkers began to question whether a street line still existed on Sixth Avenue anymore. It was an amorphous space. When you walk in the street, you're a long way off from stores or anything going on in the buildings. Not just me, but a number of architects began to feel that even very big buildings which would cast shadows, were better set right on the street, with the shops right on the street. Holly Whyte, who has written about the way people move and sit down, and pedestrian life in the city, reinforces this, that the worst thing you can do for retail and for the ambience and excitement of the city sidewalk is to break the street line, putting the leftover space in back, in the midblock. So our IBM Building is set hard up to the corner of Fifty-seventh and Madison. What action there is on the ground floor—exhibition center, and retail space—will be right on the street, reinforcing the other shops. As you go down the street, you can look at shop windows and not find something a hundred feet away, like missing teeth.

Diamonstein But isn't your pedestrian arcade within the building itself?

Barnes Yes, the pedestrian arcade in this case is the glass-covered plaza. It follows that if you put the tower—forty percent of the building—right on the street, that there must be sixty percent in back. And that sixty percent is a greenhouse structure which is really a covered plaza. It's used as a pedestrian walk between Fifty-seventh and Fifty-sixth.

Diamonstein This building rejects the glassbox design that fills most of the city. It is a five-sided, 603-foot, 41-story gray/green polished granite tower, that has a prismatic shape. What is the central theme of the whole design and how did you arrive at the prism shape?

Barnes It was bound to be a very big building, breaking the skyline in a new part of the city. Everything else in that immediate block was low. We didn't want to build a blockbuster, simply a big square building, symmetrical in every direction, very dominant. We thought there might be a way to break it up into odd-sized planes—odd shapes. One end of the building, for example, is very narrow. It's only 50 feet, and it goes up over 600 feet, as you say. Another bend is a big broad plane facing southwest, and the two on the streets are plain rectangular surfaces. As you walk around the building, it will appear to be different sizes in different lights. You will never quite realize what the form of the building is, I hope. That was the intent of the design, that from every angle, you would see a different building.

Diamonstein And each of these different buildings concerned itself with the context in which it was placed?

Barnes Yes. When you see the scale of the 50 foot width, a narrow shaft going up the building, seen against New York skyscrapers, the rest of the building will be very dramatic, very much like the Woolworth Building—kind of those steep proportions.

Diamonstein In a telling article in *Progressive Architecture,* Suzanne Stephens writes about the public amenities in your building, the AT&T Building, and the proposed building for the Bonwit Teller site. She says that it is beyond dispute that the quality of your greenhouse design is superb. But she goes on to point out that these three buildings, and many other buildings in the city now create an interiorization—what she calls the private-ization— of "bonusable" public space. She contrasts that interiorization with the street life and activity on the rest of Madison Avenue. Do you share that concern?

Barnes Well, all of these bonus public spaces have to be kept open till midnight, so I don't think they're private. The space under the AT&T Building arcade, the space in our greenhouse and our arcade, and I think the space in Der Scutt's building [Bonwit Teller site]—even though it is really entirely interior space that you can't see into—have to be kept open till midnight. The city planners' theory is that these inside spaces are part of the city. It's a little bit like Minneapolis, where they think that all those bridges are just as much a part of recognizable public space as sidewalks. So I don't agree with Suzanne Stephens on that. The quality of pedestrian movement in those two blocks is going to be extremely interesting. Whether it'll all add up, I'm not sure, but I think it's going to be very, very lively, and very, very exciting, and various.

Diamonstein As we've mentioned, IBM is next door to Philip Johnson and John Burgee's AT&T tower. On the other side, just around the corner from IBM is the immense new glass tower that is going up on the former Bonwit Teller site. How did you try to relate to your neighbors and how have they tried to relate to you? Is that possible, and are you disturbed, are you pleased, are you concerned with the results?

Barnes Our building started first! But I did call on Houghton at Corning Glass, and I worked with Genesco who owned Bonwit Teller. I tried to organize what you might call a block party on Fifty-sixth Street, because we were in the process of designing it. There was a hotel group that was going to build on the current AT&T site. I met with them, and we discussed massing, and all kinds of things. But then, for better or worse, we made the first assumption and went ahead. After that, the others had the responsibility to check with us—they had a reference point. And I think within limits the pedestrian flow has been checked through. There are some things that we all agree could be done better, but there is an arcade in the AT&T Building, which is not too far off from lining up with our arcade, and there is another arcade going through Bonwit's which will lead the pedestrian flow all the way to Fifth Avenue. Der Scutt came to me when he was designing his building, and he worked very hard to form his mass as a foil to ours. The best success will be at the pedestrian level. When we all get through, the relationship between those three towers is going to be very odd. We have a model in the office which shows them all. It is really three disparate towers, all of a sudden growing like mushrooms in the night, over 600 feet high, almost twice as high as the adjacent buildings, and looking totally different. I think it's going to be exciting, I think it's going to be provocative—I think it's going to represent this transient quality of life that I'm talking about.

Diamonstein But will it be good?

Barnes The more basic question is, would you say it was absolutely a calm, serene space? I don't think so.

Diamonstein What about relationships between materials—all the glass in the Der Scutt building and Philip Johnson's effort to bring granite back? What do you think of the color of that glass? When last I heard it was bronze.

Barnes Yes, I hope it doesn't remain bronze. I think that the brown color, to me, is too personal. I would prefer to see it a silvery green, or something more like Kevin Roche's UN Hotel.

Diamonstein Have you communicated that to the architect?

Barnes I've told him. He's not the only architect who likes brown, and there are a lot of brown buildings all over the country.

Diamonstein You've talked about your interest in education, and what you foresee happening in the future. You have a special right to do so, because for a very long while, your office has been very much a breeding ground for creative younger architects. They've included people like Jack Robertson and Robert Siegel and Charles Gwathmey. Can you hazard a guess as to why this has happened? Is there a particular kind of environment that you've sought to create?

Barnes I find it difficult to guess. I've been lucky to get very good people. At the same time, I have not wanted to indefinitely expand. If you have an office, and get the jobs to just continually expand, and there have been times when I could, then there's a future for everybody in the office. There's always a brighter future ahead, more jobs, more people, more jobs, more people. But whether the quality would hold is something that worried me, and whether my own lifestyle, or my own nerves would hold up, worried me, too. So somewhere along the line I concluded that an office of over fifty was beginning to be a problem, and that an office of a hundred is a different structure. So there has been kind of a growth ceiling. With very, very talented people in the office, and without the option of being in a continually expanding office, I think that a number of bright guys have been forced out to swim on their own. They've been very successful, and I've tried to encourage them and help them. If you're organization-inclined it's fun to build a huge organization, like General Motors or something, but I don't have any interest in doing that at all. So there's a kind of self-limit to the whole thing, and definitely, at a certain point, a number of young people—I see some here—have to think about their own careers.

Diamonstein Do you find that younger architects are interested in going out into their own practice? What advice would you give to younger architects?

Barnes Well, I feel that there are some things that you always wonder why you didn't do. If there's any chance of that happening to a young architect—I hope that the people that are here in my office won't all leave tomorrow, you understand, but speaking as a friend, and not as an employer—I think that if you're going to feel, why didn't I ever do it? then for goodness' sake, make the move. If you like to work in a team, and if you feel that an office such as mine is loose enough so that there's fulfillment for a designer, then I think it's probably reasonably satisfactory. But in all honesty, you never know all the business of finding out about yourself, until you're thrown on your own, and you have to make decisions, and so on. It's not quite the same in somebody else's office. That's not a prepared statement, but I think I'm trying to be honest.

Diamonstein We appreciate that. I guess it's accurate to say that you really don't have what is referred to as a quote, style. Your work has never quite fit into the mold of orthodox modernism, and yet it hardly belongs in the category of the new post-modernism. How would you describe your style? Do you feel that you have a style?

Barnes I suppose I do think that I have a style. When I went to school, there were words like "clean." It was a word used in architectural circles, "clean designer." Nowadays that word is out, and all kinds of other words are used, metaphors, symbolism, this kind of thing. But the idea of being simple, clear-headed, doing work which has clarity, has always appealed to me tremendously. It happens, however, that we've had all kinds of projects—college jobs, schools, banks, office buildings, museums, theaters, and if you really do a functional building, each one comes out looking quite different. But I like to think that at the base of each of these designs there's some sort of clarity of thought. If you are working with people in the office, and you are not interested in completely dominating every aspect, it is essential that you share a basic schematic idea. Then you have a kind of armature that people can work within, or around.

Diamonstein How can you design in so many different styles?

Barnes I don't think there are that many styles. There are different materials. The Haystack for example, shows great interest in volumetric form, as does the Walker and IBM, too—but if it looks that way, maybe you're right.

Diamonstein I'm probably wrong! You mentioned that when you went to school the word used was clean. Well, you are back at school as a visiting professor at Harvard. In a recent speech you commented that as a result of that encounter, your vocabulary has expanded considerably. You referred to words like eclecticism, historicism, pluralism, dichotomy, analogue, metaphor, syntactic, semiotic, and of course, complexity and contradiction. But not clean. What do these terms have in common? How do they all relate to urban development and the future of architecture?

Barnes Well, as opposed to all of that, I certainly have a style. The kind of expression that you get in architectural school, I think, and in the wind today, is definitely pluralist. Definitely. You find that both in school and in practice, there's no compunction against having a building look one way at one end, and one way at the other. You find some historical element absolutely grafted on to modern media so that the eclecticism, even with one building changing styles, is not a shocking event. As nearly as I can make out, that is very largely a reaction against what must seem very, very barren. The architecture of the modern establishment must seem tired, routine, and just plain boring. Take something like O'Hare Airport, which is just a routine, terrible building that weighs on the soul.

It's just miles and miles of third generation Mies van der Rohe architecture. A young man is not going to be impressed by that, whereas I can continue with examples of all kinds of routine architecture and routine thinking. It's not much fun to do what I would call systems architecture, to continue to develop modular architecture. So there is kind of a reaction, that something else has to be said, and I sympathize with that. Then I think that architects often are not concerned with mood or with the real feeling of a site or a space. Often a routine system solution to a school or something is just implanted on the site, and it's kind of a heartless affair. In school, I found students thinking a great deal about the exact ambience of the site, and exactly how you approach the building, and exactly what it would look like in moonlight—a lot of romantic stuff. They were not too much concerned with the functions. Gateways are big in school—gateways and gazebos are focal elements. Now that means that it's much more poetic. It's also partial. I mean it's not complete. I was on a jury for the American Academy, and we saw a number of these routine, cliché-type, everyday modern solutions—what I was taught, and what was taught continually down through the sixties. The way those juries work, you have a hundred submissions, and a bunch of architects. The jurors sit around, and pass them along. I saw one come by, and it was sort of a Miami pink building, with a moon. It was like a child's drawing of this strange pink building with palm trees in front, and it definitely caught you. So I just put it in the hold file. Then the drawings went round and round and round, and then it came by again. I put it in the hold as the pile got smaller and smaller, and smaller. Everybody said, well, I'm not going to throw that one out, and it kept going by. This was an absolutely incompetent architect, a person who obviously didn't care about the plan, or the structure and so on. But the drawing was provocative. It was like looking at a painting, and that drawing came down to where it was being compared with a very slick top designer from I think Minnesota. We ended up giving both of these two people fellowships. One on the basis of being a good solid, well-trained, reliable architect, and the other, because she—in this case—was saying something poetic, as simple as that. I had a student at Harvard, who did that kind of thing. A number of my fellow jurors were picking on it, because it didn't work, the building couldn't be built. You couldn't get into it; it just didn't make any sense. But it also had mood and it had a plaza with nobody in the plaza. Since architecture is a social art, I guess a plaza is supposed to be full of people. But this plaza was like a Salvador Dali painting, with lines just going to a vanishing point, and one figure here, and one figure there, and two empty buildings, looking at an empty plaza. We spent so much time talking about this—why it was so offensive to these other architects. When it came to my turn to criticize, I said that I thought that it was very, very artistic, and very moving, but I questioned whether the person was in the right profession. And that is true. It is true of some of Graves, it is true of a number of tendencies in architecture. They're painterly, if that's the word, the instinct of a painter. People are just plain bored with problem-solving.

Diamonstein Besides the art functions that we are familiar with in the Asia House gallery, there are non-art purposes to the Asia Society, namely diplomatic and trade functions. Please tell us about the design of the new Asia Society, particularly its context and location. How was the site selected, and why did you choose that color?

Barnes Well, the site was selected because we looked for two years at a number of sites, and none of them were available, for one reason or the other. We finally backed into a site which admittedly was too small. But we took it, because it was a good site, although a little bit small for the building. So the building has been really tightly corseted to fit. The site is on Seventieth and Park, and it faces Park, which is one of the great volumes that you spoke about—this great hallway running through New York. It seems to me absolutely proper to reinforce the wall of Park Avenue, and so the building is very, very strong. It's up against the sidewalk line as hard as it can be, defining Park Avenue, and lining up with all the other Park Avenue buildings. The building is fairly big, equivalent to a ten story apartment building, and it faces little brownstones on Seventieth Street. The design question is how to accommodate Park Avenue and also to come down to earth—to be a good neighbor. It is this context kind of architecture that I've been talking about. You would never design this building free-standing, but it would be perfectly clear to you when you see the site, what we're trying to do. The building on the side street suddenly shrinks back and there's a garden in front of it. It immediately moves to the back of the lot, and the adjacent house then sets forward, free. Our whole building is kept back fifty feet away from the sidewalk. That's a good example of this question of paying attention to the spaces on both sides. As for the color of the building, there was a brownstone there, the old Milliken House. . .

Diamonstein . . . which some people admired very much.

Barnes So did I. I thought that it would be nice to use the brownstone. Brownstone has almost vanished as a building material now. You can't get brownstone, not enough of it; because all the quarries have run out. In puzzling about how to get brownstone, we looked into importing some from Germany. John Rockefeller, who is the great benefactor of Asia Society said, Why don't we get it from India, why don't we get Indian sandstone? And so the Asia Society made contact with the prime minister, and went through all the motions, and we immediately started to design the building, using Indian sandstone.

Diamonstein It's a reddish color?

Barnes Yes, we wanted to mix it with a polished red granite, so that you would have two kinds of reds, a polished and a dull, and then inlay them in the building, sometimes checkerboard them like an inlaid box. And that's what we're doing, with one important difference. Somewhere along the line the Indian sandstone fell through. We had to shift to two kinds of granite finishes, but we're still using a dull pink against a polished red. It still looks like an inlaid box, and we are getting enough of the red sandstone for the paving. So there'll be three kinds of stone. The stone will be going up this summer, so you'll have to see what it looks like.

Diamonstein You mentioned that you, too, admired the Milliken House. Were there any elements of that house that you'd have retained to incorporate in your current design?

Barnes We didn't find a way to take chunks of Victorian brownstone and incorporate them in the Asia House, I think partly because it would have been confusing. The Asia House gallery is full of Asian art. I think if you're going to incorporate anything, it ought to be something from that part of the world. But in another context, that would be a reasonable thing to do, if you were building an apartment house or something.

Diamonstein I thought there was once a plan to incorporate an existing arch as part of the entrance to the garden.

Barnes That went the way of the brownstone.

Diamonstein Let's talk for a moment about the Klein Building, a 36-story skyscraper on the northeast corner of Madison and Fifty-fourth Street. It's 495 feet high, 420 thousand square feet of office space squeezed out of the last inch of that 420 thousand square feet. The material is a light-colored aluminum similar to the silver satin finish of Citicorp. There is an 80-foot-high arcade with a diagonal pedestrian walkway from Fifty-fourth Street to a large urban park behind. It is no accident that there is a greenhouse in IBM, that there is an urban park behind the Klein Building, that you are the person who recycled the Bronx Conservatory, because of your long-standing interest in landscape architecture. What do you see as the inter-relationship between the design of the IBM Building and the Klein Building? Were any elements adapted from the IBM to the Klein Building?

Barnes Well, in both cases we reinforced the retail line on Madison. Happily, the line of shops goes unbroken up and down Madison in both cases. And the leftover bonus space is put in midblock. This is worth fighting for. This is worth concentrating on, that in New York City the high masses be on the avenues, and the low masses be on the streets. That would give the whole city a grain which is absolutely clear, like a piece of wood. It's logical that the wide streets get the high buildings, the narrow streets get the low buildings. You get light into both. As you cross the city, it gives a kind of a sense of history and scale, to go leaping up the big buildings framing the avenues, and down to a scale low enough to accommodate the brownstones on the side streets. The Klein Building does that. The park is on the midblock side, and faces two brownstones. So all of a sudden, there will be a sort of Paley Park-scale garden. The other thing that we are currently very interested in—I don't know whether it'll come off or not—but we are playing with interesting materials in that building. For the aluminum, we're trying to get a gunmetal finish in the aluminum—an ice color, gray with a slight blue. And the glass, which is very slightly mirrored, will have a blue/green cast. In the garden, we are playing with a fountain which we're designing in the office with the help of a brilliant young guy who works for Corning Glass, doing glass sculpture.

Diamonstein What's his name?

Barnes James A. Carpenter. We hope to have a fountain of glass brick and water—more ice colors, more water and glass and cool colors. We keep doing this; I hope it'll have a cumulative effect.

Diamonstein You say you have been energy-conscious in all of your construction, particularly in the IBM Building. What assistance did you have in the design of that building, and how do you know that your claim is an accurate one?

Barnes Well, because IBM is absolutely dedicated to this. If the architect was completely goofing off on energy, IBM would straighten him up. They are computerizing everything—when the heat goes on, when the heat goes off, when the lights go on, when the lights go off.

Diamonstein How about when the windows open, an important feature in that building?

Barnes They've asked us to use windows that open. But there is a difference of opinion between the architect and IBM, as to whether that really is going to save energy, or whether it's going to be misused and let all the heat out. So that the windows will have locks on them in case that assumption doesn't work. But the thought on opening windows is, everybody in this room would say, why can't we open windows? A person on the street says that. The thought is that at the half seasons, when you don't need air conditioning or heating, you can simply open windows to get fresh air. In the case of a big building, you're talking about only the outside 15 feet. There are acres of space inside that aren't affected. But there is a possibility that having open windows will get misused.

Diamonstein Which opens for use first, the Klein or the IBM Building?

Barnes The IBM will top out first, but the Klein will be finished and occupied before the IBM is finished.

Diamonstein Since there is that prism top, and other similar elements in the two buildings, how will that affect public perception of either building?

Barnes I haven't even thought of that. I think that the IBM Building will be seen as a steel frame first. Actually, it's quite different from the main shaft of the Klein tower. I think most people will think of them as quite different buildings, and I do, too. One is stone, and one is high tech. Except for the things I've mentioned that are alike, the siting and so on, they are different.

Diamonstein Charles Moore claims that his clients are the starting point for all of his designs, while Kevin Roche says his best clients tell him nothing at all. Where do you fit in on the scale of all or nothing?

Barnes I am definitely on Charles Moore's side. If I count the good buildings and the bad buildings that I've done, the good buildings usually have someone like Martin Friedman, or a good client. I think that the relationship between an architect and a client is so much mixed up with the quality of the building, I can't imagine isolating myself from the client and doing a good building.

Diamonstein Has the work of any particular architect inspired you?

Barnes When I was in school, and for long after, I liked, of course, Le Corbusier, and Mies van der Rohe, and the Chicagoans like Frank Lloyd Wright—those three great pioneers. And I've never been able to come off it quite, but I have almost as high a regard for Lou Kahn. I think that given his period, and what he did, and so on, he was an absolutely remarkable architect.

Diamonstein Do any of his museums, and the use of the light within them affect your work?

Barnes Yes. I looked very carefully at his Fort Worth Museum, the Kimball Art Museum, and I went to see the Salk Center recently. I thought it was absolutely marvelous.

Diamonstein A last question. You are associated with the so-called Grays. In fact, you are referred to as their dean. They contrast with architects like Moore and Venturi who are concerned with context or vernacular, historic association. They're architects like the New York Five, who have formal interests that stem from Corbusier. How do you feel about this division into camps? Is it artificial?

Barnes There is a connection between the New York Five, and Le Corbusier, when he was White. There was a whole section of Le Corbusier, when he was Gray. *When the Cathedrals Were White* is such a romantic title. . . . And a great period in the twenties, when he was White, now has tremendous nostalgia, like Art Deco. It's very much easier to be romantic about something which is just not next door. And that certainly unifies Meier and Gwathmey, and certainly Graves. All of them seem steeped in the romance of that period, and I understand it perfectly. It was a great period. I once made a tour of Paris trying to see all those buildings.

Audience To what extent did IBM's energy management system affect your architectural design?

Barnes The size of the windows was limited. The amount of glass was restricted. You'll see in the Klein Building a higher percentage of glass, and that's what you'll see most of all. You also will see these little windows which may or may not be opened in spring or fall. And I hope you'll see the lights go out. It won't look like the World Trade Center at night. The cleaning cycle is arranged so you don't have to turn everything on to clean. I tried to get them to fix it so the lights would move around the building during the cleaning cycle, and keep the cleaning people— women—moving, but I didn't get away with that.

Audience Are you designing the interior?

Barnes Yes, we are doing all the interiors, all the furnishings, the partitioning, and everything in the whole building, working on it now. The ground floor spaces you can begin to see, the cantilever on the corner, and the great hall that runs through the building to the park. The upstairs space, that odd corner had to be proven to IBM before they would allow us to do it. We had a number of furnishing studies to find out whether that odd shape was plain usable from their point of view. It's on a five foot module. There is that one obtuse corner, and then it gets right back on the five foot module. The lights will avoid the partitions in all of the usual things you do in a building, so that you can bring partitions into glass walls. It's very standardized except for that one obtuse angle, where you turn the corner, and that does make a special condition.

FRANK O. GEHRY

Frank O. Gehry
Born Toronto, Ont., Canada, 1929
B. Arch. University of Southern California, 1954
Graduate School of Design, Harvard University, 1956-57

Diamonstein Frank O. Gehry may be the most provocative, best-known, California-based architect in the country. His eighteen-year-old firm, Frank O. Gehry & Associates, is located in Santa Monica. He is renowned for his close ties to West Coast artists as well as his conception of building as incomplete structure. He is also especially interested in the use of industrial materials, and in making his art from such everyday materials as chain-link fencing and plywood.

Frank, you are a spokesman for what you call in a rather dramatic exaggeration, "cheapskate architecture," the art of using inexpensive industrial materials, such as corrugated aluminum, steel mesh, raw plywood, and cinder block to enrich interior spaces. When and how and why were you first inspired by the idea of using these materials for aesthetic effect?

Gehry I had a lot of poor clients. I guess the first turn-on for me was at the Jewish Museum Show on primary structures in '67 or '66. I ran into Carl Andre's work, and I first got interested in Don Judd's work, and the idea that you could make a work of art out of anything. Of course, it had been done by a lot of artists before that, but that work really interested me. I'd done some work with inexpensive corrugated metal. I didn't really know what the idea was when I was doing it. But looking back now, I kind of understand. I was trying to work more hands-on with material, and those materials were easily available to me. The best example that's all neatly packaged is the cardboard furniture I did in the late sixties, where I got interested in the material, and actually built structures myself in the office with my guys. More like a sculptor works. Directly, rather than doing a drawing and having it made. We worked with the material. But I'm not saying that I build my own houses, and so on.

Diamonstein Was your first expression of that idea in an exhibition for which you designed the installation? As I recall, you did the installation for Billy Al Bengston in the Los Angeles County Museum around 1968.

Gehry Right. There, I was interested in breaking down the institutional look of the Los Angeles County Museum so that it would be a nice environment for Billy's work, which grows out of motorcycle racing. His whole aesthetic comes out of his involvement with the motorcycle track. And the Los Angeles County Museum's institutional quality just fought it. So, I did a series of rooms using just raw plywood, and the museum officials didn't like the raw plywood. They wanted to paint it. They threw me a curve and brought up plywood that had already been used in other shows. It was already partially painted. They thought that would throw me.

Diamonstein What did you do?

Gehry I just left it the way it was, and used corrugated metal to make some of the walls to hang some of his paintings on.

Diamonstein And the first job that expressed that aesthetic was a small hay barn, I think, in San Juan Capistrano. Would you tell us about that?

Gehry The program there was sort of negligible. It was just a structure to cover up some bales of hay and the form it took could have gone anywhere. The budget was tiny. So I used a bunch of telephone poles. I tilted the shape. I became fascinated with tilted forms, and roofs. I think that grew out of my fascination with Frank Lloyd Wright, actually. The way he played with roof structures was a very important part of his architecture.

Diamonstein Was your intent to build a building, or to create what you have referred to as a minimal sculptural element?

Gehry I hate to use the word sculpture. I've used it before, but I don't think it's really the right word. I'm not comfortable using it.

Diamonstein What would you prefer?

Gehry Just an architectural element of some kind. It's a building.

Diamonstein It was a building like none we had seen before.

Gehry When I tilted it, the reflections of the sky and the metal made the building disappear sometimes. Then that proportion of the San Juan Capistrano hay barn came back in a small house I did for Wagner. That's not going to be built, I guess. It's a similar aesthetic, and a similar design. It keeps recurring.

Diamonstein Some architects enriched their early training with stage design, or furniture design, or graphic work. After you came from Toronto, where you were born, you worked your way through architectural school as a truck driver. Has too much been made of that, your Jack Kerouac-California funk connection? Is that really what you're all about? Does that persist in your work? Or rather, is it a poetic reference to some of the tough materials that you use?

Gehry I don't know how to answer that one. I'm working on a show at the Los Angeles County Museum of American-owned constructivist paintings and structures. And I decided that work feels so much like home that maybe my Polish-Russian background is coming out. That might be more of me than the truckdriver. Maybe it's in the genes.

Diamonstein DNA.

Gehry Yes.

Diamonstein You describe building as an unfinished journey. What does that mean?

Gehry Well, that's recent. I always find that I start out to do things only with the idea of doing a good job. I don't have any notion of the direction. It's only after the fact that I somehow find words to describe it. I guess I was interested in the unfinished—or the quality that you find in paintings by Jackson Pollock, for instance, or de Kooning, or Cézanne, that look like the paint was just applied. The very finished, polished, every-detail-perfect kind of architecture seemed to me not to have that quality. I wanted to try that out in a building. The obvious way to go about it was the wood studs, the unfinished wood studs. We all like buildings in construction better than we do finished—I think most of us agree on that. The structure is always so much more poetic than the finished thing, that I started working with the studs exposed, and leaving them that way—encased in glass, and encased in my house. It was just that kind of idea.

Diamonstein As we discuss the genesis and evolution of your work, it seems obvious that your intent is certainly not elegant and hermetic architecture—

Gehry But I like marble, you know. Don't get me wrong.

Diamonstein We're going to come to those very serious projects of yours soon—those sixty-million-dollar projects. Happily, you have one going on right now. But for now, I'm contrasting the kind of elegant and hermetic architecture that we generally associate with the East Coast, or with Europe, to the kind of zingy California quality and Oriental flavor of the West Coast that your work reflects. Does part of this contrast relate to regional differences in taste?

Gehry I would guess so. I would think that there's a regionalism in my work. But I'm not sure how to characterize it. I would think that if I tried to do my own house in New York, I would have a lot of trouble.

Diamonstein You had a little bit of trouble out there, too. Is the East Coast more knowing and the West Coast more experimental, while the Midwest, as the cliché goes, is more traditional?

Gehry I always thought the East Coast was more open. I mean, there are more ideas floating around here, more ideas being thrashed around. In L.A. I don't see anybody. We don't get together. There isn't the kind of close, tight circle of architects that you have here, where you're talking to each other every day.

Diamonstein Is that important to an architect's work? Do you think you've suffered as a result of not being exposed to that kind of critical mass?

Gehry Well, I've found it in the L.A. artists whom I had a social relationship with. It was like a support system. It wasn't everybody chopping away at you and making you struggle, like you have here.

Diamonstein Is that one of the reasons that you spend more and more time here?

Gehry I like it here, yes.

Diamonstein We're glad that you do. You mentioned that you don't like the kind of architecture that has every ashtray in place, every Mies chair in some rigid—

Gehry I didn't say I didn't like it. It's only that it is very different from what I think I do. I don't intend to say I don't like it. I absolutely do like some of that work, when it's well-done. There are a lot of people doing it, and doing it well. I felt that it was lacking a kind of spontaneity that possibly was worth exploring, and that's what I've been trying to do. In other words nobody else was doing it, and it looked like something that would interest me. I guess I approach architecture somewhat scientifically—there are going to be breakthroughs, and they're going to create new information. It's adding information to the pot—not necessarily regurgitating other, older ideas.

Diamonstein And part of your pressing forward to that cutting edge is your belief in flexibility. Do you think all spaces should be available for architectural improvisation?

Gehry Well, I've found that the idea of building everything so that it was all set is hard to do with clients. I'm enough of a voyeur that I like to see how somebody responds to what I do—that is, how they respond to it even if they shriek.

Diamonstein Do they?

Gehry Sometimes. My whole architectural growth has been in the area of commercial architecture—shopping centers, speculative office buildings. It's not been in high-budget institutional work. The theater work I do is outdoor stuff.

Diamonstein What a contrast that is to what we're talking about now. Obviously those are not structures that can evolve in response to the needs of the user.

Gehry Well, they do in the sense that they create a shell. Then the user comes in, and puts his junk in the shell in some way. The house I did for Ron Davis was that idea. I built the most beautiful shell I could do, and then let him

Frank O. Gehry Residence,
exterior, Santa Monica, Calif.
Picture Credit: Timothy Hursely/
B. Korab, Ltd.

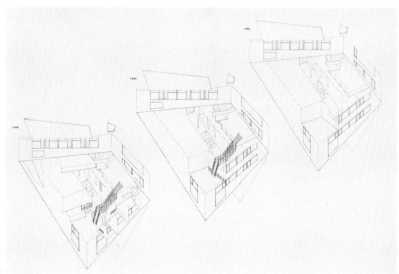

Ron Davis Studio/Residence,
Malibu, Calif., axonometric
drawing

Santa Monica Place, Mall,
center court, interior,
Santa Monica, Calif.
Drawing by John Reinwald

Ron Davis Studio/Residence,
exterior, Malibu, Calif.
Picture credit: Tim Street-Porter

bring his stuff to it, and convert it to his use. Theoretically in its optimum, it is kind of a confrontation between the client's aesthetic and values and my aesthetic and values. I'm idealistic in thinking that there's a value in that interaction.

Diamonstein You're referring to the house that you did for painter Ron Davis, in Malibu. There are certain aesthetic ideas that are present in Davis's work that you extended into the architecture which, in turn, has led Davis onward in his work.

Gehry If he was in the audience, he'd shoot you right now.

Diamonstein Well, how would you reply to that? Perhaps you should comment on the relationship between you, the artist, the house, and the work.

Gehry I did learn a lot from him, I admit it, and I feel very strongly about it. I thought he did, too. But I think it's not as clear.

Diamonstein What about the nature of collaboration between artists and architects? Is that a fruitful alliance? Is it a possible one?

Gehry Well, as soon as you say that, you separate architecture and make it not an art, somehow. I think that in the collaborations that I've had, our intentions have been exactly the same—to create a beautiful object, and to transcend the functional and programmatic issues. They tend to create false security of some kind—the building works for a certain period of time, because it solves a particular problem. In the case of the Ron Davis house, or the work I'm doing now, when you start to think of the building as a shell, and as an object that somebody else comes into, then the intentions are no different from Richard Serra making up a piece. . . . I mean, there's the same kind of intention. And so I think that it's like collaborating with anybody.

Diamonstein It's not different from collaborating with another architect, or an interior designer, or an engineer?

Gehry With an engineer it is different, yes. But I think there's an interesting exchange of ideas. The hard thing is to keep both egos intact, as you go through the process.

Diamonstein That's hard.

Gehry Well, I worked with Bob Irwin on the cardboard furniture, and we still talk to each other.

Diamonstein The interior of the Ron Davis house is a flexible and mobile interior space. Is it true that that house has been reconstructed inside several times—that it has evolved? I assume that was very close to your original intent.

Gehry It's not been reconstructed. It's been constructed in two or three moves. I built the shell. Then he came in to live in it with one set of needs. And then they changed. So we had to build rooms in the shell. The intention was that stuff that went in it would be aesthetically different from the shell, so there would be a kind of a confrontation between these two ideas. What happened is that Ron asked me to do the insides. I thought he would do them himself, but he was, I guess, insecure about it. He asked me to do the insides, so now the inside looks like it's part of the outside. It's very hard to change your aesthetic—I mean, just constantly. I don't know how to do it. It's kind of an elusive question.

Diamonstein Do you want to change?

Gehry Yes. Within a project, I do. Very much.

Diamonstein The house is a trapezoid that in some way mirrors the long and uneven hills that surround Malibu. Was the trapezoid to reflect the hills or was there some other influence that generated the shape?

Gehry Well, the trapezoid grows out of his painting. The tilted roof grows out of my preoccupation with the tilted roof. The idea of forced perspective grew out of Palladio. I was nervous about that project, because I thought that the extent of the angle, the degree of the angles might be too large, and it might get bizarre, and make you feel uneasy when you're in it, and so on. In fact, it was very restful. That building unlocked a whole lot of other possibilities for me, and I spent a lot of time there, sitting and looking for a lot of days and evenings, just looking at it, watching the reflections. That helped me in my house.

Diamonstein What were some of the possibilities that were unleashed?

Gehry Because nothing was parallel, you couldn't predict any of the—I mean, this was obvious after the fact, and I should have known it—but you couldn't predict where the shadows and sunlight and reflections would fall. If you've got a rectangular box, and the windows are rectangular, and everything is straight, you pretty much sense where things are coming from. But if they're not, then you get a different take on it, and that became an interesting part of my work. I'm using it in my vocabulary in my new work. I am playing with those reflections in a predictable way.

Diamonstein Earlier, when I mentioned the barn in San Juan Capistrano, I referred to it as some sort of minimal sculpture and you were reluctant to use that word. But in the past, it's a word that you have used.

Gehry I know. I don't know what else to use. I used it badly.

Diamonstein And you've used it frequently. You've said that you are a frustrated sculptor, that you work in model form and scale models, and you cut away, like a sculptor does with clay. Does that still hold true, no matter by what word we describe it?

Gehry I don't know how else to describe it. But I do work that way. That's true.

Diamonstein Do you still think of yourself as a frustrated sculptor?

Gehry I'm not frustrated.

Diamonstein How do you define the difference between the way an architect works, and the way an artist works?

Gehry The process of doing architecture is to work through a set of ideas, a set of finished drawings, and give them to the field for construction. Everything's got to be on that drawing, or else you get killed with extras. So, process forces a kind of precision. I can see why architecture tends to be so precise and finished, because the idea of building in the unfinished is very much against the system of building, unless you get out there, and work hands-on with the materials. It is something I've been urging students to do, rather than go to work with a big office and become cynical in two years. It would be much better, I think, to go into the field, and build hand-on. It's a more positive and optimistic kind of attitude about work.

When the artists and sculptors I know work, there's sort of a free play idea. You try things; you experiment; it's kind of naïve and childish; it's like kids in a playpen. Scientists work that way, too—for example, genetic scientists that I've been involved with, through a genetic foundation that

I work with, seem to work similarly. It's kind of like throwing things out, and then following the ideas, rather than predicting where you're going to go.

Diamonstein You said that you press for a predictive quality now in certain parts of your work.

Gehry I did say that. That is a contradiction. What I was saying about the reflections is that I am aware now that I have a different attitude about them. So I sort of deal with it. But then there's infinitely more there than I'm aware of in advance. I'm always surprised.

Diamonstein You mentioned earlier that you spend a great deal of time talking with artists and sculptors in California—perhaps in a social setting, but nonetheless you were finding ideas. I assume you meant larger ideas, not ones for specific projects.

Gehry No, we rarely talked about our work. It's very interesting. It really was ninety-five percent social. But it was like a support system. People whose work I respected would come to look at my buildings.

Diamonstein To the work of which artists do you most respond? Who has the greatest influence on you?

Gehry From out there?

Diamonstein From anywhere.

Gehry Ed Moses was a very important person in my work only because, I guess, we spent a lot of time together. He has an attitude towards his work that appeals to me. He is a good role model.

Diamonstein There are a number of artists in California with whom you are closely involved. At one point you were going to collaborate on a house with some of those artists. For whatever reasons, that did not come to pass. Were there some barriers, some obstacles to collaboration between architects and artists, if not in general, specifically in that project? Would you care to talk about it?

Gehry I don't remember the project. Oh, God, conveniently I didn't remember it . . . Jesus. A guy came to me, and talked about building a house, and then he went to one of my so-called best friends, who told him that he would do the house.

Diamonstein I thought the artists decided to dispense with having an architect involved in the project at all.

Gehry They're doing it, and I think it may even be built. It was just a friendship thing, where I said, look, if you want to stay friends with me, I want to do a piece in the house. And so he said, okay, you do the stairway. But the more we got into it, the more it became clear that there was a different standard for me as an architect.

Diamonstein What happens when the roles are reversed? Do you have different standards for artists?

Gehry I've never tried to get an artist involved. I feel like it's an insult to ask an artist to do a piece in front of a building. So I never do.

Diamonstein But you're currently involved in a collaboration. Does that work?

Gehry So far.

Diamonstein Do you want to tell us about that?

Gehry Well, it's an Architectural League project where teams of ten artists and ten architects are working together on a realizable project. I've been working with Richard Serra on a project to build a bridge. It's kind of a fantasy, but Serra has done a spectacular film on a bridge. He asked me to work with him on this project, not as a technical consultant. Then this Architectural League commission to do a collaborative project came along, so we fit into that. We're not sure where it's going to go. The idea is that we are going to work on what a bridge is—and a bridge is everything. A bridge is talking and a space between, a very Oriental philosophy. It's mind-boggling what a bridge is. Our hope is eventually to find a specific site and design a specific bridge for it.

Diamonstein Have you located a site?

Gehry No.

Diamonstein One of the works of art that you did manage to create, however, is your very own house. It has been described as suburban anonymity. The original structure was a two-story gambrel-roof clapboard house. You proceeded to build a one-and-one-half-story-high wall of corrugated metal around it, but behind the wall the original structure pokes up from inside the new structure. Can you tell us what your intentions were there?

Gehry It had to do with my wife. She found this nice house—and I love my wife—this cute little house with antiques in it. Very sweet little thing. And we were having a lot of problems finding a house. We bought in Santa Monica at the height of the real estate boom. We paid the highest price possible.

Diamonstein A hundred and sixty thousand dollars, I read.

Gehry A hundred and sixty thousand.

Diamonstein A lot of money.

Gehry A year earlier it was forty. Talk about desperate moves. I always do that. And we could have lived in that house fine. There was enough room in it and everything.

Diamonstein A pink house with green shingles?

Gehry It was all pink asbestos shingle over white clapboard. It had several layers on it. It was already layered, which is a heavy term these days, layering.

Diamonstein That's part of the appeal to you.

Gehry Anyway, I decided to get into a dialogue with the old house, which is no different, you know from what I was saying about the Ron Davis house, where the interiors would join in a dialogue with the exteriors. Here I had it easy, because the old house was already a different aesthetic, and I could play off of it. But I wanted to explore the relationship between the two. I got fascinated with the idea that the old house should appear to remain totally intact from the outside, and that you could look through the new house, and see the old house as though it was now packaged in this new skin. The new skin and the windows in the new house would be of a totally different aesthetic than the windows in the old house. So they would constantly be in tension, or whatever, with each other. I wanted each window to have a different aesthetic, which I couldn't accomplish at that time.

Diamonstein So, the old house was the core, and the new house is the wrapper. Of course, you've used a number of the materials that are familiar in your own vocabulary—metal, plywood, glass, and chain link fencing—all very inexpensive. On one hand, the house looks unfinished and rough—

Gehry I'm not sure if it is finished.

Diamonstein You're not sure?

Gehry No.

Diamonstein Is one ever sure?

Gehry It's confusing. I was wondering the other day what effect this had on my family. I've noticed my wife leaves papers and stuff around on the tables, so there's a kind of chaos in the organization of how we live in the house. I was beginning to think that it had something to do with her not knowing whether I'm finished or not.

Diamonstein There might have been another cue that you have given to the occupants. When that house was photographed, in contrast to most shelter magazine photographs with three perfect lilies in one place, and two books in another—you had soap powder for the kitchen sink on the kitchen sink, and some of the cupboard doors open. It was very much a lived-in environment. It seemed evident that this was a deliberate structuring of the photo to reflect an environment in which real people lived real lives.

Gehry Actually, it wasn't structuring the photo.

Diamonstein It was taking a photo of the way you live?

Gehry Yeah. Well, what happens is—I've had a lot of photographers there now. Each one comes in and has a different idea of how the place should look. So they start moving the furniture around. If I get there in time I start putting everything back.

Diamonstein That's contrary to what you originally wanted, this flexible room, but here you're the user, and they're not.

Gehry Right.

Diamonstein So, it really should respond to your needs.

Gehry I like the comfortable feeling of just carrying the stuff all around.

Diamonstein How did you feel about the reaction of some of your neighbors who felt less than comfortable, somewhat startled and sometimes even angered by what you had done to a house that was the pride of their neighborhood?

Gehry I was disgusted with myself. There are only a few people—there was an architect down the street, whose house is covered with fake stone, who tried to get the building department to put me in jail.

Diamonstein They didn't want to give you a certificate of occupancy—

Gehry There was a lady lawyer down the street, who has a cute little modern house with columns and pediments. She's very avant-garde.

Diamonstein Except she did it thirty years ago.

Gehry Yeah. And she said she'd try every way possible to sue me. I got very angry at first. I felt like I was misunderstood, and being abused, and all. But the lawyer down the street stopped me dead. She said, "I don't like your house, and I tried every way I could to sue you, but I can't do anything now. You're totally legal." And then she said, "Quit yelling at me." I called her all kinds of names. And she said, "Just stop. I'm going to be your neighbor. Explain what you were trying to do. That's all I want to know." And that stopped me short. I realized that I owed them that. So, I did. Whenever anybody asks, I explain it to them, I take them in, I show them views, show them what I thought I was doing and why. It has defused some of the anger and misunderstanding, and it's made me feel better, because it's sort of childish not to explain that I'm not totally in touch with the rupture. It looks great to me.

Diamonstein Did you explain your intentions to your family, when you placed the dining room in the driveway?

Gehry It always comes out like I'm being funny. Actually, I like that idea, because it means people think I'm not taking it so seriously. But I'm very serious about everything I do.

Diamonstein I guess the dining room relates to, again, the inside versus the outside—the former driveway is now the existing dining room in-between the first structure and its wrapper. Why don't we go on to your more "serious" work? Because while we are talking about some of these smaller and more experimental projects—

Gehry Why do you say "more serious"? I guess I invite that.

Diamonstein Really, because of the reference that you've used, now and in an earlier conversation. Would you care to change that reference?

Gehry It's all of one piece, actually. It's just that the larger-scale commercial work requires more compromise by its nature. When you do a shopping center, you have to put a department store at each end. There are rules of those games that I'm not allowed to tinker with. If you accept those projects, which I do.

Diamonstein You've said in the past that the larger the scale of the work the more one is forced to compromise, and that's why you need and enjoy these smaller projects.

Gehry Right.

Diamonstein But your practice has always struck a balance between the straightforward and the experimental, between large-scale and small-scale commissions. In fact, you are in the process of doing your largest work yet. It's the sixty-million-dollar project that I referred to earlier. Can you describe that briefly?

Gehry The program is a typical suburban shopping center, only it's in town, and so all the parking is in parking decks. It's just a tight little ten-acre thing with two department stores, and three levels of shopping, and two thousand cars, all jumbled together. I was interested in changing the scale of those amorphic, formless shopping center interiors, where you go from court to narrow to court to narrow. I wanted to try to make different architectural statements along the way. Those are hard to do, but I was able to get the central corridor as a separate building. The outside has small vest pocket parks, I guess you'd call them. The entrances are set back, and each one has a different character, or tries to. One of the things that the client did agree on with me about this project was that maybe in a suburban location it made some sense to make the architecture homogenous. Although I'm not sure, even there it couldn't be done differently. But downtown, where there is a mixture of old and new buildings, I wanted to keep the shopping center in the texture, the language of the existing downtown. A series of separate discrete structures.

Diamonstein What material did you use?

Gehry Chain link. There's a garage three hundred feet long and six stories high that's covered with a curtain of chain link. It's just hung like a curtain in front of it. The rest is stucco, and one of the garages is covered with metal—not corrugated, just plain.

Diamonstein You've referred several times to the cardboard furniture that you designed in the early sixties. That is particularly striking, because for a very long while you have been interested in both the economically and aesthetically affordable. The furniture fits in with your use of cheap materials. I think this line of laminated cardboard is quite splendid, and I don't know if it's ever reached a wider audience. I saw it long before I ever saw you, only in one place quite a long while ago. What has happened to it?

Gehry Well, the idea still exists. It was shown at Bloomingdale's, and they were selling a lot of it in retail.

Diamonstein How durable is it??

Gehry It's held up very well. Ten years, fifteen years. I started in about '68, '69, and pieces are still around. There's a piece at the Museum of Modern Art in the basement. I hope everybody will make a run on the place, and request it. They don't like it, when you come and ask them for it. It started to have a life of its own, and the life of its own would have taken me away from architecture. It's just that simple. If I had made an arrangement where I got a royalty, the thing would have worked. But the people that backed it didn't want that kind of relationship; if they were going to put in money, they wanted me to be more personally involved. It was frightening when I got to Bloomingdale's, and saw people buying it, and coming at me from all sides. I couldn't hack it.

Diamonstein You don't feel that way when they use either your shopping center or your building?

Gehry No, because I don't have to continue in the involvement. The furniture could have become a fairly big business, at least for a short time, judging from the way people wanted to support it and back it. I think that it could still be done. I'm surprised that somebody else hasn't used it, or done it. I hold the patent rights.

Diamonstein Do you see your work be it furniture, or building—as part of a larger, stylistic trend?

Gehry Well, I think that of necessity we're probably going to have to build cheaper and cheaper—at least I will with the clients I have.

Diamonstein Has your work been imitated by other architects?

Gehry I hope not. I haven't seen any imitators. Oh, you know, people use corrugated metal. People use chain link. But I didn't invent chain link, and I didn't invent corrugated metal. I'm not trying to start a school of architecture. I am trying to respond to a particular time, because I don't think you can escape. I don't believe you can jump out of your time. Maybe there's some relevance in terms of the economy now—in terms of understanding that things don't have to be quite so completely finished, and they have a value in terms of livability, in terms of people being able to bang nails in the wall. Everything can survive and be strong, without needing all the perfectly organized furniture.

Diamonstein Is that what you mean when you refer to invisible architecture?

Gehry Oh, God, you had to ask me that one. I had a funny notion that you could make architecture that you would bump into before you would realize it was architecture. I deluded myself with that idea for a long time. Obviously I haven't been able to do it. I'd love to do that. Probably Venturi gets closer to doing that than anybody else I know.

Diamonstein And how do you compare your aesthetic and your way of using everyday, familiar materials to the way he does?

Gehry I think it's quite different. He's into kind of a story, a verbal polemic. I don't know, it doesn't fit the same groove. I'm really interested in this hands-on thing, and not in telling stories . . .

MICHAEL GRAVES

Michael Graves
Born Indianapolis, Ind., 1934
B.S. University of Cincinnati, 1958
M. Arch. Harvard University, 1959

Diamonstein Michael Graves is among the most influential architectural educators in the nation. Professor of Architecture at Princeton University for eighteen years now, Mr. Graves has helped define Princeton's identity as a strong, self-assured school that is deeply committed to aesthetics. His design work, which includes residences, medical facilities, cultural facilities, and town plans, has won nine design awards from *Progressive Architecture* and two from the national American Institute of Architects. Yet he is as well known for his murals as for his buildings, and his architectural drawings have been even more acclaimed.

Michael Graves, it has been suggested that you've rejected modern architecture as a social instrument. Your view, it seems, is that architecture communicates with individuals, not classes. Thus, the architect is more than a technician who solves functional problems; he is also an arbiter of taste. Like the modern painter, he is called upon to say something new, and to propound a philosophy. To understand your work, what is it we have to know?

Graves You begin with a premise that I think is not true, of having something to do with interest in the individual rather than in class or society. I suspect that architecture only succeeds as architecture when it does both. It is curious to me that anyone would think that if one attends well to one, the other is excluded. Certainly, architecture has to be read both by the collective society and by the individual. You asked about the architect as an arbiter of taste. I've just read Bob Gutman's review of my monograph, and evidently that notion is in the air. But I don't think the architect really is the arbiter of taste. I think that the kind of session we're having now has more to do with levels of taste and understanding than any one person setting the standards. For instance, there must be people out there doing interesting work, more interesting perhaps than that by some of the better known people you will talk to in this series. But because you've talked to some people, or because others write about them, they and their work become known. Those particular points of view have become part of the culture at large, because they become part of the critical domain. They're discussed; they're understood; they're denied; they're accepted. Whatever. I suspect that there is a consciousness of taste that is first held by the society. As the architect fits into and confronts that prevailing taste, there is a kind of give and take. As their ideas become known, the architect, the artist, the poet, the scientist, whatever, are assimilated. In that critical debate, they become a part of the culture; and in that sense there is some shift going on constantly in the way we look at things, the way we see things. I'm avoiding a fixed definition of taste. But, I suspect that this kind of session has more to do with taste than the building itself.

Diamonstein You talk about shift. In the past few years, your own work has drifted from abstraction toward cultural symbolism. A few years ago, your work was generally white, complex but rather austere. Through the joint publication of the book, *Five Architects,* your work was also associated with the work of architects such as Richard Meier and Peter Eisenman. In the past few years, however, you have emphasized classical architecture, and your work reflects an unusual mix of classicism and cubism. What provoked this movement and its dynamics?

Graves   That for me is a very interesting question. To the layman, a building done ten or twelve years ago and a new building might seem as different as night and day—diametrically opposed. But even though the shift was enormous, it was very, very gradual. The difference comes about, I suppose, through reaction, both my own reaction to my buildings as they're built and the reaction of readers of one's architecture—the layman, the client, and, most of all, the critics, who for me play a very important role. When I read criticism of buildings that I was designing in the sixties, I felt that I was not just losing readers, but that they were not reading into my abstractions what I expected. There is a difficulty in any abstract code. Of course, architecture, being geometric, uses the abstractions inherent in geometry. How is the architectural language understood when the surfaces of the building are neutral? When the textures, the chiaroscuro, the idea of the building have been abstracted to the point where they're non-figural? The kinds of attitudes I had about my architecture in the sixties are similar to the ones I have today, in terms of making a plan, making an enclosure, understanding the rites of passage relative to the dimensions of movement in a building. However, in the early work, I did not stress the more familiar and associative symbols of the culture. It seems to me that the problem is overcome to some extent when one accepts the abstract language which is necessary to any art form. We have to be, to some degree, abstract. We can't have any purposeful ambiguity in our language unless there are abstractions. But at the same time, we run the risk, if we are not figurative enough, of losing our audience. There has to be some balance between what is figurative, what is associational, what is understood as symbolic in terms of its figural association, and what is multifaceted in the sense that the abstraction allows the several readers of the composition to read what they want to into the composition. And so, over the last ten or fifteen years, there's been a gradual shift in my work because I've attempted that equity between the figurative and the abstract.

Diamonstein   Were those early white buildings meant to be colored?

Graves   In fact, they were; some of them are colored inside. We were five architects whom the press named the Whites, primarily because we had done more neutral abstracts, work based on early Le Corbusier, rather than work out of natural materials. However, from the first, John Hejduk and I placed a very strong emphasis on color. In my first two buildings, however, the clients felt that the color proposed was too much for the context. They said, "You're welcome to paint the inside of our buildings. Leave the outside alone." But more important, at that time, we were taking a kind of Neoplatonic stand about the idea of architecture being derived from general principles rather than from specific ones. The so-called Grays, the group of architects which included Venturi, Moore, Stern, *et al.* were seen as people who were deriving their compositions, in the conceptual stage at least, from an emphasis on the particular rather than on the general, as we did. Since that time, most from the "White" and/or the "Gray" school have seen an equity between those two positions. I'm not quite so feisty about being so overly general that the specific attitude of a local region can't play into the organization. Nor do I think that they, on the other hand, would disallow the general framework of their compositions to be more actively read.

Diamonstein You said that you felt your public and your critics were not reading your intent before this shift in your work. Did you doubt the validity of the earlier work? Or did you want to move closer to what you felt was the mood of your time?

Graves Well, I thought that even though I was convinced that it should be bloody apparent, that all those things that I was trying should be apparent to everybody else, I thought it was going to be a pretty lonely world out there for me, if I continued to speak what seemed to be a more or less private language. And the privacy of my language was not what interested me. In fact, being by nature a generalist, I very much wanted to include the mood, not just of the society but of the culture at large.

Diamonstein Is there such a thing as an architectural spirit of the time? Is that a simplistic notion?

Graves I think it's a pretty simple idea. There is no doubt, however, that we are influenced by the time. Mies van der Rohe said that architecture has to do with the will of the epoch. I doubt that Picasso had to do with the will of the epoch. He changed the way we saw by virtue of including the way we saw in a new way of seeing, a new series of ideas—cubism and other discoveries he made in the way we see. It seems to me that the artist or architect is required to understand the current condition of the society, his historical context, and then to take a critical view.

Diamonstein Both your architecture and your painting can stand on their own merits. They also inspire one another. Could you discuss for us the relationship your painting has to your architecture? Is it a hybrid?

Graves My painting is an extension of my architecture. At least it started that way. Painting allowed me to explore things I was not able to do in architecture, because of meager budgets, and so on. However, spatial and thematic ideas, which were endemic to both, allowed me to make a correspondence that otherwise would not have been possible. In painting, where I was my own client, I was able to express a richer dimension of those ideas. Lately, however, the painting and architecture have come together much more closely, as I suspected they would, and had wanted them to. Not so much because the budgets or the projects are more generous, but because I am more frugal with the gestures, both in architecture and in painting. I am now able to make references from one to the other which I think are more positive and engaging.

Diamonstein To the work of which artists do you most respond?

Graves That's very difficult. I'm an avid looker and reader of almost everybody's work. I read once that Robert Motherwell felt very guilty on Sunday afternoon when he did nothing but look at his picture books. I do the same thing. I look constantly. I look and draw what I see. And if I were looking at a painting by Matisse, or Morandi, or Mantegna, I would probably end up fixing the archetypal conditions of the painting in my memory by drawing them. So it's difficult to say there's one attitude, or one person that I would look to. There are attitudes in painting and architecture, however, that are extremely important. And they have less to do with classical ideas than with painting classifications.

Portland Public Service
Building, view from park,
Portland, Oreg., drawing

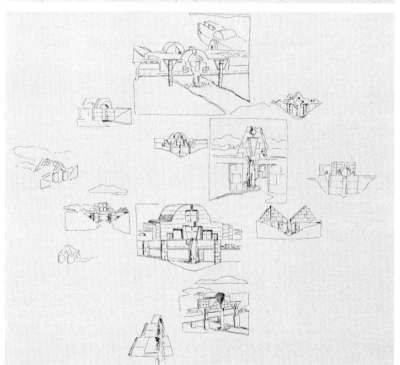

Fargo-Moorhead Cultural Center
Bridge, Fargo, N. Dak./
Moorhead, Minn., sketches

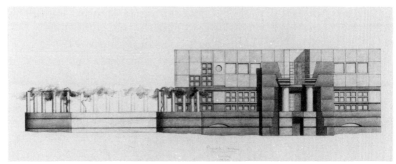

Plocek House, street
elevation, Warren, N.J.

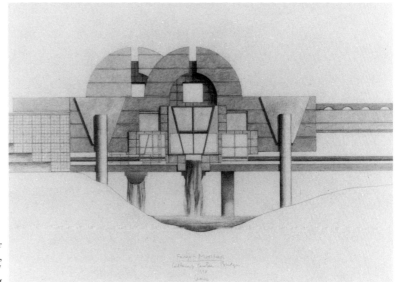

Fargo-Moorhead Cultural Center
Bridge, south elevation bridge,
Fargo, N. Dak./
Moorhead, Minn., drawing

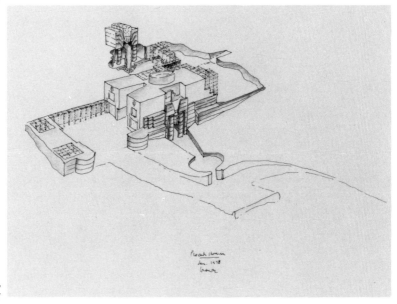

Plocek House, Warren, N.J.,
axonometric study

An essential role of painting and architecture, it seems to me, is to talk about differences, and ultimately to bring together, in a single composition, the classifications and hierarchies of elements and symbols which give the work thematic significance. Those are the kinds of paintings and architecture I look at most. I could mention the Cubists, but then, I could mention a good bit of the sixteenth century. It's not an easy thing for me to say Picasso, Raphael, Mantegna, to say Greek low-relief sculpture, antique sculpture. I can say those things, and they're the things that attract me; but the edges of those worlds are such, for me, that they tend to blur and meet in-between. I really look at everything I can.

Diamonstein Your most recent project that seems to bring together both your architectural and painterly concerns is the plan for a bridge, the Fargo-Moorhead Cultural Center that links the twin cities of Fargo, North Dakota and Moorhead, Minnesota, in a single structure spanning the Red River. I guess it's three buildings rather than one. A number of people have said that it is a project, a building, that shatters a lot of ideas about what a building should be like. How did you get the commission? Will it be built? and when?

Graves I got the commission by giving a lecture at the University of Virginia. (I always knew it would pay off, all that talking.) There happened to be a young man from North Dakota in the audience who later, after graduation, was asked by the city of Fargo to put together a list of one hundred architects across the country. But that was after they had asked this young architect, Royce Yeater, to show them the work of the three best architects that he knew. He said, "In what category do you mean, the three best architects? It's an interesting question." And they said, "Well, there's a Frenchman; there's Frank Lloyd Wright; and there's a Scandinavian—we've forgotten his name." I thought that was pretty good.

Diamonstein One out of three.

Graves He explained that there was a problem with all three of these people. And then they said, "Well, the next two or three that we know are the people who have been on the cover of *Time* magazine." There, you see, you strike again. And he said, "Who's that?" And they said, "Ed Stone and Yamasaki." And then he did a kind of soft-shoe shuffle, and said, "Well, maybe we ought to go to a larger list." He suggested that he do some research and put together a very pluralistic list. He evidently got the list from a publication by Charles Jencks, who's known to make lots and lots of lists. I asked Royce at one point how he knew, how he was able to develop this list. He said he took one from each camp, a Chinese menu. At that point, I suspected that we were all in trouble. But anyway, they showed work from that list to the Joint Cities Citizen Task Force. They selected a group of twenty, to whom they sent letters. From the responses to how we would go about making a composition for this particular place and function, they selected four architects to interview: Charles Moore, Hugh Hardy of Hardy Holzman Pfeiffer, Stanley Tigerman, and myself. We were lucky to win such a strong competition.

The project has been going on now for over two years. It's surrounded by local political controversy out there. Mayors have come and gone. Various funding agencies have been very generous to us and to the

Task Force. After we had done a kind of master plan for all three buildings, the "history museum" on the Moorhead, Minnesota side asked us to do the design development drawings, which we completed just last week. Presumably the working drawings will be done in the next eight or ten months. At least that third of it is going ahead in the next year.

Diamonstein In this instance, you have been able to transform your masterful, painterly collages into three-dimensional buildings. How close will the actual buildings be to the drawings?

Graves I think drawings are drawings and buildings are buildings. When I draw, I try to represent the idea of the building. The drawings, however, are in watercolor, or prismacolor, or graphite on paper, and therefore they cannot be a building. They can only be a representation of a building— critical intentions. They don't try to imitate reality. I don't expect my drawings to imitate my buildings any more than the reverse. Perhaps that is going too far. But nevertheless, I think that the point is to represent ideas of mass, of polychromatic value, of light and dark, of chiaroscuro, of the sense of space within a drawing, and to do the same within a building. There is a general tradition in architecture that sees drawings as tools for buildings. Those are our working drawings, with detailed specifications. But they don't try to represent ideas the way a conceptual drawing might.

Diamonstein Can you encapsulize your intentions in the Fargo-Moorhead project?

Graves Originally, we had wanted to defuse the competition between the two towns, Fargo and Moorhead, which are separated by the Red River of the North.

Diamonstein It's not a very wide river.

Graves No. Except when it floods in the spring, it's a very pleasant, canal-like river—about half the Tiber, I think. However, it is the traditional boundary, symbolizing competition and separation between Minnesota and North Dakota. Because of the size of those two towns, it was inappropriate to build two cultural centers. So, they did decide that, for a shared institution, perhaps a single architectural composition could reduce that problem of separate identities.

At first, we wanted to change the line of the river itself, to dam it up and make a centralized water garden that the buildings could surround. The water garden would become the focus, a center on the line of the river. That, as a formal strategy, simply wasn't possible, because of structural problems of the soil. So, instead, we focused the building over the river. It is a kind of linear gallery, a link between the history museum on the Minnesota side and the concert hall on the Fargo side. Each of the separate institutions is identified with its respective community. But the present art museum is not identified with either city and therefore we established it as the linking element in a single span over the river. Technically, that's not difficult. The idea of the Ponte Vecchio, or a bridge-building, is familiar from Palladio and others. Here, however, we made an enormous window, facing north, representing the permanent collection of the museum. On the southern side, there is another, similar window which opens to southern light, to a public porch on an upper level of the bridge. It looks down on the river, and the concert hall and its adjacent amphitheater so that people can lunch and hear noontime concerts from the bridge. Presently, they close the street and have chamber group concerts on the bridge at lunch (though I understand the trucks don't like it much). The association with the shoreline, the river, and the porch itself, was my way of describing volumetrically all those things which brought us there in the first place. So, the symbol of linkage was probably more important than the individual pieces.

Diamonstein Besides the cultural center, you have also designed museum spaces in New Jersey. What do you feel is the architect's role in designing display spaces?

Graves Well, I've been terribly influenced by other museums. The way to show objects has to do with putting them in rooms, not spaces. One should create an ambience around the object that encourages associations with the object. Without making period rooms, one can give an identity to a place that heightens the rhetorical value of the artifact to be shown. Of course, that is different from the neutral display that some modern architects seem to regard as essential. I would take the opposite point of view, and say that there should be a kind of debate between the room and the artifact, so that they both become more.

Diamonstein Have you employed that theory in the design of display spaces?

Graves Very little. At that point in any project, the budget is usually dwindling, so one can only make suggestions. In the Moorhead, Minnesota history museum, I have, however, described a linear series of rooms that take a kind of linear path through the chronology of the culture of that landscape. It's an agrarian-based society. I have described a series of rooms that will encourage that chronology. That isn't the case in the Union County [New Jersey] Museum, which is one of my first buildings. The work that I've done for the Newark Museum has had to do with education rather than with display.

Diamonstein Do you always create murals and interior works of art for your own buildings?

Graves I usually offer murals. Sometimes they're accepted, sometimes not.

Diamonstein About the converse of that situation: how do you feel about the use of works by other artists in the spaces you have designed?

Graves Well, occasionally, we've been asked to do interiors for private collections. Regardless of whether it's a modern collection or an antique collection, I would use the same principle.

Diamonstein How do you feel about doing a building for a collection of works of art that you don't like?

Graves It's a reasonable question. Though my taste is pretty inclusive, there are probably certain things that interest me more than others. For instance, I would rather make a museum for artifacts with a broad base in the culture, like the Moorhead museum than make a museum of pop art, because pop art, to me, is not inclusive enough to develop the kind of architectural ambience that interests me.

Diamonstein In a round-about way, we have been talking about the relationships between art and architecture. How do you view the possibilities of collaboration between artists and architects?

Graves As my work has been more widely published, I have gotten requests from several artists to collaborate on various projects. I am absolutely bowled over by the amount of common interest. I have to admit that I am not overwhelmed by much of what I see in the art world. But the people who have sent me slides of their work, in reaction to my own, have in many cases been interesting.

Diamonstein Have you ever collaborated with another artist?

Graves I haven't. No.

Diamonstein Would you like to?

Graves I think we probably will do it soon. We're doing a public project in Portland, Oregon in which one percent of the construction cost is given to art.

Diamonstein What about that project? I think it was awarded to you within just the last several days. It's also the largest commission you have ever received.

Graves I have mixed feelings about talking about it tonight, because the City Council is receiving the decision of the jury today. Since they're three hours behind us, I'll be on the phone this evening to find out what happened. This was a limited competition for what might be regarded as the city hall annex, called the Public Service Building. It's a twenty-two million dollar building which will collect the various city offices now scattered throughout Portland into a single building next to City Hall. It is a fine, turn-of-the-century, American Beaux-Arts building with some Ledoux-like episodes. The other competitors were Mitchell/Giurgola and Arthur Erickson. The jury recommended our scheme, but the local architects were furious. As I understand, the competition was originally the idea of Neil Goldschmidt, who is now the secretary of transportation. He was then mayor of Portland. He was a young, active mayor who used his eyes and traveled a lot. Although he knew that Portland's major office structures were amongst the best we have of modern architecture, he felt that there was something else going on in architecture as well, and that Portland was not getting its share. There was a worry that only the city's largest firms would continue, as they had in the past, to get all the major commissions, and that Portland might be foreclosing on other possibilities. So, before he left Portland, I understand that he suggested the competition and a number of lay citizens were selected for the jury. He then asked the jury to select an architectural advisor and they in turn asked Philip Johnson and John Burgee.

Somehow, our building is threatening to the status quo or the prevailing machine aesthetic, to the extent that the FAIA and Portland's professional old guard have joined together to protest to the City Council. So, today's vote is extremely important for us. Though we won the competition, the jury recommendation may be thrown out by the City Council. I'm not sure. My building is threatening because, as I said earlier, it attempts to make classical classifications. It suggests that the building has a base, and in the city the base is anthropomorphically understood as the foot. It's different from the shaft or body of the building which, in turn, is different from the head, or cornice, or capital. The local press has already labeled it "The Temple." At first, I guess, I did not want that to happen. But on reflection, that's really what one is after—making a building stand for something. The building is no longer primarily a metaphor for the machine: it instead has to do with the classical relationship between man and nature. Our building really does have a foot, made of a commercial street level shopping arcade, and then, just above, a number of public meeting rooms. The head of the building reflects the requirement that approximately a third of the building be rentable space. There is a break in the building at the tenth floor—this is a fifteen-story building—so the top five rental floors are supported by the city services below. So there is some literal symbolism in the building in terms of the idea of support; the structure of the building is represented in a somewhat anthropomorphic language.

We have used our one-percent allocation for art to redefine the city symbol, which is a woman holding a trident in one hand, and a wreath of wheat in the other, thereby saying something about port and land. She's been located above the doorway, to monumentalize the entrance. But we have evidently upset the local architects by using art again in some rather expansive garlands along the side of the building to give a traditional welcome to this new garden. That's how garlands or swags are traditionally used, not only in Manhattan but also in classical Portland. But this, too, is unorthodox—it's seen as frivolous, upsetting the prevailing hygienic aesthetic. I find that aesthetic so incredibly alienating that, I suppose, if I were bound to do that the rest of my life, I'd rather practice law.

Diamonstein It should have come as little surprise to that city, since your architecture has always dramatized everyday experience; entering a building has been a ceremonial drama in each of your buildings. Although it's immediately engaging, I've often wondered if there was a particular theoretical intention behind that drama. Is it the raised doorway, or is it the visual connection between the sky and the building, for example?

Graves Well, it can be all the things you say. But it came about in my work, I suppose, as a negative reaction to the simplified or stripped down idea of the "modern" threshold. Modern architecture sees space as primary. And I make a difference between the two, because, if you look at drawings and buildings by Mies van der Rohe, or Theo van Doesberg, or De Stijl, you see their influence on today's way of looking at the world as undifferentiated, homogenous space. Of course, space is continuous. But our culture needs separations between one point and another—outside versus inside. Now, in a way, we have the technical capacity to dissolve those differences. But if we do, we also dissolve the difference between the private and the public, the sacred and the profane. We destroy enclosive realms that have helped give identity to our society. We could say that in the passage through a building, there are a series of thresholds, of doorways, if you like, or even conditions of aesthetic framing as we pass from place to place, which enable us to label, understand, and identify those particular places. I try, in my work, not to suggest that closed is better than open. But to use one system without the other is, I think, limiting to one's palette. Just as we speak to each other face-to-face, there is a surface between us. Language is our way of making the window between the two of us. In making a conversation, we connect our differences. That mimetic and verbal interchange is a surface understanding that society requires. We have to find ways to get around that problem of homogenous, singular spatial sameness; and so, in my own work, I amplify that passage, the door, the window, the simple elements of which the architectural language is made—floors, ceiling, etc. Perhaps I go too far, for I'm also criticized for keeping these elements somewhat too separate.

Diamonstein You often describe architecture in terms of the sacred and profane. Are you suggesting that architecture is a kind of secular religion?

Graves No. I only mean it in the sense of cultural identity, that there are familiar places, as opposed to new, threatening, and "primitive" territories beyond them. If we make, or idealize, a place, in a sense we sanctify it—we identify with it. We regard our presence in it as central to it, and that is one way to differentiate the ideal from the primitive.

Diamonstein Your concern with architecture as the language of symbolic and functional elements is quite clear. What about the larger-scale symbolic elements? Many of your projects have been additions. Do you consider the additions, or the old houses, (the original structures themselves), as elements or fragments?

Graves Obviously, one must regard one's own contribution not as the last thing that will be done but, rather, as a fragment that becomes a part of the context. However, the difference between old and new is still felt within any composition, because we see certain things as representing newness, while other things represent earlier traditions which may, in turn, incorporate even earlier traditions. But it seems to me that all architecture is both a continual and fragmentary thing, and that an architect can express that fragmentary nature in his own work.

Diamonstein Your own work has incorporated many historical quotations. You've mixed elements of streamline design, Beaux-Arts classicism, futurism and constructivism to produce an unexpected combination of past, present, and future. Perhaps you could discuss a little more elaborately the tension between the notion of fragments and your underlying structure; that is, the general approach versus the specific solution to each project.

Graves The belief that every problem has its own solution is something that, though I didn't know him personally, was the basis of the work of architect, Eero Saarinen. My work is just the opposite, in that my works are related, one to the next. There are generalities and particularities that hold from one project to the next. That's not to say that one project will look like the next. But my general attitudes about human habitation don't change dramatically from one scheme to the next. However, there are obviously certain exaggerated programmatic requirements, certain functional or institutional requirements, that we fulfill which do require specific, not general, decisions. But that's not the norm. I tend to see my work, and architecture in general, in classifications that are primarily thematic and hierarchical—themes that are part of the ritual of passage, if you will. But the various aesthetic concerns that you suggested are embodied in my work are indeed there. I don't try to collage them into one inclusive composition. Instead, different attitudes or themes dominate in one area, while others dominate in other places. Isn't that the nature of narrative?

Diamonstein One interest does seem to stand out consistently in your work—its attitude toward nature. You assign meaning and hierarchy to colors by relating them to nature: sky, earth, and foliage. You use earthy colors like dark green and terra cotta at the base, and blue sky tones above. Why and how has representational color worked for you?

Graves As you have said, I don't attribute the same formal density to the coloration of a building as I do to other formal constructs. That's not to say that the color is additive. But the labyrinth of color does have a density that goes, I suppose, beyond the individual surface of a plane or volume. My color sense is very childlike in that the kind of description that you just made can be easily understood. I don't try to upset the code. If I'm to represent the ground plane, let's say, not only on the ground, but somewhere else in the building, as a new or transposed ground plane, one can imagine how that ground and the lower, "real" ground can be thought of and elaborated by color, by texture, and of course most importantly, by position. But without those thematic and formal designations, we run the risk of using a singular language. So, if your aesthetic is inclusive, then you have to question yourself about making the composition around a color code as well as a formal code. Those two things should identify and amplify each other.

Diamonstein It's been said that you are lovingly and painstakingly inventing a different language of form and meaning, which leaves the post-modernists behind. How do you react to statements like that?

Graves I don't think vocabularies are invented. I don't wake up in the morning trying to do so. I was surprised to read that.

Diamonstein Were you pleased?

Graves No. Though it was meant as a positive assessment of my work, I took some exception to the idea of my making a "different" language. I think that any language is only worth its salt as its general meanings are understood. Changes to the language are only the kind of changes one would experience from, say, prose to poetry. One can of course subvert or invert the language, but one must first have the common language to speak at all. So that, as you said earlier, the base to my building is terra cotta, or that the soffit is azure blue, then you are, as I am, expressing meaning within our accepted formal language. But if at the same time I make an inversion, I want you to be aware of the way that I have used the language. However, without a common language, architecture is finished.

Diamonstein Do you expect the viewer to respond that way? That list-maker that you mentioned, Charles Jencks, once referred to the Snyderman House in Fort Wayne, as a cross between a Gris and a Mondrian, a stucco box waiting to get out of its cage. Do you intend the viewer to interpret things that way?

Graves Well, I always expect Charles to label things, though some of his labels are not my labels. He is, nevertheless, one more "viewer" and as such, his take on the object is as valid as the layman's. I do think that he often tries to put himself in the layman's shoes and thereby "reads" the work somewhat simply.

Diamonstein How would you describe the Snyderman House?

Graves About the way he did. The building was first designed in 1968, and finally finished in about 1972. The building is a little over-zealous, but it was one of the first times out, and I did what I thought was appropriate. It is a kind of Neoplatonic frame, if that's what Charles means by

Mondrian. It's based on the gridding found in the Maison Domino of Le Corbusier. Within it, there is a freer play of the surrounding and enclosing surfaces, the walls and the plan that is engaged by those walls. These rooms are not trying to escape the grid, but are in a kind of debate with it. One could play the neutrality of the structure against the particularity of what I was then attributing to the various sides of the local conditions, the entry against the view, the west light against the north light. And then, as I turned up the rheostat on those surfaces, they moved relative to the neutrality of that frame. I thought that by using a standard language, I could then put the poetic language against it, and the contrast of the two would be worthwhile. However, it was one of those buildings that has had very few readers. Modern Architecture's last stand.

Diamonstein There are certain constant themes and motifs in your work, such as the keystone. What is the significance of the voided keystone?

Graves Well, in the Fargo project, the keystone was my attempt to use an architectural element that is in the public domain. The window and the door are similar elements. Of course, the architect used the keystone as symbol. The keystone is not necessary to the actual construction of that building. If you eliminate the pragmatic value in any form, you tend to heighten its symbolic value. So I voided the keystone, in a sense made a window out of it—hence Mrs. Huxtable's references before concerning a different language. But if the window and the keystone remain, though superimposed, it seems to me that I could heighten the identity of that center portal of the bridge.

Diamonstein Which of your unbuilt buildings brings you the most pleasure?

Graves Oh, my. The next one.

Diamonstein And which of your built buildings?

Graves I really don't have favorites. It would be simple to say the one I am working on or the one that's under construction, because one is constantly engaged in the present. But in my case, I guess that's not true. I don't mean to be saccharine about this, but there's a different lesson in each. I regard them as very important to me, and the way I reinterpret them is part of my own education.

Diamonstein In your reassessments, other than your self-effacing comment on the Snyderman House, are there any that you would build differently now?

Graves Yes. I think that in the early houses the language that I used was overly abstract. As I remember, Jack Robertson called the Benacerraf House a kind of hay thrasher in the garden—perhaps tough criticism—but the building was a bit frantic. At the time, I didn't see it that way. But if I were to put it next to buildings I am designing now, I seem to be slightly more clear and economical in my intentions. However, I still have enormous interest in certain passages in buildings such as the Benacerraf House, and still lecture about them because some of those things have not been played again, simply because the place or the situation hasn't been right. But in no place else have I been able to construct a kind of garden metaphor as literally and as abstractly, with that kind of equity, as I did in the facade of the Benacerraf House. Though other parts of it, perhaps, aren't as I would have them today, that particular part of it is still instructive to me.

Diamonstein How lasting do you think the architecture of the seventies will be?

Graves I have a hard time with such a temporal question. I just don't think that way. Looking the other way, though, my general criticism of the work of the sixties or the fifties, when I was being trained, as well as of my own work, becomes extremely important for the next thing that I do. But I can't tell what the future will bring. I am, in that way, not interested in the future. I don't believe in progress in art, and therefore tomorrow is the future. But tomorrow is also simply very much like today. I tend to think of my work not so much as based in the past either, at least not in the sense of stylistic references. I do think of my work as using archetypal conditions of the past and present. By the emphasis of the archetype, I would try to skirt the stylistic problems found in present versions of modernism.

CHARLES GWATHMEY

Charles Gwathmey
Born Charlotte, N.C., 1938
University of Pennsylvania, 1956-59
M. Arch. Yale University, 1962

Diamonstein Charles Gwathmey is widely known for his elegant houses and thoughtful solutions for institutional buildings, as well as his fine interior design. Gwathmey Siegel and Associate Architects is now one of the city's leading architectural firms, designing new housing for Columbia University and Roosevelt Island, some office buildings, and several large houses. You were once a member of the so-called New York Five, otherwise known as the White Architects. But unlike your colleagues Richard Meier and Michael Graves, your work was never pure white. Does that have to do with the fact that after studying at the University of Pennsylvania, you graduated from the Yale School of Architecture? That school has fostered a nominal respect, at least, for the specifically American context and the practical necessities of construction. The point is, how did you manage to go to Yale, and then become a White, instead of a Gray?

Gwathmey Well, you don't plan your life that way. I mean, I didn't know the New York Five was going to exist. I didn't know I was going to go to Yale. And I didn't know it was going to mean anything now. Let me just clarify about the New York Five. It's not a school. It was a publication that Peter Eisenman, who's the head of the Institute of Architecture and Urban Studies, decided to do. The most important thing about it was, I think, that it began the whole discussion among architects, teachers and students about the ideas of architecture. For the first time in a long, long time, people began debating and talking about buildings again—and buildings as ideas, and buildings as art. From that point of view, it was a very pertinent document. Afterwards, many people saw it and decided to make separations, and began putting people in schools or groups, and talking about people being grays, or whites, or whatever. I don't know about the gray.

Diamonstein Is there any real distinction between the two groups?

Gwathmey Oh, yes. I think the original five architects—and certainly other people could be included—were really interested in the European intellectual basis for architectural ideas. The other so-called group was more interested in the American vernacular and that tradition. I think the two points of view are different. They overlap, but I would say the American point of view was very literal, and the other tended to be more abstract. One was representational, and the other was not, and I think that was the difference. It made a lot of people very upset, which I never understood.

Diamonstein Did you ever quite fit into that New York Five group, which was six before it was publicly proclaimed five? By the time that the book was published you had taken a partner, Robert Siegel. Did you ever really fit into that group, since you were always profoundly interested in built work?

Gwathmey Like I said, it wasn't a group. We were all associated through teaching, and we've been friends and not friends over the years.

Diamonstein What is the current status?

Gwathmey The current status is that we all communicate. It's essentially looking at the work, and criticizing. About a month ago, we all had dinner together to celebrate John Hejduk's show. It was a marvelous evening, because John and everybody told stories about how and why it happened. In retrospect, it's fairly amazing that it ever got to be. We all laughed about it, you know, because it was a kind of time and incident that provoked enough interest to make what's happening today available—meaning that there's a huge debate about architecture and its relevance, and post-modernism and how it relates, if it does, and so forth.

Diamonstein So you never really expected the media or the profession to proclaim what you were doing as a specific school?

Gwathmey No. I think it's interesting that it did. I think it shows that there's an insecurity about identity. People like to identify groups. Code names are efficient and seem simpler. But I never thought the names or any of the work were very simple, either.

Diamonstein We have been talking with Frank Gehry. As you know, his interest in industrial materials and the aesthetic of the incomplete contrast very sharply with your great concern for expensive and rich materials. The wood of your cabinet work, the glass of the walls, the metal, the detail—all seem to celebrate these materials with very great precision. Why do you choose those materials? What are you trying to convey by them?

Gwathmey I disagree. I think that historically our work has also relied on available industrial materials and products. We've tended to reinterpret their value, and developed a kind of an aesthetic in the process. The materials may appear refined and expensive, but that's not the intention. For instance, glass block, metal pan ceilings have historically been used in kitchens, restaurant kitchens—all of the metals that you said looked so refined are all available products that have had other aesthetic value implications imposed upon them. We have tried to take these materials and reinvolve them perceptually, put them in a different context where they take on a new life. Therefore, you identify them as being fancy.

Diamonstein I don't know if that was exactly the word I used.

Gwathmey Refined and rich.

Diamonstein Paul Rudolph says, and I would agree with him, that your work can be read in many ways. Is there a single theory or ideology that would de-scribe your style?

Gwathmey I think our work really has to do with being intensely responsive to the program, to the site constraints, to an idea that a building must first perform its role. Then the building transcends that, and becomes a work of art. Now, that's not so much a style as an idea—it's an attitude about architecture. Our process begins with understanding the problems, and trying to establish hierarchies and priorities in the problem, and then legitimately trying to solve that problem with a certain, I hope, clear attitude about the manifestation of the problem as an object. So how it gets to be what it looks like is as pragmatic as the process of constructing. We learn as we build, and we believe in building.

Diamonstein Are there any architects to whose work you especially respond, and who have heavily influenced your work?

Gwathmey I respond a great deal to Frank Gehry's work, and to him. I think Jim Stirling, the English architect, has had the most influence on me—not necessarily stylistically, but as someone who believes in the building ethic, and has used what, again, I would call industrial materials, or industrial systems. He has been able to put them together in a most unique and, I would say, pragmatic way. And of course I look back to Le Corbusier and Frank Lloyd Wright as great influences on the way we think about space.

Diamonstein How has your own basic design vocabulary evolved in the ten years that Gwathmey Siegel has been in practice?

Gwathmey Initially, when we began in the sixties there was, at least as I look back on it, a great gap between the ideal and the condition of the times—in other words, the Vietnam war. I was teaching school. Students were upset. They couldn't face the rigors; they couldn't understand the discipline of architecture while we were having assassinations and problems with the political system. All those things made me pull back from that kind of identification with the system. I think architecture was very, very Jesuit as a result. It sort of stripped itself. It became extremely abstract, relied totally on its own self-exposure and was, in fact, minimal. As time has gone on, and as one learns and continues, I think we're at a point now where architecture is being reevaluated, both by us, and by people that work with us. We're interested in the reenrichment of the work—making it more complex—but also maintaining the clarity and the rigor of the spatial order. I think the two things are consistent. The old work is not illegitimate, and it has a very strong influence on the present work.

Diamonstein One of your buildings still has a strong influence on houses of our time. It was your first really major construction and perhaps your first major project, and that is the house and studio that you did in Amagansett in 1967 for your parents—your father, the distinguished easel painter, Robert Gwathmey, and your mother, Rosalie Gwathmey, a photographer. The house itself is a composition of cubes and cylinders, with slanted roofs, and vertical wood siding. How does it look to you now?

Gwathmey It looks terrific.

Diamonstein What do you think of its imitators?

Gwathmey I don't think about that. If you start thinking about imitators, then you start thinking about problems. It gets insidious, and you stop doing what you're supposed to be doing.

Diamonstein How differently, if at all, would you do that house now?

Gwathmey That's an impossible question. I think that house is strong, because it's responsive. It was so clear and so small. It's a composite of a whole education and a whole experience I had, and it was the perfect opportunity. My parents were perfect clients. They really wanted me to make a work. They were supportive.

Diamonstein As artists themselves with singular points of view, did they collaborate with you?

Gwathmey Not at all. They were actually more removed from the participation than most clients. We had a piece of land, and they had a certain amount of money, and no contractor on Long Island would touch it. I wound up building it myself with some workers from Brooklyn. We all went out, and built the building. It cost thirty-five thousand dollars.

Diamonstein That's twenty-six houses and thirteen years ago. You are currently building a summer house in a neighboring community, a summer house for a client at a cost of approximately one and one-half million dollars. Do you consider this house a summary of your other work?

Gwathmey No. That's interesting. It's hard to talk about architecture, and not see it. What happens, I think, when you teach, and when you have an opportunity like this to reflect on what you make, you always consider houses buildings—in other words, our houses have a tendency to be more general about ideas. They talk about orientation and view and site and weather, and how they're built, and so forth. They tend to have less to do with identifying the specific personality of the clients.

This house has afforded us an opportunity to make a summary, having gone through a sequence of learning and building other buildings. It's very rich programmatically. The two people working with us in our office are young and energetic and smart as hell, and they are making us push all the time to confront all the issues that we've touched, or missed, in our history of buildings. It's become a very valuable growth period. In that sense, I hope it's going to be, if it's worth it—a summary of all the other buildings.

Diamonstein   Can you describe some of the issues including the programmatic ones that you are confronting, as well as this rich program to which you refer, this spatial, horizontal layering plan?

Gwathmey   What interests me is that in the past we were very interested in architecture as an object. That was clearly and more precisely expressed when the program was smaller. You could really compose a building—you could make a composite object that was highly articulated. Going through the process we have found that we've had to pull the building apart sometimes; sometimes the building no longer holds together perceptually as an object, but it does something else—maybe it makes a place. I have felt a kind of need to return to the richness and the clarity of the object, while simultaneously making it complex as a place. With all of the complexity of program—a greenhouse in the building, five bedrooms, a library, a sitting room, a projection room—it's a fancy thing. You put all this together intending to make an object, like in my parent's house, and that's what's terribly exciting about it. It's also very challenging. Every intersection, every layer, every spatial move, both vertically and horizontally, has an amazing impact on how the building develops and how, finally, it's perceived. That's a great opportunity.

Diamonstein   You speak about the opportunity of the ideal client—like your parents— which, I assume, doesn't happen very often. What about the relationship between architect and client—particularly in a project like this, a part-time summer residence?

Gwathmey   I don't think you should make a value judgment about that. If you say part-time residence, summer residence, that implies, at least to me, that it's less pertinent somehow. Right? When one says you're building a summer residence, then it's extravagant. That's a value judgment, and I don't think architecture should ever carry a value judgment.

Diamonstein   I was referring more to location than to price and extravagance.

Gwathmey   Okay. But you know what I'm saying?

Diamonstein   I do.

Gwathmey   I think a work of art is a work of art, whether it's used in the summer, or whether it's perceived by people walking down the beach, or in an airplane. The idea, the process is critical. The fact that the object is perceived by however many and whether it's summer, winter, or year round should not be an issue. At least it's not an issue to me.

Diamonstein   Let's talk about the client, and the issues for him or her. How much of the job should emerge out of the problem as the client has defined it? How much of any such project is the result of a preconceived style or notion? How responsive can you be to a client's needs in doing a house without really compromising your intentions as an artist?

Gwathmey Well, two things. One is that I believe that clients come to an architect like us, because they're familiar with the work, and have an affinity to it.

Diamonstein Initially. . .

Gwathmey It's been fairly consistent that people who don't know our work are either shocked immediately and disappear, or they stay. There's really no middle ground. So, this client did know the work. What we tend to do to make the piece of art, since we do teach, and since we do feel that we're obligated to talk about the art ultimately, is we find out all the programmatic issues, all of the client's likes and dislikes, all the hates, all the preconceptions—we really want to know. Sometimes it's more or less extreme. We make that a body of information. Then we talk about the site, the whys and the wherefores of the view, privacy, and so forth. We talk about basic, organizational possibilities, which I see as very factual things. They're not preconceptions; they're not things that are automatically going to make a design, but they're things we have to understand. When you put this together with a point of view, which comes from that body of information and the site—where it is, and how you build—you start to make a work. Our tendency is to be very informative, maybe over-informative to the client, as to why we're doing something. I think it's part of educating the client, and I don't mean it negatively, because he, she, or they participate in the process—in the sense that they are ultimately the initial user. They deserve the experience of learning why something got to be what it got to be, when it's something that's so private, yet not treated necessarily as private. They tend to become terribly supportive, and terribly involved in the ultimate expression. They want it to go as far as we can make it. They want us to extend ourselves, because we're extending them, and it becomes a mutual support system—which is the only way.

Diamonstein You are especially interested in the inside versus the outside. One of your houses, the Kislevitz House in Westhampton, New York, is referred to as a renovation, although it is essentially a new building. It's also an interesting lesson in assemblage and in fixed elements and the intricate interpenetration of space.

Gwathmey Well, we take any problem that offers a design opportunity, and that building was one of those old Spanish-style, neo-neo-Colonial white elephants that was literally dropped on the Sound in Westhampton. It had no view of the water and was totally dark inside. It was really a very strange assemblage of Spanish-tile roofs and configurations. The real pertinent part of doing that building was first to understand how it got to be put together the way it did, to find the organizing principles of the basic building, and then to literally reweave a brand-new program, a brand-new building within it, and also around it. I mean, extend it, and also work within it. I think constraints are very important. They're positive, because they allow you to work off something. The constraint we established was to keep all of the different roof configurations, and the original foundations. We planned to work off of those two items to intensify the basic strength of the original building, by modulating it with a new environment, and new forms. It's really the most intense kind of juxtaposi-

Gwathmey Residence,
exterior,
Amagansett, N.Y.
Picture credit: Charles Gwathmey

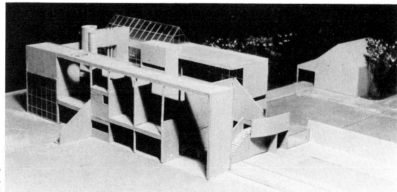

Long Island Residence,
exterior,
Long Island, N.Y., model

Kislevitz Residence, hall
from second level balcony,
interior, Westhampton, N.Y.
Picture credit: Norman McGrath

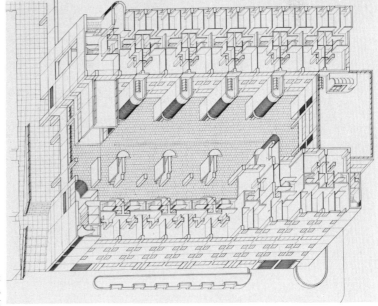

Columbia University, East
Campus Housing, New York,
N.Y., axonometric drawing

tion that one could have. I always said, if I didn't make that roof, I could work off of it. You're doing two things at once something which I would be more hesitant to do if I were starting from scratch.

Diamonstein I know you are interested in an architecture of permanence. But in a project such as that, why wouldn't you start from scratch?

Gwathmey Because his wife liked the building. She liked the old Spanish-style roofs, and she had a vision of a Southern plantation house, which is not bad. So that was fine.

Diamonstein What did she get?

Gwathmey She got a Southern plantation house.

Diamonstein On the outside?

Gwathmey No, no. She got the whole thing. It's terrific. You know, Southern plantation house only means that it's a building that establishes a sense of place. It has a certain presence. It has a program which is accommodating; it participates with the land, and it offers itself to the user as a rich establishment. I don't mean rich, money rich, I mean rich perceptually. Reinterpretation is all art is, anyway, and all architecture keeps doing is reinterpreting history. So, I think she got it and so did we.

Diamonstein What's the difference between building and architecture?

Gwathmey By definition, building is making shelter. Building is construction. Architecture is design, and hopefully art. So there's a big difference from my point of view.

Diamonstein What is the historical responsibility of the architect?

Gwathmey From our point of view, the responsibility is to understand the principles of the history of architecture—not necessarily the stylistic implications, but the reasons why buildings or towns or whatever were organized, and how they were organized. It's interesting when you think of a courthouse, which is the oldest organizational idea you know. You go to Pompeii, and then you go to the Renaissance palazzo, and then you keep going, and if you just sort of understand why they are, and how they got to be, that principle can be reinstituted today, redefined, yet with the same logic and the same consistency. In other words, it would be a very valid proposition to design a courthouse, if the site, and if all of the other constraints implied that was a legitimate solution.

Diamonstein But you are *not* implying that historical quotation is the legitimate solution for today's—

Gwathmey I'm not interested in historical quotation, *per se,* as a stylistic idea. I like to understand historical styles, but I prefer not to apply them.

Diamonstein It's been said that in part, your firm's success is due to your relationship with your partner, your classmate and chum from the High School of Music and Art, Robert Siegel. Did you know way back then that you would share such common ground? How did the partnership come about?

Gwathmey Well, we played ball together in high school. He went away to school, and I went away to school, and we came back together at Edward Barnes's office. He was an associate and was very happy with that state of his life. I always had the fix to open up my own office. My parents' house came along about that time, and I left Ed's office. Sooner or later, there was some work, and I went and talked to Bob. The amazing thing about the partnership, I think, is that we're both highly competitive and goal-oriented people, but we're not competitive with each other. It's a fantastic relationship, because I really think we complement each other and work together. It's an amazing kind of condition.

Diamonstein Well, that's nice. It's interesting to refer to it as a condition. When you and Siegel designed the Thomas and Bett Building, the vice president of the company said, "Sometimes Charles Gwathmey would make what I thought were pie-in-the-sky proposals, but Robert Siegel and I would modulate them, and make them work within the budget." Is that the way your relationship with Siegel often works?

Gwathmey No. That's press. That's the Five Architects people.

Diamonstein How does it work? What's the reality of the situation on an ongoing basis? Are you both involved in the design of each project?

Gwathmey We're both involved in the design all the way through. We work with the other people in the office, and the more involved they get, the better we are, I think. The real difference between us is that my energies, as opposed to Bob's, can go off on tangents. I tend to think about a lot of things at the same time. Happily, he likes to concentrate on a single thing at a single time. What people say about how people work is really funny. We both come and work, and we love to do buildings, and we work well together. He may modulate the vice president from Thomas and Betts, and I may modulate the president from Columbia University in another way. Right?

Diamonstein For the last three years, the project that has been engaging your interest and energies is the eighteen-million-dollar residential and academic cloister that you have designed for the Columbia University campus. You had an entirely new notion of how to deal with students; your intent was to deal with students as individuals instead of as categories. Did you have to modulate the president of Columbia University, and in what respect?

Gwathmey That's an interesting project, because it's our first major New York urban project. It's terribly intense, because of the constraints and the existing conditions of the Columbia-Morningside Park fabric. It's a very complex program. Columbia is a very, very dense client with layers of authorities. What we really tried to do is understand that the dormitory *per se* was no longer a viable building type. A student needs and should have the same amenities as someone who would go out and rent an apartment—basically, it's that simple. So the building was organized around privacy, with the idea that four students in private bedrooms share a common living room, dining room and kitchen. The idea was to give the student identification, a sense of place in an architectural organization that was at once small—a college or a building—and then relate to the larger university. All of those things were important. When the design, which was the first design, was approved by the board of trustees and the president, Bob and I got drunk one night, and looked at each other, and both said that we thought Columbia was awful.

Diamonstein You mean, the project you had designed.

Gwathmey Right. We felt that we were pressured falsely into proposing what we had. We felt like we should redesign it. And when we told that to the president, we were almost fired. Instead, a new platform was elevated off of the street level to make the connection between the Columbia campus level and the New York City level. All the implications about neighborhood, and Columbia opening itself up to the neighborhood, had a very critical part in determining how the building was organized. The group of buildings, is really a complex that is at once an edge to the New York City grid on Morningside Park, and a gateway to the campus. It ties together a lot of separate buildings and entrances that previously had no identity of place; you just sort of found them. It also really does make a major outdoor space on its own—a court space, which organizes the entire plan. And it speaks to issues that run the gamut of the urban scale, from underground parking to safety, to security. When you look at it, it looks very simple; it's really about a cloister. The notion of a cloister is that you enter it, and you are then in your own domain, and all of the entrances, all of the houses are working off of that central space—both actually and perceptually. That's a device which is not new.

Diamonstein What is new is that this is the first dormitory Columbia University has constructed in over twenty years.

Gwathmey *That's* new.

Diamonstein It's also the kind of job that usually goes to larger, or more commercially-oriented architectural firms. How did you get that assignment?

Gwathmey Jim Polshek was the dean at the Columbia School of Architecture. I think an architecture school should have a practicing and design-oriented dean, because not only does the school become involved in the idea of design, but the dean has a certain impact upon the building decisions that a university makes. This has been the first time, I think, in a long time that the architecture school participated in the choice. He made a list of the architects that he thought would be responsive and we were so charming, that we got the job.

Diamonstein At Columbia University, and at your very important renovation—in fact, an award-winning one—at Princeton University, the university setting provided a specific kind of opportunity and a particular obligation for design. In your design for the burnt-out Whig Hall, you worked out juxtapositions of old and new scales and old and new monumentality. Tell us about that building and about the obligation/opportunity that you think an architect has, especially when working in a university setting.

Gwathmey If you're a teacher, you're also a student, because you learn from students and you learn by teaching. You also learn from what you make. The Whig Hall opportunity was wonderful, because it spoke to the classic sort of precedent for a building organization—a temple. In 1970, a brand-new program came about. The problem was to reconcile, not restore the old building, at least internally, to what it used to be, to literally build a new building within the old building, saving the critical pieces to speak to the relevancies of historical precedent. We wanted to use the opportunity to try to develop a dialogue between the possibility of maintaining the critical pieces of old, and the critical pieces of new, and to have them work satisfactorily. Also, being in a university, there was obviously the opportunity for students to learn from that possibility, both during construction, and later when the building was used. The university gives the building a kind of exposure which it ordinarily wouldn't have. The university is a laboratory and, I think, therefore, a wonderful, challenging place to build buildings.

Diamonstein It is not only a challenge, but obviously didactic in nature. I have often wondered if the fact that your father was a painter, and such a widely-recognized one, had any influence on your own work.

Gwathmey I don't think it has an impact on why my work looks as it does. But he and my mother certainly had a powerful impact on me. Since both were in the visual arts and always had their studios in our house, I was constantly exposed to that life. I think I understood that the idea of creating something was pertinent and satisfying. My father taught at Cooper Union, and I watched and lived a way of life. They forced me to be exposed. They made me go to every museum and every cathedral in Europe with them when I was eleven, sometimes against my wishes.

Diamonstein You preferred to go alone?

Gwathmey I preferred not to go at the time. But that had real meaning. I don't know if I understood what I was looking at. But I certainly had a different sense about it, and a remembrance of it, because I documented it. I drew; I bought postcards; I made notes; I remembered just from my own sort of recollection. My parents have always been terribly supportive of the idea that I be something else besides an artist. I still do have roots, and a certain amount of passion for the South.

Diamonstein You were able to satisfy Mrs. Kislevitz's need for plantation architecture with some ease. Have you ever collaborated with an artist yourself?

Gwathmey No.

Diamonstein Would you like to?

Gwathmey I'm not sure. I sort of agree with Frank Gehry about that. I thought he said it very well that collaboration automatically implies a compromise. As I think I told you one time, the reason that sculptors put a piece in front of a building is to sort of make the building more relevant. That's really why they do it. That's why clients buy art. The architecture is not what it should be, so the art makes it more acceptable.

Diamonstein That's an especially cynical view, particularly for an artist's son . . .

Gwathmey No. The cynical view is why people purchase art in that context. I don't think the Picasso in Chicago's Hancock Building had to do with collaboration. I think one person built the building, and another person bought the object. And there they are together. It's fantastic.

Diamonstein But in the future, either by gentlemen's agreement with the General Services Administration, or by mandate in approximately seventeen cities and about twenty-one states, one-half to one percent of construction costs will be earmarked for art. So, willy-nilly, that process of collaboration could/ should/ must take place. What do you envision as its future and its possibility?

Gwathmey Well, as an architect, I have to say that if that's true, and if one believes in the artist participating and enriching a space, which certainly one can believe in as one designs buildings and thinks about perception, I would have to consider the artist's contribution as an integral part of the program and design process. Almost in an architectonic sense, one can understand that that could be a possibility and a reality, and think about it in those terms. Right? I don't want to sound like it's compromising. But I don't think that I could ever design a space simultaneously with an artist for the sake of collaboration.

Diamonstein Could you envision any relationship with an artist?

Gwathmey Oh, sure. I think an architect who designs a museum or gallery or apartment or house that will contain art has to think about it positively. That doesn't mean collaboration should exist on the initial level in the design. I find that problematic.

Diamonstein Because you don't want to take external cues from someone else's intention?

Gwathmey No. I think that I really don't think that way. I'm not saying that I couldn't think that way. Let's say I haven't thought that way. The buildings that we're making are objects on their own terms and have many, many implications about form and sculpture and everything that we would identify or define as art. I never thought that they would rely on, or be necessarily beholden to a collaboration.

Diamonstein Circulation seems to be at the heart of your design, the spaces in-between. I suppose that includes the process of layering space. Would you say that, in general, your spaces are becoming more densely layered?

Gwathmey I think as the programs become more complex, the opportunity to layer space is more available. I think there are different ways of talking about layering of space. Space is three-dimensional in the volumetric element, and layering *per se*—at least the way it's being used by other practitioners—has a different implication. You can layer space, but you can also layer planes or surfaces. We try to enrich the space, rather than the surface. Spatial interpenetration, overlap, and intersection interests us. Our buildings are volumetric. They are space-reliable. They are less about the so-called applied surface notion of enrichment than they are about the nature and the whys and the wherefores of the space.

Diamonstein One of the ways that you extend that enrichment is with your very skillful use of interior design. Do you ever conceive of doing interior and exterior design simultaneously as was done during the nineteenth century?

Gwathmey We do—yeah. We don't think that the eye really separates. If a building is talking about transparencies, and talking about inside and outside simultaneously, one could not but design them simultaneously, and perceive them simultaneously.

Diamonstein But you have done fine interior designs exclusive of the exterior.

Gwathmey Right. We've done extensive interior designs. The opportunity there is very much like the Kislevitz House—working within constraints, within a given reference. The idea is to really explore the notion of one's perception of space, to make environments, to use that opportunity as a kind of learning laboratory about things we would not tend to initiate in a new building. The design of interiors has been another piece in the puzzle to help us, again, understand how to enrich and make more complex the new buildings that we're doing now. They feed upon and support one another. . . .

Diamonstein Do you feel restricted, when you have to respond to the client's demands in that kind of situation?

Gwathmey No. I'm glad to have it. I think the most impossible problem is to design in a vacuum—no program, no site. That would be almost impossible for me to conceive. The more information and so-called constraints we have, and the clearer the opportunity and the references, then the more clear, supportive, and accurate the design is which will be built.

Diamonstein What are your best unbuilt projects, and why weren't they built?

Gwathmey I don't know. The best unbuilt project probably started with a house we did in Malibu, which sort of reinterpreted the whole notion of the strip and the edge, and of making a layered building. It started to deal with the oceanside and the roadside and that whole notion of strip architecture, which didn't happen. We tried to reapply the same principles about a year ago on another house that didn't get built.

Diamonstein You abandoned that plan?

Gwathmey No. But all buildings have references. Some buildings that are detached have urban implications. In other words, a building on an ocean, on a dune, where there are a lot of buildings all lined up for the specific purpose of the view and the edge are really no different conceptually than row houses. If you conceive of the urban implications of that, you would tend to design a building in a line differently than you would design a building in the middle of a field. But I don't think about unbuilt things. I think that when you go through the process and design something, it's just another important piece in one's development. You always want to build them, at least I do, but I'm also happy that we had an opportunity to go through the process, because it still informs.

HUGH HARDY

Hugh Hardy
Born Majorca, Spain, 1932
B. Arch. Princeton University, 1954
M.F.A./Arch. Princeton University, 1956

Diamonstein Hugh Hardy is a partner in the New York firm of Hardy Holzman Pfeiffer Associates, one of the most closely-watched younger firms in the nation. Besides actively designing new buildings, the firm has been a leader in attracting attention to the need for the preservation and reuse of older structures. Hardy Holzman Pfeiffer has led the way in renovation of historic and many non-historic older buildings, ranging from the Carnegie Mansion, which now houses the Cooper-Hewitt Museum, to schools, hospitals, residences, train stations and community centers across the country. Among the firm's best-known buildings are the Mount Healthy School; the Columbus Occupational Health Center in Columbus, Indiana, that remarkable town full of unusual architecture; the Firemen's Training Center on Ward's Island in New York City; new symphony halls in Minneapolis and Denver, and the recently dedicated Civic Center in Madison, Wisconsin.

The firm is headquartered far away from the lush uptown quarters of such offices as Johnson-Burgee and I. M. Pei. Hardy Holzman Pfeiffer occupies a floor in a Park Avenue South building in the low-rent East Twenties. The offices are full of loud-patterned carpets, bright lights and memorabilia-filled walls, including numerous awards for excellence. It's obviously not Skidmore, Owings & Merrill, but then again neither is the firm's architecture. In fact, Hugh, most of your firm's renovations are by no means the understated, spare, well-bred restorations that one might expect from the Cooper-Hewitt. Far more often, they are brash and bold, full of primary colors, big patterns and bright lights. Two of your projects in New York City are museums. One is the Children's Museum across the river in Brooklyn. It is almost the perfect opposite to the Cooper-Hewitt. How is it that your two New York museums are so very different, or are they in fact different?

Hardy They are both a transformation of an institution. The Cooper-Hewitt was privately funded, and it took a long time to renovate. The Cooper-Hewitt grew out of Cooper Union into a new identity, a new building with new support by the Smithsonian, a new perception about its collection and its role in the community. All this was due to a large extent to its director. The Children's Museum was in a condemned building and was moving to a new environment thanks to a new director, new resources, and city funding. The two are certainly, in terms of the vocabulary used, quite different. But they also have similarities, although I guess it's somewhat forced to say they are the same. Our design for the Children's Museum—which was designed about twelve years ago—was an attempt to buy the maximum volume of space with limited resources and to achieve as much spatial variety as possible, without a clear definition of the program. At the Cooper-Hewitt, we had a fixed series of volumes, a very clear definition of program, and again limited resources. It was built in phases over a two year period. Both were very difficult projects technically, because of the problems of a phased construction sequence. So I suppose they're the same and they're not.

Diamonstein Your firm has designed many buildings for the arts, including the performing as well as the visual arts. Often, the interaction between art, artists and their public, and flexible spaces appears to be a part of your design philosophy. I am thinking not only of the museums we have just mentioned, but also the Adelphi University Theater, an environment that emphasizes the relationship between the performer and the spectator, and the multipurpose Performing Arts Center in Artpark, in Lewiston in up-state New York, close to Niagara Falls. There you managed to turn a chemical dump into a contemporary arts center. What do these projects have in common from an architectural point of view?

Hardy Artpark is sort of a miracle. I think it shows a lot about the architectural process. It came into being in a crisis in which the basic facility had been politically funded. It was a question of me-tooism. The people in that part of the state said, "How come Canada has this glorious culture across the river? We ain't got nuthin'." So in honor of a local politician, a huge performing hall was built—huge, at least for the region. No one quite believed it was real until halfway through construction, when the state discovered (through the Parks Department which administrated it) that indeed it would have to be used, and it should be well used and people should appreciate it, like it. But it was completely unprogrammed. There was really no precedent for such a structure in that part of the state. So people involved with the program invented the idea that on a temporary basis there should be a single opening season which combined the visual arts with the performing arts. No one was sure what would happen to a ballet, opera or symphony performance by the Niagara Gorge. But since there are so many tourists who arrive with their kids in trailers to see the Falls, it seemed that there ought to be an experience during the day that would draw tourists. The idea was a little like an art zoo: you could come and see artists at work. Out of that has grown something quite different. Now it's a permanent institution, I suspect, although it's all designed in that tinker-toy way so that it could come apart. It was a wonderful excuse to be fanciful, like World's Fair architecture. It is now becoming perma-nent, and each year another layer is added to it. The whole thing is growing parts that were never originally envisioned, all of which is per-fectly consistent with the first premise that it should change and grow. It's remarkable to see how the state funding has led to some highly creative works. One tends to think that bureaucracy can't handle such matters, but it's really made an enormous difference in the visual arts field. There is a certain badge of honor in having worked at Artpark. And the en-vironmental arts now have a whole palette. They have that wonderful physical site to work in.

Diamonstein You referred to the design premise. How does an architect design space to promote the making and experience of the arts? Where do you begin?

Hardy Artpark was based on the premise that it could all come apart and go away. It was also based initially on small-scale work, on crafts, pottery and things indigenous to the community. It was only later that the larger-scale professional works came. Therefore, we tried to create something that would give a sense of variety and an assortment of places, in an experience that is constantly changing. So there were open places and closed places, made of angles and dissimilar materials and industrial ob-jects. We even made a log cabin for one of the enclosures. You don't really know when you work that fast what the final outcome will be. We tried to provide as many possibilities for enclosing space as one could imagine.

Diamonstein Does the architect serve as the agent provocateur, and should he? How assertive should either the architect or the architecture be in designing the program for a place like that?

Hardy In that case, what was absolutely essential was some kind of framework upon which people could hang whatever they chose, and against which they could react. I can imagine circumstances in which that would be the wrong premise, where you should make something as neutral as possible. But the words "neutral" and "flexible" are very dangerous.

Diamonstein How do you decide—when is it presumptuous and when is it necessary?

Hardy Well, architecture is nothing more than making conscious decisions, so you have to make them from the very beginning. The process involves big choices and big questions, all the way down to the final paint colors. The room we sit in would be radically different if it were a different color (and it wasn't the present color originally). That's an important choice about the character of the New School Auditorium. But whether this place should be here at all is decided at the beginning of the process.

Diamonstein Who wrote the program for Artpark?

Hardy A wonderful series of accidents brought together people who gave us a range of assumptions, but it wasn't an architectural program in the traditional sense of so many square feet for so many kinds of activity. The basic idea was to have as many kinds of places as possible between the range of a parking-lot and an eight-million-dollar performing arts center. The Artel, as it's called, was envisioned as the bridge that brought the automobile and the audience together.

Diamonstein What's that Artel like?

Hardy It's a wooden series of platforms covered by the trusses that you use for making barns, all bolted together. Now it's gotten gray. It had petunias the first year. I don't know if they are maintaining the petunias. It even had topiaries. It's a fairly gentle work, because it was conceived so as to disappear altogether. Temporary isn't always temporary, like the buildings from the First World War on the Mall in Washington, which disappeared only about five years ago. Artel was meant to be something that could change, could be adjusted, was malleable. I think that's a radically different premise than something like, say, Cass Gilbert's St. Louis Art Museum, where our design is as tyrannical it could be. Every single molding, every square inch of the place must stand and be a certain way. The reason why they are different comes out of the perceived need on the client's and the architect's part.

Diamonstein Before you became an architect, you were a card-carrying scenic designer. I believe you still are a member of Local 829 of the United Scenic Artists. You've worked on stage sets for such productions as *Gypsy* and *Sweet Bird of Youth*. You were an assistant to scenic designer Jo Mielziner for four years, after spending several years in the Army Corps of Engineers. How did you first become interested in scenic design?

Hardy I was stagestruck. It was that simple. I just thought that theaters were magical, wonderful places. It was a little bizarre to be that way in the fifties. Most educational institutions didn't have courses in the arts, except in history. You could go to a drama school, but there was no general educational institution that had much to do with the arts. I found that the theater was extraordinary fun. Relations were very intense, and I enjoyed it all.

Diamonstein How did you get that first job in the theater?

Hardy I just pestered. Jo was my cultural hero. He was, without question, the finest scene designer of the period. He really transformed what people think of as a Broadway production. His influence in Europe is beyond telling. He was also a man who used light as a basic element of design. He was really a kind of three-dimensional painter, only scenery and Postimpressionist performers became part of the whole thing. I wanted to work for him. I just had to work for him, so I kept after him.

Diamonstein How did you go from three years of that to establishing, first your own firm, in 1962, and then several years later Hardy Holzman Pfeiffer? What marked the conversion from theater to architecture?

Hardy It was another cultural hero. It's strange, because I think we are fortunate to live in a time without heroes. They make me very nervous. When someone announces that the second coming is at hand in any given sphere, I get very apprehensive. But I will confess that without the second extraordinary conversion by exposure to Eero Saarinen, I don't know that I would ever have become committed to architecture. You see, Jo and he were designing the Beaumont Theater. I think the battle between them is still going on. The theater is reviled currently. It's said that it's a rotten theater. A lot of that has to do with Joe Papp and his perception of what the theater should be. I think it could be an extraordinary room. But in any event, there was this collision of values between Jo Mielziner, who represented the best of Broadway theater, and Eero, who was constantly talking about evolution and change and exploring and challenging things. He had been to Canada and seen the Shakespeare Festival there, by Guthrie. He was obsessed by the idea that you could have an audience and performers in the same space, instead of an audience in one room and performers in another. And the two of them came together like this. I was operating sort of as translator between two perceptions of theater.

Diamonstein You and Malcolm Holzman and Norman Pfeiffer are the principals of your firm. It's obviously a partnership of complementary talents. But you might tell us just who performs what functions. Who and how many are the associates?

Hardy There are three associates at the moment, although, like everything else in our firm, the number's in a constant state of change. Tomorrow it might be more. Relationship among the partners is very hard to explain. We're very fortunate now that we got together when we were young. I don't know that you could forge such a thing out of the kinds of beings we now are. We are probably too protective and too self-aware. But we really grew up together and did the thing that kids do with their parents. We rejected everything. We rejected the fifties, we rejected the AIA, we rejected midtown, we rejected contracts, we rejected working drawings, we rejected design. We rejected everything but clients. We tried to invent clients, in many cases, which is a hopeless exercise. You can never do it. But the surprising thing is that the partnership has survived. Each of us really perceives himself as capable of doing what the other does, yet we are not competitive in the bad sense. We certainly are in the good sense.

Diamonstein How do you differentiate between good and bad?

Hardy Well, in the bad sense, you attempt to overtake somebody else. In the good sense, you challenge the other person and say, "That's the stupidest thing you ever did—why?" There's a great deal of what I think is healthy combativeness. The problem with the firm is that as it grows, the contact among us is less.

Diamonstein Are the three principals always involved in the design of a project?

Hardy Yes—I can say that with equanimity—but to greater or lesser degrees. People who see the office in operation probably aren't aware of some of the thought transference that goes on in airplanes or during cab rides. There actually is collaboration. Sometimes it's very abstract. But because we have worked together so long, we have a very efficient means of communication which allows ideas to pass around. It's great fun to be able to work interdependently, because I think that architecture itself is collaborative. No architect in his right mind thinks he does it all. I suppose that the theater gave me that imagery, because the theater is all based on interdependence.

Diamonstein How do you select the type and the number of jobs that are undertaken at any given time?

Hardy We never have been able to say no.

Diamonstein Oh, no. I can think of several things that you've turned down.

Hardy We tell clients that we are highly selective and that we've limited the size of the firm because the principals must be involved. And I think that's true. But we are now suffering the problems of discovering that if you are going to grow you have to be challenged by more and more difficult things, which in architecture means larger projects. In a large-scale project, it's much harder to achieve what one can in a small project. The failure of modern architecture is that there has been a breakdown about the scale at which we can control the environment and the results. Large-scale projects are usually grim beyond comparison, and we'd like to try and do something about that, but is it hard. I can now see why large-scale firms and large-scale projects are organized in a military structure, with somebody in charge here and somebody subordinate there, and then lots of subordinate somebodies and then a whole sea of somebodies, and a chain of command that works only one way.

Diamonstein Well, in today's world, with inflationary pressures being what they are, it seems to me that clients would be more interested than ever in the reliable and responsible services of large firms. How does a smaller firm manage not only to produce large and artistic projects but also to do them in a businesslike manner?

Hardy It's a game of tug-of-war. Really, architecture is impossible. It is an attempt to resolve conflicts which are impossible. The difference between the outside and the inside has never been resolved in any building ever. The great ones only come very, very close. The struggles between architecture as commerce, which it has to be to get itself made, and architecture as art, which I am positive it *is,* are very, very difficult. But it's no worse than any of the other struggles that one needs to resolve. There are always money problems. There's never been enough money to do what the clients want. How does one make those choices? There are problems about time, because architecture takes so long to do. Over the weekend I was in Madison, Wisconsin, for the dedication of the Civic Center. There

I was looking at something that we were working on six years ago. What were you in 1974, what was I? Where were we all in 1974? The measure of all that is now built.

Diamonstein Well, consider how the people in Madison, Wisconsin, feel about it. I guess it was the longest-running sideshow in that town's history, 132 years from the time that an early mayor announced that they needed a civic center until February 22, 1980, when it was finally dedicated. Let's discuss that project in more detail when we talk about your renovation work and your new construction projects. Let's go back to the theater for a moment. How much does your life in the theater and the stage-set continue to influence you?

Hardy I think it was very good experience, because I know what scenery is. I don't think architecture is scenery at all. In theater work we have spent a great deal of energy trying to get architecture out of the way so that scenery could fill up the rooms. There is a movement now in architecture to make buildings as scenery in a kind of transient, quite pleasant, wonderful way. But it seems to me that there is a difference between the two. The other thing is that the fifties were the frame of reference for my education. It's hard to imagine the fifties sitting now in the eighties. It really is. You have to do a lot of work to conjure up what that time was like. It was a world of black and white drawings and ruling-pens and very hard edges were everywhere in architects' minds. There was no color, while the theater, scenery and so forth, is nothing but color. There was little use of natural light. Everything was conceived in fixed artificial light. In the theater you discover all there is to know about light; that it has intensity and color and direction and that you can change those things. In the fifties, there was no real discussion or interest in the problems of scale, what makes things big and what makes things little. There was more concern about technology. And so exposure to all those things through the theater was just super.

Diamonstein *Architectural Record* has gone on record as saying, in a complimentary way, that some of your techniques are closer to scene painting than contemporary architecture. They went on to say that the buildings represent an architectural approach which lies between science and scenery, and extended it by accepting the juxtaposition of the old and the new. Is it fair and accurate to place you on that continuum?

Hardy I think we're all doing the same thing in various ways. It always happens that when you look back at a period of architecture you can see how remarkably consistent, not uniform but consistent, the work is, due either to reaction or to action. I still think that we are reacting against the fifties, even those who were never there. A certain license to misbehave comes directly from that impetus.

Diamonstein Your colors, those sometimes playful and brash colors, is that a reaction to the fifties?

Hardy I can't state strongly enough how narrowly architecture was then defined. It was a very specific and mechanistic type of problem-solving, and part of the reason was there were extraordinary new problems to solve. No one had ever made an airport at the scale that was then called for. It was pre-freeway. Los Angeles existed and [Robert] Moses was building highways here, but they weren't considered part of the realm of architecture. That jump in scale was beginning to happen, and one had to work very hard just to solve the basic organizational problems. There wasn't much left over for the consideration of the rooms and the places themselves.

Diamonstein Do you really think that purple columns and exposed orange ducts please or excite people?

Hardy Oh, sure, that's all the decorative arts. When we started carrying on about what buildings are made of, in part it was the moralism of architects saying, "You must let the building express itself," which is a fifties, forties, thirties notion, that architecture must be honest. Looking back on it, I think we were not aware of the extent to which we *had* paid attention in school. A building had to be honest in that sense. It had to express its structure. And the other thing was, by grabbing hold of all the parts of the building, the bolts that hold the columns together, and the ducts and the wires and the conduits, and using them, one had a kind of rudimentary form of the decorative arts. It also helped with the geometric juxtapositions that we tried to make between different materials. There was an awful lot going on there. We have since learned, I think, that you don't need to do so much. The early work looks like early work. Not that it's bad. It just looks like early work.

Diamonstein You have often expressed the view that your work is known too much for the very things that we have just discussed, the exposed duct work, the primary colors, the brashness. What would you prefer that it be known for? In other words, what do you think Hardy Holzman Pfeiffer stands for?

Hardy We've always consciously avoided answering that question, and I won't go into why. I hope that people just become curious to see what is going on in the buildings themselves—not in what we say about them, but in the buildings themselves. And I hope it is understood that we don't approach each project the same way. I know all architects say that, but we've tried very hard to explore each concern on its own. If you are given somebody else's building which happens to be quite ugly and sort of boring, one might take that ugly, boring thing and use it as an element of the larger whole, and we have had the fun of doing that. We have had the fun of blitzing other people's buildings, too.

Diamonstein What does blitzing mean?

Hardy Demolishing them outright, or making fun of them. But one has to be careful about that, because history has a funny way of making fun of the person who made the fun.

Diamonstein You stated unequivocally your view that architecture is art. I wonder if we can explore that a bit.

Hardy That could go on for some time. I think that architecture is a language of communication in the same sense that any really fine art can be. It's a two-way kind of communication. What you do, in part, is to try and figure out what some client is after. A client may not be an individual. It may be an organization, in which case the job is more fun, because it's more abstract, and you need to translate that want, which is something psychic as well as monetary, into a result. Then there is the larger question of where the users of the building—the society it is built for—will be by the time the project is made. That's a guess, that's a hunch, that's an instinct, that led us to support restoration as an idea before it was conventionally interesting. There are lots of hunches and guesses in the work at Cooper-Hewitt which are not perceived, because what was originally there is now forgotten. It seems to me that that reflection of the energy and the sense of what's happening in the larger society at a given time is a part of what creative acts do. But in a sense, none of that is important, because I think that the buildings are their own measure. Architecture is a hybrid art. It's troublesome. I think when it becomes completely re-solved, it turns into sculpture and becomes fine art. And we don't think of ourselves as sculptors.

Diamonstein Some architects may not think of themselves as artists. But certainly one subject of increasing awareness and concern is the relationship between architects and artists. We've asked each visitor how he views the state of that relationship, and how he would evaluate the nature of the collabora-tion and its potential in the future.

Hardy The nineteenth century divided art into two kinds. There were crafts, the useful or applied arts, and then there was art, with a capital "A." The distinction was made that crafts were things that you used, and art with a capital "A" was for contemplation. It wasn't something you used; it was Fine Art. It hung in museums. Those distinctions have been fairly well broken down. But even the National Endowment, if you apply for fund-ing, still has two categories for buildings using artists. In Eugene, Oregon, we are involved with both. The distinction is arbitrary, and yet it's some-how useful. Really splendid Beaux-Arts buildings—think of the Public Library here or Grand Central, or the University Club—had an extraordi-nary combination of architectural order with a lot of blank spaces, that craftsmen filled in, in collaboration with the architect. There were, for instance, giant ceilings which clearly had to be frescoed. I don't think the architects cared that much about the details, as long as it represented the sky and had something flying around up there, and had some kind of high-toned symbolism that you could sell the client.

Diamonstein The collaboration did not permeate the project from its very beginning.

Hardy Insofar as craft is concerned, no. I think that the craft was perceived as subordinate to the larger vision of the architect and that's fairly tradi-tional. That idea still goes on. The terra cotta details around the build-ings here on Twelfth Street, were the products of craftsmen working within an architectural frame. I think that's perfectly valid, if attention is given to graphic art, to craft, to video, photography. Part of the problem is it's damn hard to do. It takes longer. It muddies up the process that the architect envisions. The architect never has any time, either, and never has the right fees, and on and on and on. The last thing he wants is to have something all neatly organized and then have it all come apart, because artists are questioning it.

Also, when I romanticized about the Beaux-Arts, there used to be a sort of house style that everyone could relate to. That tends not to be the case, certainly in our work. So it's much harder for the artist or craftsman to have a common idea about what it is he would do. There tends to be competition.

Diamonstein Your own work is so assertive that it is sometimes difficult to see how a successful collaboration could take place. Perhaps it requires a more neutral combination. Yet you have worked with some very well-known artists. How did that work out? What are the ingredients of a successful collaboration?

Hardy Obviously, part of it is just whether people enjoy each other's company. In the case of the soon-to-be-revealed Best Products Building, Jack Beal, who is a fine artist in his own right, collaborated on the design of carpet, based on a triptych he did that, amazingly enough, is in the Madison Civic Center. It's a borrowed image of water lilies, enlarged and repositioned and then Rorschached and then divided and made into an endless pattern for the carpets. The fact that you walk on a patterned surface which is directional one way and nondirectional the other is absolutely essential to the building. It's a concept that he understood. The fact that he chose water lilies and worked them the way he did was his doing and his contribution. But, it had to fit within the concept of the larger building. So I suppose that's a fairly ancient, traditional idea of the architect providing the framework within which things happen. I suppose if one did a museum for a single artist's work, you could have a true collaboration from the word go. You could consider the work itself and all the problems of exhibition and light and handling crowds. But that would be rare.

Diamonstein I didn't want you to get away quite so easily when you talked about the long sweep of history in selecting buildings. Which of your buildings do you think will be most remembered?

Hardy Couldn't care less. I think that's history's problem. I just don't think it matters. And besides, whatever I thought would be wrong anyway.

Diamonstein Do you think any of them will be forgotten?

Hardy Oh, sure, they'll be torn down, although that doesn't mean the building is forgotten. Penn Station is remembered better now than if it still existed.

Diamonstein Are there any that you would like to have forgotten?

Hardy Oh, sure.

Diamonstein For example?

Hardy I'll never tell. No, they all represent an effort to do something, and it's wonderful to see buildings after the fact, after a while, because then you discover that your own perception of them changes. Therefore a scorecard is relatively meaningless. And besides, you don't do them for history. That's not why you're an architect at all.

Diamonstein Why *is* one an architect?

Hardy Because you enjoy building buildings. If you're an architect, it's the most wonderful thing there is to do. It's an impossible game. The mere fact that you can do it all makes you want to try again. It never comes out right. It *never* comes out exactly right. And so you have to do it one more time.

Diamonstein In what was certainly intended to be a cynical note, you said many of your buildings will be torn down. Well, not if there are future Hardy Holzman Pfeiffer firms around.

Hardy God help them, anybody restoring our work.

Diamonstein Obviously, many of our best buildings escape from us each year, and obviously, too, that doesn't have to happen. Long before it became the thing to do or fashionable, or even considered appropriate—I guess it was only recently that you could reuse a building without losing your standing in the profession—your firm was turning warehouses into museums, barns into schools of the performing arts, and almost anything into theaters. I think that it is commonly accepted that Hardy Holzman Pfeiffer is one of the foremost proponents of recycling. You have redone the Galveston Grand Opera House, the St. Louis Art Museum, the Cincinnati Playhouse, at least in phase one. Almost everything you have done has been a recycling of one project, with another structure added to it. An example in New York is the 1901 neo-Georgian, perhaps better described as Victorian wealthy, Carnegie Mansion, that became the Cooper-Hewitt Museum. In practically every instance, you tried neither to preserve the existing buildings intact, nor to alter them so radically as to lose their good qualities. You call what you do "interpretative restoration." Can you tell us what you mean by that?

Hardy I think it's absolutely essential to understand that scientific restoration is physically impossible. The bulk of restoration is conceived in those terms, in this very simple-minded idea that architecture is science and enough technology applied in restoration can turn the clock back. Therefore, you could fix all the paint colors by analysis and repeat them as they once were. You could find the original structural drawings and recreate them, on and on and on and on.

The thing that you cannot recreate, at the rate we are changing, even if it was last year, is what the people were like who perceived and used the environment and how the place was thought of. I am certain that the level of light in this room would have been unimaginable to the man who designed it. And yet we now accept extraordinarily high light levels as not only reasonable, but the law has required them for public spaces. So that when you restore a building, if you put back gaslights, not only would they smell bad but they would be illegal. The most absurd example of this is the Ford Theater reconstruction, which is not really a restoration. It's conjectural, because it came out of photographs that Brady took for the trial of John Wilkes Booth. The Park Service, being of the pseudo-scientific bent, prepared drawings saying, this is what the room was. And they were almost built. The only problem was that the seats were so narrow and the aisle spacing was so tight, that it was illegal for people to occupy the chairs. So the Park Service said that it would be used as a tourist room. People would be ushered into it, twelve at a time, and there would be a sound and light show on stage about Lincoln.

The thing cost—I've forgotten now, I think about eight million dollars—and that was to be its use. That's the sort of ludicrous extension of the assumptions of scientific restoration. And I suppose Williamsburg is, too.

Diamonstein That's a reconstruction.

Hardy But the illusion that you could reproduce kitchens, and then reproduce fat, wonderful people in slave costumes polishing brass is ludicrous in the extreme. It's really physically and conceptually impossible, and morally indefensible, to think about turning the clock back. Only a rich society would even consider it. What always has to happen is some interpretation of the way things were. It's the spirit of the work that's most important, anyway, not the detail.

Diamonstein Let's talk of the spirit of the National Museum of Design, the Cooper-Hewitt Museum. How feasible was it to turn a private house into a public museum?

Hardy We were fortunate because of the original plans, and the fact that Carnegie used that house for the public, in the sense of guests. The two biggest changes are the circulation, which had to permit the public to stream through and use all five floors, and the way in which all the services have been handled. Carnegie had furnished the house somewhat pretentiously, but in a really remarkable kind of overstuffed, upper middle class way. The walls and the details and the standing bridge-lamps were completely impossible in a museum setting. So we had to find some approximation for the way the house looked, without the furniture, without the rugs, without the lighting, without the potted palms. The more basic thing we had to be ruthless about was how people moved through the building and how to solve code problems. We had to have fire-stairs where there weren't any before. But those things that were radical were pushed into the background, so that the things that were the best about the house would shine.

Diamonstein I thought the best part of the house was that Carnegie was so interested in technology that he had mechanical servants.

Hardy Oh, they are wonderful. Yes. I think that in time the house will become a museum in its own right. It's a museum of technology, basically. You can see Andrew Carnegie on his way to founding Carnegie Tech. He had air conditioning, for instance, in which air was drawn through cheesecloth, which had water sprayed on it, and then, as the water evaporated, it cooled the air. The present systems do exactly the same thing, only they do them mechanically instead of through natural evaporation. He also controlled the humidity in all the guest rooms, and in his own.

Diamonstein Tell us of your efforts to recreate the Galveston Grand Opera House.

Hardy Well, that's clearly an example of interpretive restoration.

Diamonstein And scenery. . .

Hardy Together. The 1900 hurricane blew the thing away, all but about three walls of it, so when it was rebuilt it was changed. Then in the twenties it was remade again. We have some photographs of that. Then Cinemascope came and blitzed the interior so it could hold the big wide screen. So what was left was really only a memory. That building is being restored out of nostalgia in a state that now realizes it has lost a great deal of its past. It's very hard work, because it's all a matter of judgment and feel. You don't really know what you've done until it's in place. We had to reconstruct the boxes on the sides of the stage, but we also had to provide modern lighting instruments, and the two collide with one another. We have to provide for all kinds of performances on the stage, including rock groups, and that collides with the requirements of the sound system.

Diamonstein Some of the symphony halls that you have worked on have some of your philosophy, color, psychology, and something that I feel is central to your work, which is the use of the rotated grid.

Hardy The Minneapolis Hall has a slightly rotated grid. That was done for emphasis. The building is really very small. It's only four stories. It sits in a portion of that city that is going to grow, clearly. High-rises are already appearing around it. And it seemed as though something should be done

Spirit Square, interior,
Charlotte, N.C.
Picture credit: Norman McGrath

Spirit Square, exterior,
Charlotte, N.C.
Picture credit: Norman McGrath

Mt. Healthy School, exterior,
Columbus, Ind.
Picture credit: Norman McGrath

18 West 11th Street House,
exterior, New York, N.Y.
Picture credit: Cervin Robinson

Willard Hotel, Washington, D.C.,
drawing
Picture credit: Neil Dixon

Mt. Healthy School, exterior,
Columbus, Ind.
Picture credit: Norman McGrath

to make the hall maintain its importance, as city growth happens. Therefore, we set it back from the main street, and rotated the hall itself slightly. We had the fun of working with Cyril Harris, who is an autocrat about acoustics. He demanded that the hall be separated from everything around it by a one-inch gap. Nothing must penetrate that. There are only two places—where a rain leader has to go through and where the electrical conduit comes out—that there are any physical connections. So we had this wonderful problem of the clear necessity to shape portions of the building in dissimilar ways. And we also had the pleasure of a client who said, "Musicians are first-class citizens, and there is no reason why they should be treated differently than the public." So the architecture consisted of a kind of inert lump turned and surrounded by a profile of very open, almost office building-like stuff, which contains public spaces, the musicians, and support spaces. The backstage vocabulary and the audience vocabulary is the same. The color scheme is the same, the materials are the same, because Minneapolis didn't want to have you think that its musicians were just the paid help. It was an extraordinary client that way. Also, that hall was designed and built in a year and a half.

Diamonstein That's the only fast-track symphony hall that exists?

Hardy Ever. And it is to the community's credit that it all happened. It's an extraordinary accomplishment. On the other hand, it produces some sort of ragged results that an architect would like to have different, once he sees it. The curtain wall, especially, isn't what we intended. That wall reads, strangely, vertically instead of horizontally. It looks too much like an office building, not an interpretation of one. Very small, little things would change that.

Diamonstein You remind me of the question that I've always meant to ask you.

Hardy Uh, oh.

Diamonstein That is that wall extension that I have never quite understood at the Mount Healthy School.

Hardy Oh. That's easy.

Diamonstein In that open-plan school, what is the role of that wall and its relationship to the rest of the design?

Hardy The school is very simple-minded. There is a right-angle of masonry. Packed against that, is an open plan for about four hundred kids. Running diagonally through it is a circulation spine. It's the one place you get to organize yourself. If it weren't for that spine, the interior would be so confusing you would never know where you are. The school was designed for expansion, so you would expand at the ends. We thought it was important to make clear the idea that the building was not complete just because an architect had been around to do something. The broken, open ends are an invitation to future generations to fill in some more. It would be possible to fill in some more without being slavish about the original, too. It would be fun to see somebody else tackle that problem.

Diamonstein You referred earlier to the most recently dedicated effort of Hardy Holzman Pfeiffer, the Madison Civic Center, which was dedicated 132 years after it was first proposed. In fact, it is a wonder that it was built at all. Tell us of your rather theatrical solution to that problem.

Hardy I guess it's theatrical.

Diamonstein Well, it was a movie house.

Hardy Yes, that's part of it. It's an absolutely superb project, and I will be very interested to see how it sits with critical evaluation by the larger community. I know how it sits with the people for whom it was built, because they had to lock the doors to keep people out, it was so successful.

Diamonstein Tell us something of the history of that project. There was a visionary civic center on the waterfront that Frank Lloyd Wright, the near neighbor and locally venerated architect, had first proposed. What has happened since that, is the move from the lakeshore site to the downtown State Street site. This move is obviously significant to the revitalization of the city.

Hardy Madison, the symbolic capital of the State, rises on a hill, dominating everything, but the actual physical energy of that community lies in the university. The main buildings of the university are a mile and a half, as I recall, from the state capital, down a diagonal street that cuts through the grid of the plan. Our project sits between them. The Civic Center project was proposed at the beginning of the century, but Wright's involvement didn't take place until the early thirties. He extended one of the major orthogonal axes of the city into the lake, so that the capitol's design, which is good in an imposing way, would be anchored. His axis concluded with a very remarkable Beaux-Arts scheme of symmetrically placed halls and a whole bunch of spiralling ramps—you remember the parking-garage era of Frank Lloyd Wright. The halls are all wrapped up in wonderful ramps cantilevered out over the lake. So there was that tension between the very big Beaux-Arts capitol and what was supposedly a modern solution. For the period, it was an extraordinary, stunning design, and a great poetic, romantic statement. His drawings are beautifully rendered, with boats in his fine hand sailing across the lake. The only trouble was that it was too romantic. The cost of putting the building on a lake, where the shoreline goes down like *that,* was a price too great for the constituency to bear. Every two years there would be a referendum about a bond issue. Some people were kept alive, it was said, by being able to come out and vote for or against it. Finally, when Paul Soglin became mayor, it was voted down for the last time. Paul was a student during the sixties and participated in the demonstrations that took place on State Street—the street that connects the capitol with the university. He then was elected mayor. As mayor, he did an extraordinary job of bringing the community together, despite initial fears of anarchy. He ended up wearing a three-piece suit and being quite reasonable. His conviction that the total community, not just the building, but the total community would benefit from reinforcing that major street and encouraging activity downtown led to the purchase of an old movie theater and an old department store, neither of which, in any sense of the word, was distinguished architecture. There are far fancier, crazier, more wonderful, exotic and exuberant movie palaces alive. And a Montgomery-Ward catalogue store is a Montgomery-Ward catalogue store, and that's that.

Diamonstein Of the fifties.

Hardy Of the fifties. Vaguely Georgian. I mean very, very faintly. But because of the continuity of the street, which is all two- and three-story buildings, very much Main Street America, and almost the foolishness of it, the kind of naiveté of its architecture and what it meant to the community, it seemed to us that that could be woven together into some larger design. I suspect that's why it's such a favorite of mine, because it speaks in many voices, and I think it appeals at many levels. Opening night was great fun for many kinds of people in the restored auditorium; "Restored" although we made it really far more serious than it was. We lowered the color intensity and made it much more like autumn and much less like midsummer, and toned down some of the Spanish stuff just a bit.

Diamonstein Is this a change in direction for Hardy Holzman Pfeiffer?

Hardy Well, it needed to be. That room was a little schizoid. We arrogantly thought we were helping it out. We never claimed to factually restore it.

Diamonstein But I thought that one of the things you liked was a contrast between disparate elements in any design.

Hardy Well, that's what I am trying to say, that in this case it was extraordinary on opening night, with conflicting perceptions. Some people discovered that they could recall the room and it made them feel good. These people would say, "You could never do something like this with a modern architect. You see, *this* is really nice." In fact, they had just come through a public space made of fluorescent-lit modern architecture and not seen it because they rejected it. It wasn't pleasing to them. And the same thing will happen in reverse, because other people will say, "Oh, you know, how could anybody do this? What a waste of money. The twenties are better forgotten."

Diamonstein How much did the entire project cost?

Hardy Well, that's a game of numbers. Some days they say it cost twenty million, which includes everything in sight. Some days they say it cost about twelve, if you don't include all the furnishings.

Diamonstein The *Capital* says it's the best bargain they ever had.

Hardy It costs half of what a new construction would, although that's a little slippery, because if it were new construction, the last thing on earth you'd do is imagine a 1927 somewhat Spanish movie house interior.

Diamonstein With a red, white and blue lighting effect.

Hardy It was built at a very good period by very good movie-house architects. It happens to have wonderful sight-lines and a very direct relationship especially between the stage and its one big balcony. You feel very good in there. Performers feel very good in there, too.

Diamonstein I suspect, like most creators, your last offspring is always one of your favorites. Your next project to be dedicated is Spirit Square in North Carolina.

Hardy Yes. We have had the wonderful fun of practicing in many communities, as well as in the various parts of this one. It's astonishing that when you go to North Carolina and discuss reusing a building, you are looked at askance, as if that's a very peculiar thing to do. When you think of the traditions of the South and you see how many of the homes are covered with moldings and dripping with reproductions, you would expect some continuity there. Not at all in the public sector. Progress means shiny new things.

Diamonstein But not until the 1960s and urban renewal.

Hardy They tore it all down. There is almost no old downtown Charlotte, except a few little places.

Diamonstein But that is the most cohesive part of that whole urban sprawl, is it not?

Hardy That's why this project is so remarkable. It is a change in the local thinking about what buildings are, of what a community is, of what a downtown is, of what a main street represents.

Diamonstein How did you arrive at the name of Spirit Square?

Hardy I didn't. It was decided by the arts groups there, themselves, a combination of professional organizations and local artisans. They felt that it was a matter of spirit, and they wanted to say so.

Diamonstein I thought it was because the Baptist Church was one of the recycled buildings.

Hardy It was originally a Baptist Church. Again, you never know. It's startling, to me, that on both sides of the auditorium are stained-glass windows, and there is the Lord God Jehovah coming down on a shining beam. I assumed that they would think that was blasphemous and the windows would have to go. Instead, they became house lights in the auditorium. Everyone thinks it's great. The baptistry, which is where one went to conduct the basic business of the church, is all marble. It has been taken apart, reerected in the lobby, and it's the box office.

Diamonstein Among the cities you have worked in is Washington, D.C. Recently you signed the contract for a very major part of the Pennsylvania Avenue Redevelopment. You have a particular preference, it seems to me, Hugh, for 1901 buildings. I'm talking about the Willard Hotel that was designed by Henry Hardenburg, the same architect of the Plaza and Waldorf* hotels in New York. This building was minutes away from the wrecker's ball, and was saved only after a lengthy and heated court fight. Nonetheless, your firm won a competition to design the renovation. Your renovation—I think you are calling it a remodeling—of the Willard is an inspired work that places a new building at the site between the two old ones. Again, the new hotel is built on a shifted grid. The old Willard follows the diagonal of Pennsylvania Avenue, and your new hotel is on a rectangular grid. Will you describe the new building to us? You referred to it in an interview in the *Washington Post* as post-modernist. Can you tell us exactly what you meant by that?

Hardy It's a complicated project to discuss. It's probably the best example of Malcolm, Norman and me in collaboration that I know, because the fact that I am here speaking about it in no way means that I designed it or that Malcolm, who is closest to its origin physically, designed it, or that Norman did. Competitions are strange. They are sort of unnatural creations, because you don't really ever know what the ground-rules are. We invented an image, not a serious thought-through piece of architecture, an image based on a different geometry for the new building, which was built out of elements taken from the old building. And we provided a design which said, in fairly imprecise terms, somehow the vocabulary that we use will be very similar but not the same as Hardenburg's. If you go to the south side of Hardenburg's Plaza Hotel here, you'll see an extension by Warren & Wetmore, which is a twenties version of this same pos-

* not the present Waldorf Hotel

sibility. But by the nature of a competition we didn't have to explain what it was made out of. We only had to say how much it cost. And in the course of development, it's clear that we still have not resolved what it's made out of. It's a fascinating problem. We have said that maybe it's terra cotta and masonry, in which case are we using Hardenburg's vocabulary all over again eighty years later? That doesn't make any sense. It's publicly immoral to even consider it. Wolf Von Eckhardt, who was a strong supporter of the design, was remarkably helpful in securing us the commission. He wrote banner articles on the front page of the *Post* and said in essence, "Thank heavens we've come home again." Contemporary architects can pick up the threads and the raveled sleeve and we can have some continuity. Hardenburg was right so let's have more of this. I hope Wolf isn't here, because I am exaggerating. But clearly he had the idea that our drawings were intended to say that we would pick up and continue somebody else's vocabulary from eighty years previous. But even if we had the resources to do it, I am not sure that it would be appropriate.

So what should it be? I don't know. We are now struggling over that. It couldn't be glass and steel, because the approximation would be too ludicrous, and it would look like a joke. So it's clearly in the masonry tradition. But what is that? How would one use terra cotta, and is terra cotta even a plausible thing to use, when you know how it's made and what energy costs are? There's only one place left in America that does it, and it's in California. It would all have to get carted here, not on railroads, because they've broken down. It would have to be by truck. So, I am trying to say a key question is unanswered. The imagery is clear. But we don't know what it's made out of. So it isn't yet architecture. And of course it isn't built, so it can't be architecture.

Diamonstein I remember you once said that computers were like light-bulbs, tools that can be used to extend your senses. Do you use that tool? Have you used computers to any extent?

Hardy Only indirectly. I often think, when you watch the aspirin commercials and things revolving through space and the titles for NBC, and all that stuff, which is all computer graphics, what fun it would be to be able to use those techniques to study things in three dimensions. Or the illusion of three dimensions. Because we are always turning plans over and inside out and having people spend time to do things that I think a computer would do.

Diamonstein I am about to bring up the saga of Eleventh Street, which is close to where we are now, and was close to you, both as client and architect, for more than six years. I am talking about the house at 18 West Eleventh Street. The house is located in the Greenwich Village Historic District, and it was bombed in 1971. There was nothing but an empty lot. Neighborhood residents, however, were reluctant to see a contemporary design replace the former house, which was in the middle of an excellent row of Greek Revival townhouses. That debate, and it certainly was an impassioned one, lasted for six years, with you again as both the potential client, and ultimately the architect for the building that filled that space.

Would you discuss some of the issues involved and deal with some of the questions raised about the nature of preservation, about recycling, and ultimately your efforts to relate the building to its neighbors?

Hardy That project represents a very specific point in time, when much that we now know collectively about the uses of the past had not even been considered. The Landmarks Preservation Commission had never reviewed a new building in a row of landmark buildings at all. There were really no guidelines for it. My first response was we could just sort of wallpaper in the hole and be done with it. It would not be a restoration, because none of those houses is the original. We were not going to put slaves back in the basements built before the Emancipation Proclamation, and we were not going to reproduce the life of that period. The problems that we got into were very difficult because no two buildings in that chunk are the same, although they clearly were built in the same period. There was also another difficulty. It was something that I never spoke of at the time because I thought it was too loaded an issue. But I did think, personally, that something special had occurred there. I did find it strange to take history and deny the community knowledge. It seemed to me that it was somehow a special place, and that one shouldn't just make all of that disappear. Also, it seemed as though a new building had its right to think through the problems of the relation between indoors and outdoors that the previous buildings had done. The previous buildings are very well ordered and contained rooms that are joined in a very logical way, that end up with the facades that you see. There is a direct relationship between them. It seemed to me wrong to put a piece of scenery in front that had no relation to a new and different room sequence behind. One of the solutions which I think would have been more acceptable to the community but unacceptable to us who would live in the results, was to do just that—to replace the plane of the world in the facade and do whatever you wanted behind it. In other words, you would adopt one pose in public and another in private. You can do what you want to in the bedroom, but don't do it in the street. The problem is that of course it's an extraordinarily limited, tiny little piece of land. Any trading back and forth had to somehow advance on the street. The logical plan was that, by turning it diagonally, you could create long dimensions in a space that's quite narrow. I think it's an extraordinarily successful inside that way—you are not conscious of how small the physical volume is. But it's why cities are so wonderful, because there's this compact contract between the life of the street and the life in the building.

Diamonstein How does the building that was ultimately designed differ from the building that you originally designed, when you were the client as well as the architect?

Hardy One window moved four feet, in honor of the fact that the current client is short. Before the original approval was given, it did not have the stoop reconstruction that is now in place.

Diamonstein This is the first approval?

Hardy No. The first approval included the design as you see it, with the exception of this one window moved. But the original thought did not go so far as to restore the stoop the way it is now. That was because of the conflict which the Landmarks Preservation Commission has now resolved: you were not allowed to restore a stoop because it was on city property and you were not allowed to build privately on public land. Which shows you how far we have come since then.

Diamonstein How much do you think one should follow context in such a situation and how much regard, do you think, should be given to the community's opinion and the government's, or the Landmarks Preservation Commission's opinion, in determining the design, particularly in a country that prides itself on private property rights?

Hardy It's an insoluble question, but clearly there needs to be a discussion back and forth, especially in landmark districts. Until the current discussions on the East Side, a landmark district has traditionally been thought of as a homogeneous neighborhood which represents a place in time. And that's something that the residents support by living there and enjoying what they perceive as benefits. So one has to be aware of that. On the other hand, it's startling in a city to find people standing up in public and saying, "Your house ought to look just like mine."

Diamonstein Both in candor and in defense, I should say that I was a member of the commission for both the first and second approval of that design. But now that all is said and done, would you have done this project otherwise? Do you think of it as you have described other works of yours, as a collage of sorts?

Hardy Yes. It's a fairly three-dimensional one. But it is a collage or an assemblage or a multiplicity of sorts, because it's impure. The design is made out of three parts: it accepts the idea of an accurate restoration of the part that was the base, and then it does something else in the middle. Then it "restores" the top. I still think it troubles people because of its impurity. If you could restore the cornice, why couldn't you restore the whole thing? Or if you could think up an idea which would interrupt or make a play upon the idea of the wall, why not be consistent and do the whole thing? All of the criticism on both sides was based on the idea of a pure solution from top to bottom, so that we succeeded in offending both the preservationist groups and the modernist groups, who said that "It isn't modern," while the preservationists said "It isn't pure." I think that has been its most troublesome face. From my own point of view, I find the collage perfectly valid for the time in which it was built. It certainly wouldn't look that way if we started over in 1980. I have no idea what the result would be, but I know it wouldn't be the same.

Diamonstein Do you approve of the idea of architects as civic activists?

Hardy Insofar as they're architects. If they become politicians, that's another matter. We have to be responsible to what we do. We are always working in the context of the site, so we are always affecting the city.

Diamonstein To whom is the architect ultimately responsible, the client or the community?

Hardy In the past, I think the architect has had his mind too much on being responsible to the client, making the client happy. You know the wonderful story. The consultant architect said about the Pan Am Building, "Well, I know it's awful, but it's better than if I hadn't done it. I helped. I made it better. I put that shape in it, because it was originally just a box." That sort of rationalization seems to me very bad for the profession. It denigrates professional responsibilities.

Diamonstein While we're at the Pan Am Building, we should talk about the fact that you and your partners have been leaders in the battle to save Grand Central. Would you comment on the fact that a large body of opinion felt that the Terminal had already been ruined by the Pan Am Building and by all the advertising within?

Hardy Well, that opinion is true to an extent. It's wonderful to watch it get mirrored now by the wavy glass facade of the Commodore. The terminal is without question one of the most extraordinary structures in the city. It created midtown, and its problems are one of success. Its problems aren't that it didn't do its job; it almost overdid its job. The great lure, though, in this part of the city that it invented, is that there are millions of square feet of unused air-rights sitting invisibly, above it.

Diamonstein You did a project to fill in that space, perhaps you could describe it. How could you justify designing a building to fit into that space, considering the fact that you publicly opposed the Breuer design?

Hardy The rationale is now gone. At the time when the buildings were still owned solely by the bankrupt railroad, and included almost a dozen buildings that go from forty-second Street way up practically to the Waldorf, there was a possibility of redistributing those air-rights through the surrounding blocks. It was tried. When Jack Robertson was working against the design of the tower over the terminal, there was an effort to transfer air-rights to the Biltmore site. If one had been able to consider the whole, instead of just one to one, it seems to me that the advantage would have been the marketplace producing taller, denser, in some cases revitalized structures, within a coherent urban plan. Now it's happening haphazardly anyway, because the Post Office Building is being rebuilt, a Canadian developer is taking 466 Lexington Avenue and so forth. But they are being dealt with higgledy-piggledy, and the total resource isn't being properly used.

Diamonstein Could you briefly describe the scope of work in the Grand Central renovation?

Hardy As part of the Commodore deal, in lieu of paying taxes to the city and the state, Donald Trump and the state agreed that sales tax money would be put into a fund for the restoration of Grand Central. This spring that money—roughly two million dollars—is going to be used to clean the exterior, to repoint the masonry and to clean and repaint all the windows. So that the building will sit, as it should, cared for. The only problem is there isn't enough money to fix the roof. The viaduct, which is now being repainted, should be rebuilt, and so forth. But what's most important is that there is a precedent for private development tossing off funds to care for public structures. And one hopes that this can be built upon so that other companies as they take from midtown to put up their structures, will give something back. And one hopes that will go on, because there is much work that needs to be done there.

Audience What about the question of tearing down buildings that are considered landmark quality in the proposed Times Square redevelopment?

Hardy It's exactly the kind of question that we should collectively consider for the next three hours, because in it lies the whole subject of the future of that part of the city. The theater district and its identity are the reason why someone wants to have development there. It's also why there are so many problems in the entertainment district area. Portman's hotel is perceived by this administration and the previous one as the salvation of that part of town because it will create interest in development there. Along with the Convention Center, one sees a giant upgrading of the whole West Side of town. It's believed that the East Side is being overbuilt, so you spread that pressure over to the west, and you create there a whole new wonderland. The problem, forgetting for the moment about the theaters, is that the scale of the Portman hotel juxtaposed to what's around it is going to be so brutal that there is going to be very little left of Times Square as we think of it. In addition, of course, you have to toss away the theaters and buy the hotel. Now, whether that's good or bad is an act of fortune-telling. It could be a wonderful thing for the city to have confidence in reconstructing some part as important as that. It could easily be a disaster. The theaters themselves are quite wonderful, but they are a small part of a much larger issue.

RICHARD MEIER

Richard Meier
Born Newark, N.J., 1934
B. Arch. Cornell University, 1934

Diamonstein There is probably no more orthodox and visible practitioner of modernism in America than Richard Meier. He is an architect best known for white houses, although he has increasingly designed public buildings of varying sorts. He belongs to the group dubbed the Five Architects, but unlike some members, he is an active builder as well as a theoretician. His best known works include the Douglas House in Harbor Springs, Michigan, a white frame and glass box set on a dramatic cliff overlooking one of the Great Lakes; the Bronx Developmental Center in New York; and the Atheneum, in New Harmony, Indiana, a building which opened in the fall of 1979 to great national acclaim.

Perhaps we should begin by determining just who the Five are. What were the group's origins?

Meier It goes back quite a way to 1964, when a group of then young architects and teachers, under the heading of CASE, Conference of Architects for the Study of Environment, met in Princeton, and these were people who were teaching all over. There was Henry Millon and Stan Anderson from MIT, and Tim Vreeland from Philadelphia, and Peter Eisenman and Michael Graves who were teaching at Princeton. I was teaching at Cooper Union. Oh, probably six or seven others whom I've forgotten. At any rate, we thought it would be a good idea to meet to talk about architectural education, and architectural ideas as they related to architectural education. Between 1964 and 1969 we had a series of meetings, at which different people would present different projects, either that they were actively interested in writing about, or working on. And people would be invited to comment on the presentations, as well. I remember Cedric Price came from England and talked about his Think Belt, which he was working on at that time. But those first meetings were rather *ad hoc,* and in 1970, we decided to create a structure. Each of the participants who came would present one building that they were working on or had recently completed. We would also invite so-called critics to comment— much like the jury system in architectural schools. We were no longer students, but we felt that this would be a healthy atmosphere. There would be open criticism of work being done, not by the architectural press, but by one's contemporaries in a rather informal setting. So in the fall of 1971, the Museum of Modern Art was kind enough to lend us its conference room on the top floor. I presented a project, the Smith House, which I had recently completed; Michael Graves presented a house that he was working on; Peter Eisenman presented an addition to a residence in Princeton. John Hejduk presented drawings and Richard Henderson presented the house that he and Charles Gwathmey had designed for Charles's parents. And we had a very good discussion—it was very open, and very lively. After the discussion someone said that we ought to put out a little pamphlet. We have the tapes from this meeting; let's make a publication of this wonderful event. And we said, oh, that's a good idea, why not? Like most publications it didn't happen overnight. It took so long that instead of just the works that were presented at that meeting, someone said, why not present something that is happening now. This was two years later. So each person presented two works for the book that became the *Five Architects* book, which came out in 1975.

Diamonstein By that time, was the group still a group?

Meier	There never was a group. You see it was rather a coming together of people with similar interests, who happened to be teaching together at one time. I taught in 1963 with Michael Graves at Princeton. I then left and went to Cooper Union, where I taught with John Hejduk, and Peter Eisenman. The next year I came to Princeton, and worked with Michael, so we all knew one another. We taught in similar institutions, we went to one another's juries, but there was no official group. It was simply a group of people who talked to one another at that time.
Diamonstein	So you really never functioned as a group?
Meier	No.
Diamonstein	But was that interaction part of the common search for the meaning of form, or the belief that architecture is high art?
Meier	I believe that architecture is high art. I won't speak for the others. But I think that the intention was really to create something that hadn't existed in this country in our time. It was based on the model of CIAM in Europe. In 1959 European architects got together at Otterlo, presented works, and had an open critical discussion. They had a lively debate among themselves which had a profound influence on younger architects, and on the teaching of architecture. We wanted to create a vehicle for the airing of architectural ideas, in an open and friendly atmosphere. There was no attempt to work as a group, to teach as a group, or to have any kind of propagandizing influence. I think all of the discussions published later about the so-called Five Architects have attempted to make us into something that never existed, and still doesn't exist. It happened that we knew one another; we respected one another's work. I think we still do. I think of it as what any group of young architects can do, and probably should do. Otherwise, when you get out of school, you're often working on your own, in a vacuum. You don't have the opportunity to really criticize and have your own work criticized by your contemporaries.
Diamonstein	You are known primarily for "white" houses. Does that label do you justice?
Meier	Well, one of the things that *I've* learned as I've turned gray is that you really have no power to control or even influence the labels that are attached to you, and the stigmas which are related to your work. The houses I've done in the late sixties and early seventies have received a lot of attention, for better or worse, and they have been widely published. But, I always get my back up a little bit when labels are attached to the work.
Diamonstein	Well, then, why don't we deal with the whole subject all at once? Let's talk for a moment about how strongly your work is identified with Le Corbusier, and buildings like his 1929 masterpiece, the Villa Savoie. They are said to be prime influences on your work. Yet your works are more picturesque, and you emphasize pleasing proportions, over the rigid grid that we associate with Corbu. At the same time you have seen the house as a white frame, not as a white mask, as was so skillfully done with the Douglas house on Lake Michigan. Perhaps you could comment on what you have adopted or rejected in Le Corbusier's work.
Meier	Le Corbusier is an important and profound influence on every architect of our generation. He certainly has been a profound influence on me, but not the only influence on my thinking about architecture. I've learned an

enormous amount from this great master, and he has helped me clarify my ideas about architecture in a way that I don't think I could otherwise have done. Frank Lloyd Wright has also had a profound influence on me and my work, as has Alvar Aalto, as has Brunelleschi, Borromini, and Bramante. One's influences are different at different times. But when I was a student at Cornell University we looked at Le Corbusier very long and hard. Later when I traveled in Europe, in 1959, I spent a great deal of time looking at his buildings, and in fact, had hoped to go and work for him. I met him in Paris, at the Maison du Brasil—it was opening day.

Diamonstein How many times did you meet him during his life?

Meier Just twice. The first time was in 1959 in the hopes of getting a job. There was a young apprentice, and he explained to me why Le Corbusier would not have an American in his office. It had to do with the past—it goes back to the League of Nations competition, when he was disqualified for using the wrong kind of ink. He thought that American intervention prevented him from winning that competition. When, in 1939, he was supposed to have a show of his paintings at the Museum of Modern Art, and that didn't come to fruition, he felt again that American business interests had deprived him of something. And there was also, as you know, the United Nations commission. He was invited here as one of the commission of architect advisors on that project. After he made preliminary sketches for the UN projects, his sketchbooks happened to have been lost for a period of time. He wasn't given the commission, but the building nevertheless turned out remarkably like his original drawings. And finally, with the UNESCO building in Paris, where again, he was part of the commission of architects, he felt that he certainly would be given this commission. But it went to an American—an architect then living in America—and again, he felt that American business interests deprived him of commissions which he felt were legitimately his. Therefore, he wouldn't have an American in his office.

Diamonstein How did you respond to that?

Meier I went home.

Diamonstein Your links to Le Corbusier and European classicism are repeatedly underscored. What, if anything, do you consider to be particularly American about your work?

Meier When I first did the early houses, such as the Smith House in Darien, Connecticut, I thought I was doing a contemporary version of a New England house, white clapboard wood, and conventional balloon framing. The spirit and the scale of the spaces are similar to the early New England houses. It was a little bit of a surprise to me that it wasn't until the European architects came to America that they said, this is really like the New England houses, and also in the spirit of some of the Breuer, Gropius houses of the early fifties. I had always thought those were important works by both of those people.

And so I think that in terms of the scale of the spaces, and the way of construction, and the kind of siding, that my early houses are related to the New England tradition of the detached single family house sitting on its site, painted white.

Diamonstein In a very recent interview you said, "What I do when I design a building is to try to take the problem beyond its old definitions. To see something new, and to make something new." Then you go on to say, "I'm reluctant to do any project where I can't take the problem to a new dimension." Are you lucky enough to have that happen each time?

Meier Well, I try. The Bronx Developmental Center is an important building for me, because it deals with all of the functional problems of a very complex program, of a facility for mentally handicapped people. It has been heavily criticized because it tries to make a kind of world within a world. It is a community which is a place to live, a place to work, a place to go to school, a place for physical education. It's like a monastery in that it turns inward to itself, and this is because of the nature of the site. The intention here was really to make a city in microcosm. It has all of the elements of an urban situation, and yet it's not related to any kind of urban situation. This was not part of the program. No one said to me, make within one building complex, a kind of microcosm of an urban complex. But I felt that this was an important thing to do, given this kind of situation, and this kind of site. You try to take a building beyond its simply programmatic requirements, and to make it something else. Whether you succeed or not is another question.

Diamonstein The Bronx Developmental Center is a glimmering and prize-winning silver structure in the Bronx, atop the Hutchinson River Parkway. It has been hailed as beautiful by nearly every visitor and every critic, but, as you point out, it has also engendered a great deal of criticism. Most of the debate has centered around whether the long low building, sheathed in aluminum panels, is appropriate as housing, school and out-patient facility for the mentally retarded. You obviously were responding to your stated concern: that huge custodial institutions were dehumanizing, and fostered sensory deprivation. As a result, to humanize the building, you built windows down to the floor, so seated children could look outside at trees and people, and used soft pastel colors on many inside walls. But there was concern voiced that the building was still institutional, and that retarded people would be far better off in small residential houses of fifteen to twenty people, or in foster homes. Some also feared that the building might be too complex for patients, and perhaps even a bit confusing.

Almost any kind of medical facility is almost obsolete in program by the time it leaves the drawing board, isn't it?

Meier Well, I'd like to think that it's not obsolete by any means. One of the problems you mentioned is that in 1970, when we were commissioned to do this project, it had been reduced from a 960-bed to a 750-bed facility because the proper funding was no longer available. As we were designing it, it was further reduced because of budget cutbacks to 384 beds. The argument, which came seven years later when the building was completed, was that there should be no institution at all, that what some of the parents of mentally retarded children wanted was a halfway house, a building in the community, a place where a dozen people would be housed. But this was not what we were about. We were about making a place which could deal with the problems of the severely and profoundly retarded. A halfway house, unfortunately, cannot do that, although it can deal with problems of the mildly retarded.

So this building became a whipping boy for people who wanted a different kind of state-financed facility. It also came on the heels of the so-called Willowbrook decree, which was fortunate after many, many years of an incredible situation out there, which I saw more times than I would like to remember as I was visiting institutions for the retarded. Willowbrook housed well over five thousand people, and the Willowbrook decree said that these people had to be housed in other places around the state, including the Bronx Developmental Center. Parents of children at Willowbrook said, no, we want them in our halfway houses or in our homes in our neighborhood. We don't want them in another institution, we don't care how wonderful that institution is, or what it looks like. And so the Bronx Developmental Center came to symbolize a place which doesn't house a dozen people or fifteen people; it potentially houses almost four hundred. I think that much of the criticism focuses on this particular problem. However, the building was designed for certain kinds of care, and it's been adapted as a much larger out-patient facility, because of changing needs, which ten years earlier one had no way of anticipating. As an architect, one is dealing with hundreds and hundreds of people who are involved in this process. The architect is not the person who makes all the decisions, much as we like to think that that's a certain power that we have. We don't have that power, you know. We have a real responsibility to the people we're working with, each of whom has input, demands, and needs. I think that in time the Bronx Developmental Center will find its proper place, and use. At present, perhaps only three-fourths of it are being used—it's not fully used.

Diamonstein It was recently used as the site of a movie. Were you aware of that, and how did you react?

Meier Well, I was aware of it. People called me daily, saying Marshall Brickman wants to film in your buildings.

Diamonstein The film is *Simon,* isn't it?

Meier Yeah, *Simon* is the film. And I said, well, you know, they're not my buildings, they belong to other people. You have to talk to them, not to me. I designed the buildings, but they're out on their own. And these people said, won't you help us, and I said, I'll call the owners and deal with them. If they want to have their buildings used as a film set, that's up to them. As it turned out, they spent I don't know how many days filming at the Bronx Developmental Center. I haven't seen the movie, so I can't comment about it.

Diamonstein The building in the film is surrounded by pastoral footage. I don't know if they got that on the Hutchinson River Parkway. If you had a similar assignment now, what kind of environment would you create for such a facility?

Meier I don't know if there's a simple answer. One thing I do know now, which I didn't know at the time, was that the no-man's land that was chosen by the state for the Bronx Developmental Center was as wrong as any site could be. Here is a site bounded on one side by the Hutchinson River Parkway, by railroad tracks on the other side—an incredibly amorphous hospital campus. I mean, it's the wrong place for any human habitation. And yet I thought that by turning the facility inward, by creating a kind of world within a world, by using large courtyards, we could make a wonderful place in spite of the site. I think it wasn't my option to say at that time to the state, go find another piece of land. But now I would make a strong stand for that. I didn't realize how difficult that site would be in terms of any kind of "normalization," and I'm still not sure what normalization means. But everyone I talk to seems to have a good idea. I can accept their point of view as to what normalization is, but I do know that that particular site is not, and therefore, is totally wrong for any kind of hospital facility. I think that a more suitable site in New York City, but one that probably you could never have, would be within a residential community, though it's been tried and we know the problems. But I think if one had one's choice, that would be preferable for that kind of building.

Diamonstein   Let's go back to your comment about taking the problem to a new dimension. This time I'd like to talk about an earlier project, also in the Bronx. Twin Parks was sponsored by UDC and it is among the very few examples of low-income housing in the city that is designed by a serious and high style architect. You completed Twin Parks Northeast in 1974 in an area which exhibits what can only be referred to as the classic symptoms of urban decay. In what ways do you think Twin Parks and housing like that can check this decay? What were your intentions there?

Meier   Architects are, by and large, very optimistic people. They think that because of what they do, things can change. We're also very idealistic in terms of what we do. Fortunately, there were a lot of people at UDC who felt the same way about the housing program in the early seventies. We felt that by the intervention of new housing in certain areas that had really become fairly run down, the whole area would be transformed. I think it takes more than just a single building, or project to do that. We had the opportunity of building more than 500 units of housing on three scatter sites—at the point of the convergence of two oblique grids in the Bronx. We tried to relate in a formal way both portions of the Bronx, the south, and the north, and in doing so to create open courtyard space, a new space which belonged to the entire community. To bring both communities into the project, we created what we felt was needed in that part of the city, and that was an open public space, a park space, an outdoor space. From our experience, people communicate a great deal, really, on their stoops. Although we were building too many houses to give everyone a stoop, we did try to create a park-like space where people of different ages could meet in different areas. We felt that this was the most important urban statement that we could make. The apartments would be okay, but they weren't going to be great apartments because of the number that we had to fill the buildings with. It was our intention to give as much light and air to these apartments as possible, and to make them as open and as livable as we could within the budget constraints. And seeing the place now, some six or seven years later, I am a little disappointed that it hasn't had more influence on the neighboring areas, but perhaps it can't. People still want to live there, but there's no way that an isolated intervention is going to transform a complete area, that already has a certain kind of character. The Bronx is a tough place to build in. I think the things which are happening now in the South Bronx are very important. They're massive in scale, and they have to be, because the problem is massive in scale. Westbeth was a different matter. There was an isolated area example, where there was no housing. It was part of a growth of the West Village toward the Hudson River.

Diamonstein Perhaps more than any other architect you are involved with artists. In fact, before you started your architectural practice in 1963, you were an artist yourself, deeply involved in painting and collage. I wonder if you would tell us how you returned to architecture. How did that transition come about?

Meier Well, I never really left architecture. In 1959, when I came back from Europe, I began looking for a job like every young architect, and carrying my portfolio around. I got a job at Skidmore, Owings & Merrill, did not have to work at night, as I do now, so I was painting at night and a friend of mine was kind enough to give me studio space.

Diamonstein You might tell us who that friend was.

Meier Frank Stella. Frank said, I have a loft, and I'm moving to another loft, and it's much bigger and I don't need all this space. Since you only come down and paint at night, and I only paint during the day, you can work down here. And so I did. I started making bigger and bigger paintings, and Frank started making bigger and bigger paintings, and finally he said, there's not room for both of us here anymore. So I went out and got my own studio, and . . .

Diamonstein . . . and proceeded to design an apartment for him.

Meier Yes. But I kept the studio for a number of years, and worked there in the evenings and on weekends. After about four years, I realized I couldn't do both properly, so I stopped painting, and gave up the studio, and spent all my energy on architecture.

Diamonstein Recently you've obviously given some of that energy back to art. I don't know if it constitutes a dual commitment, but very recently you had another show of your art works on the West Coast.

Meier That's true. I haven't given up completely. During this period I made collages, and I still do, but it's really something I do as a personal thing, and not professionally. I make collages which have to do with things which interest me at certain times. It also helps while away the hours you spend in airports. Traveling on airplanes, I carry a little box with me, and my glue and my paper.

Diamonstein How do your collages affect your architecture?

Meier I think everything one does and experiences affects one's work in one way or another. I've had the opportunity to be the resident architect at the American Academy in Rome, and during that time I had a studio where I was able to make drawings and collages, which had to do with some of the things I saw in Rome. When I took the students on a trip to southern Germany, to visit all the German Baroque buildings, I came back and worked on collages. I think that they relate—maybe not on a one-to-one relationship—but in a way that affects how one thinks about space and light and structure and how to organize space. That's why they're meaningful to me in a personal way. And probably not transferrable to anyone else.

Diamonstein Is all that sightseeing in any way relevant to a commission that you recently completed, for the design of a new museum in Frankfurt?

Meier Well, no, because that commission actually came out of the blue, like all good things. It either comes on the telephone or in a letter, but not something that you're actively thinking might happen. I was one of seven architects asked to compete for a new museum in Frankfurt, a museum for arts and crafts on the Main. Like most European museums it's an extension of an existing building, only this extension is twelve times the size of the existing building.

Diamonstein In a park setting?

Meier It's a small villa in a park setting. We've sent the drawings off. We're adding quite a large museum to this small existing villa, but the collection is all in storage and they haven't had the space to show it. It's for the permanent collection in Frankfurt.

Diamonstein And what is the new dimension there?

Meier Well, it's really taking the existing villa, which is an early nineteenth-century building of some quality—not the most distinguished building you've ever seen, but it certainly is a building of quality—and taking all of the proportions of this building, all of the way in which it's built. It just happens to be a cube—we're very lucky. Analyzing that building was the point of departure for the new building, so that the new building relates, in terms of scale, texture, and attitude, to the existing villa. It doesn't mimic it, it doesn't try to make a mockery of the villa, but it uses that villa as a point of departure, and builds around it, so that all the decisions about the new building refer back to the existing building. Therefore the existing building becomes one quadrant of the new building.

Diamonstein You referred earlier to Westbeth artists' housing. Westbeth is a residence that was recycled from the former Bell Laboratory buildings in the West Village. In that instance, many of your clients participated in the design of their own living units. Generally, do you think that's a good idea?

Meier I did think it was a good idea. I still do. I've been very disappointed because when we designed Westbeth we had a lot of help, not only from people that would be living there, but from agencies who were involved in the process. We were able to cut through a lot of red tape in order to make real inroads into the process of building with federal financing. We were able to design open space in which the resident could then create his own environment, inside the unit. We were able to make more space for each living unit. I thought this concept would have applied not only to renovation or what later became known as adaptive reuse, but to new construction as well. I've been very disappointed that this idea hasn't really been able to find expression in new construction with federal funding, because I thought that Westbeth showed not only a way, but a successful way, that it could be done. A lot of people say, oh, it's just for artists—artists are a little crazy, and they can do things that other people can't do. I don't believe that's true. The greatest luxury in New York City is space and light. This is what people want. Too often we're crammed into small, tiny spaces, because of economic necessity. But here was a way of creating more space, more light, much more open dimension: because we didn't build partitions. We didn't build rooms. We let people build the rooms the way they wanted. We provided kitchens and bathrooms, and then let people organize the rest in any way that they wanted. I sincerely thought that this would open up opportunities for other architects, for other builders in many ways. This never happened.

Diamonstein Obviously you'd like to see increased collaboration between architect and client, including the non-artistic client. Would you also like to see increased collaboration between architects and artists?

Meier Well, I think there's always been collaboration between architects and artists throughout history. It's only stopped in rather recent times, but I think that it will happen again. It's always happened in the past, and I see no reason that it shouldn't continue in the future.

Diamonstein Are there any artists with whom you want to collaborate?

Meier Well, Frank Stella and I are working on a project right now, which is a great deal of fun, because we've known one another, and worked together when I designed his loft. And yet this is something totally different. He is intervening to transform a building I designed, and then I transform his intervention in a different way. We don't know what it's going to come out looking like; it's an experiment.

Diamonstein Do you expect to have the project built?

Meier I expect to have everything built, but unfortunately most things don't get built. In this case, I don't think it'll be built, but you never know.

Diamonstein As a modernist, how do you feel about the current interest in reintroducing classical ornamentation and decoration into contemporary architecture?

Meier I think it's a very temporal situation which will pass. I think that there are legitimate reasons for change. I would like to think that one's experiences in life, and the way in which one thinks about things, are always open to change. I believe that one has to look to different ways of doing things. To pick random elements from the history of architecture, which had meaning in particular locations, in particular places, and to use them out of context, with no meaning, or to fasten on to them some new meaning, or some metaphorical connotation—I don't think this is a change which comes out of any profound notion about what it is one is doing. I think it's a stylizing of architecture as mere decoration. I'm very much against it, and I just don't think that it has any enduring quality or value. I think that one's knowledge and use of history is very important because of the principles involved. An understanding of the principles allows us to interpret where we are, and where we can go, not simply to manipulate elements used without principles. This is what I feel is being done at present. It is a stylizing, an overreaction to the fifties and sixties. I would agree that a kind of dehumanization occurred, through corporate structures, through many municipal complexes of that times, that lack human scale and quality. I think this is what people are reacting to, lack of human quality in the spaces which one is experiencing.

Diamonstein Certainly many of those finely machined images of the recent past have had little staying power over the imagination. Over the past half-century, they've had more success in charming the architectural profession, than the public at large.

Meier The economic situation which existed in the sixties and the early seventies is something which I doubt we'll see again in our lifetime. And that is a kind of unprecedented building boom. The volume of work, the rapidity with which it was done, the lack of thought that so many of these enormous projects seem to have resulted from—I think is what has led to this picking and choosing of columns and cornices. There was just too much

Bronx Development Center,
view of courtyard, interior,
Bronx, N.Y.
Picture credit: Ezra Stoller
© ESTO

Twin Parks Northeast Housing,
exterior, Bronx, N.Y.
Picture credit: Ezra Stoller
© ESTO

The Atheneum, New
Harmony, Ind
Picture credit: Ezra Stoller
© ESTO

Smith House, interior,
Darien, Conn.
Picture credit: Ezra Stoller
© ESTO

building, too quickly, with too little thought. I'm sure we're going to see a period in the future of fewer and fewer building projects on the scale that we saw in the sixties and early seventies. Those that do come to fruition, I would hope would have a lot more thought behind them than most of those we saw in the previous period.

Diamonstein Should that thought emphasize the lifestyle of the occupants, or should it reflect certain abstract notions of the architect? What should come first, the architect's ideas about space, or the client's ideas about ways of living?

Meier Except in the case of private houses, one doesn't know who the real client is, who's going to use the building. We deal with public agencies who build for whomever the alternate user is. The people who are going to be living in public housing are not directly involved in the design process. So I've never had any experience with users other than in the private houses, in which one is ultimately dealing with the "user." My ideas about architecture have to do with the quality of life, the quality of space and how one makes it. I believe that's the concern of the architect. I think that that's what the architect brings to any building project—what is the physical environment, and what is the physical organization of that environment, and how one can best create spaces which have a quality of life.

Diamonstein You've continually described your buildings in terms of abstractions, the making of space, light, the molding of forms. Rarely in any of these descriptions has there been talk about function. I would hardly argue in favor of purely functional architecture, but how much emphasis should go to the functional aspects?

Meier I think that every architect spends ninety percent of his energies making the building functional. It goes without saying that that's the role of the architect. It's what you do after this that interests me, because I think that every good architect can make a well-functioning building. The functions of a building are not so difficult at all.

Diamonstein After five years of planning and construction, a new museum and conference center was dedicated in New Harmony, Indiana. That building, the Atheneum, is your latest structure, and it's been described as a building of beauty and brilliance, and indeed it is. It certainly reflects what you've been talking about, the controlled and purposeful manipulation of light and space. Ada Louise Huxtable described it as a classic meeting hall for the nation's heartland. New Harmony is the focus of a massive restoration and revitalization effort. The town is the site of two unique nineteenth-century experimental communities. From 1814 to 1824, the Harmony Society occupied it, and after that the Owenites, the scientific and technological society led by Robert Owen. They were the people who were very influential in establishing the Smithsonian Institution. In this Owenite experiment that was filled with scientists and educators, architecture played a very specific role, the agent of social change. There is no real harmony of any kind in New Harmony, at least in terms of architectural style, nor is there any overriding vernacular. Is the Atheneum stylistically compatible with the rest of your work, but not necessarily with the rest of the town, which is a historic village of early nineteenth-century structures? Would you tell us how you came to build such a beautiful, but stark white building in such a place?

Meier I was asked by the president of Historic New Harmony, Ralph Schwarz, to go out there and take a look at New Harmony, and see if I would be interested in building the Atheneum, or designing the Atheneum for them. New Harmony is in the southwestern corner of Indiana. Now the nearest public transportation by air is Evansville, which is an hour's drive away. You get off the plane at Evansville, and you have a drive through flat farmland. I remember thinking the first time, am I in the right place? There can't be another town out here in this sort of wilderness. We finally came to New Harmony, and it was an oasis in the middle of the farmlands. It's a place that has never experienced the normal kind of suburban growth and sprawl which usually develops as two small towns grow together, where you get a sort of strip development.

Diamonstein I thought they had a declining population until the revitalization.

Meier Well, that's not true, because up until recently, farming was the major industry. In 1824, when Robert Owen was there, there were 950 residents. Today there are still 950 residents, not the same ones of course. But it's always remained about the same size. That as such is quite fascinating, because it's not a place with any one style. There are a few interesting Federal houses; there are a few interesting Greek Revival houses; there are wonderful Victorian houses; there are some reconstructed log cabins from the Harmonious period. There is a wonderful cast iron facade one block long, which is Main Street. It has a lot of quality but it's all diverse. There is no one style that is present. But what is unique about it is that whatever is there was of its time, and was meaningful when it was built. And to build a building today that looks like the log cabins would be as ludicrous as building a pseudo-Federal building. What Historic New Harmony wanted, and I think quite appropriately, was a building that they could say was of its time, and yet would acknowledge somehow the history of New Harmony. The Atheneum is a visitor's center. It's a place where people see exhibits on the history of New Harmony and a film on New Harmony's past, buy their tickets for the tour of the town, and begin their promenade through the town.

Diamonstein In some ways it is an orientation center, not unlike Williamsburg, Virginia.

Meier That's right, that's right. But unlike Williamsburg, people don't dress up in costume, and don't greet you at the door in a kind of phony way of saying, this is the way it was. People live there, and work there. It's a living, working community. The purpose is to show how a community which has quite a rich history, has a contemporary life which is as meaningful as its past. And so this building of orientation is a building which one moves through, sees exhibits, and also sees aspects of the town. It's on the edge of the Wabash River, and one comes up through the center space and looks out and sees the river, sees the point where one formerly entered the town. In the 1850s people entered New Harmony by boat, down the Wabash River. As you move through and climb up, and go on through the roofs, and walk around and go through the theater, and come back down the stairs, and down the ramp, the building propels you back into the town, and relates to the roofless church by Philip Johnson. It's got access to that roofless church, and the crown of the building points to the top of the roofless church, which happens to be a block away, as well as to the Orchard House, which is an Owenite structure, and the cemetery next to it. It also makes reference to the natural setting. It's up on a podium, too, because the Wabash River floods every year. So this porcelain paneled boatland of knowledge is sort of floating on New Harmony's shore, as the river rises.

Diamonstein Did you select the site?

Meier No. I manipulated the site, but I didn't select the site.

Diamonstein What does that mean?

Meier Well, the site—like other sites which I've been given—was formerly a garbage dump. This is not the first time we've built on a garbage dump. But it was a garbage dump; it was at the end of the town; it was outside the historic limits of the town; and there was an old foundation that had been built a number of years ago for a building that was never erected. Originally they thought, well maybe we could use that foundation and build on top of it. Fortunately, as it turned out, that foundation was decaying, so we could move the building to a different part of this open field. We had to conform to the wishes of the U.S. Department of Natural Resources, and build a podium in order to keep the building out of the river. That helped us too, because we then could have a sort of Acropolis-like setting. And then the building sort of slopes down to the woods and to the water. So when I say "manipulate" the site, what I mean is form the site by moving earth. We were allowed to keep the trees and to shape and open them to use the water.

Diamonstein You said you had to conform to the wishes of federal departments. How about the wishes of the people that live there? How do they feel about the building, now that it is there?

Meier Everyone I talked to loves it, but I only talked to the people who liked it. We have the same thing here in New York. I walk along Madison Avenue now, and see all of these buildings under construction, and I have my view of what they are, and how they're going to affect our town. And I'm very concerned about what they're going to do to the people who live here. In New Harmony, it's even more so, because it's the first new building in the last twenty years, so there's even more concern about what this new structure is, and there's nothing like it. Every night when the workmen left, the town's populace, without much else to do, came up the gangplank to see what happened that day. Everyone was very skeptical about it. But when it finally opened, and people came through it, they were really very enthusiastic. And what's interesting is that it's really in the middle of nowhere. Anyone who goes there will see that. I think it's well worth the trip. New Harmony as a place is worth going to see. But the Midwest is very different, and I had no idea about how different it was until I had this opportunity to work there. Distance is different from the way in which we experience it here in the East. I learned a lot from this experience, and I think we did the right thing.

Diamonstein In honor of the dedication of the Atheneum, you involved your own talent in a new medium, and that is the exacting art of lithography. As I recall, that cast iron structure on Main Street is also an art gallery, and the man who runs that art gallery is also a fine printer. How did your collaboration come about?

Meier I'd never done a lithograph before, and I thought, you make a drawing and someone prints it. There's nothing to it. There's a young lithographer who runs the gallery, as you pointed out, and he gave me all these big metal plates, and said, okay, make a drawing, and we'll do a lithograph. So I made a drawing, and he said, is that all you want to do, and he gave me six more plates. I made six more drawings which overlaid, and he went and got some people in central Indiana to make the paper, and we made a print. It only took two years. But it was a very wonderful learning experience for me, because of the way a group of people came together. I didn't really know very much about the whole process before it began. I know a little bit about it now.

Diamonstein Do you plan to do it again?

Meier I do. In fact, I hope that Frank and I are going to do a lithograph together. Frank Stella is making some absolutely beautiful lithographs right now, the most beautiful lithographs I've ever seen.

Diamonstein Have you as an artist ever collaborated with an architect?

Meier No.

Diamonstein Would doing that ever occur to you?

Meier Never had that occasion. But who knows, anything's possible.

Diamonstein Among the buildings that you have built is one omission, and that is—at least in this country—any building to house the fine arts. Is that the kind of commission that would interest you?

Meier Actually, I've done a number of projects. One in Florence for a museum which was also a renovation, taking the stables of the Villa Strozzi, and making a new museum. I also did a room in the Guggenheim Museum, a small reading room, about half the size of this stage. I also had the opportunity of doing an exhibition, which was really a museum within a museum, in Albany for an exhibition called "New York: State of the Art." Part of the Albany Mall is a large cultural center building, and within that building is a forty thousand square foot space, which has been sitting empty for about two or three years. I designed a museum installation for a special exhibition of the New York School of Painting and Sculpture, which was there two years ago.

Diamonstein And unfortunately, because of the size and scale of the art, it has never been able to travel. You might tell us what you did do with that forty-two thousand square feet of space that you had to play with. It's been said that the installation was an imposing presence that never intruded on the arts, and was discussed as much as the art itself at the time.

Meier I was very close to the work that was being shown there. I mean, here we had people who were my heroes when I grew up. They had Rothko, de Kooning, and Pollock, and I could just go right down the line. And great pictures. So these are all really people of the street, people who worked in New York, who really loved the city, and in the fifties made New York the center of art that it is today. So in a sense, the installation is a metaphor of the city. There are streets, there are windows, there are rooms, there are buildings within—and of course we were lucky to have this huge, enormous space to deal with. We could make an installation which not only showed the arts in an incredible way, but made a further statement about a kind of city structure within the building. It allowed windows so that one could see a work of art in an intimate setting, and then look across and see another work of art, a distance away. As you moved through the space, not only were you able to see things close up, in a normal gallery situation, but you were able to see things you had seen before, in a different relationship to other works of art. It's something I learned from the Guggenheim Museum, where you see a work, and then you go around to the other side of the ramp, and when you look across, you see it differently. But fortunately, because of the space that I was dealing with, I could do it in another scale, and make it much more intimate, without getting into rotational complications.

Diamonstein I think it's interesting that you say that, because your installation accommodated itself to the art, and I think very few people would say that about the Guggenheim. In fact, in an interview, you called the Guggenheim Museum the best work of architecture in the city. Do you still believe that?

Meier I still believe that, yes.

Diamonstein Why do you like the building so much?

Meier Well, when you go into that space in the Guggenheim, there's an uplifting quality which is absolutely wonderful. I happen to think that good works of art look good in the Guggenheim, and bad works of art fall apart there. Things hold their own, and they really have to have the strength and the power, and a poignancy. I don't think group shows work well in the Guggenheim Museum. I think a good one-man show does work well, and that you can see it, and see it again and again. It does need a kind of unified theme, such as a one-man show, to hold up. The Calder show that was there was absolutely exquisite. I do not happen to be a strong proponent of Beuys, but I thought that the Beuys show had an incredible power, and a wonderful presence, which would not have come across any place else in the same way. I've often said that—and this is a little bit facetious of course—but someday that building may not be any longer a place to show paintings and sculpture, and it'll still be a great building, as far as I'm concerned.

Diamonstein In this pluralistic moment in architecture, is there any building that you haven't built that you would like to?

Meier All the buildings I've designed and haven't built, I would like to do. But it's a funny thing—as an architect, you really put all your energy into the thing that you're working on at that particular moment, and you really think that that is the thing that is important. Then you either build or you don't build, and go on to the next thing. And that becomes what is important. But one of the reasons I did the book on my work was a certain frustration, having designed so many buildings, and having done the working drawings, and gotten them to the point where they could begin construction, and then because of the economic situation in the early seventies, so many were not built. They were simply models and drawings. This disappointment was enormous for me at that time; it still is. But, as I look back, I couldn't say that's the building I would want to build, now. At the time when they didn't go ahead, I felt a great sense of loss. It hurts, because you work and you work for a year, two years, three years, and your work is almost finished, and then it's really up to someone else to execute it. But that's the point at which it becomes expensive for the client, because compared to the building cost, the architect's fees are minuscule. And that's the point at which many things stop. You realize that you've spent all of this time, and this energy, and the commitment, and a certain part of your life is taken—put into that building, and the fact that the building isn't realized is an enormous disappointment.

Diamonstein What's the most important thing for us to know about your work?

Meier It's a good question. As I pointed out earlier, my thoughts and my concerns really have to do with space and light, and the ways in which one manipulates them. And it's something which I think I pursue with a kind of direction, or perseverance, in terms of the quality of the space. That's really what concerns me the most, to get the maximum quality that is humanly possible. In working on my first house, and working in the Northeast, one thing I learned was that inside space is different from outside space. Wright always talked about the continuous flow of space from the interior to the exterior. The minute you put up a glass wall, you define the space, whether you want to accept it or not. That doesn't make the space go away. And just because it's a glass plate doesn't mean that the inside space and the outside space are contiguous. Even if the material on the inside wall which penetrates that glass plate is brick, which for the most part would weather less than any other material, the appearance and the understanding and the reading of that brick on the outside is different from the brick wall on the inside. The way in which the brick wall encloses the space on the outside is not the same as on the inside. This I learned very early on, and I guess this is why Le Corbusier became more and more important for me. In Le Corbusier's work there is a clear definition in terms of interior and exterior space. And many of the things which Wright preached which we loved so much when I was a student, aren't quite that way in reality. I think that in terms of light though, Wright was a master. You go and visit any one of his buildings, the way in which light comes into that building is uplifting. Le Corbusier was different, but he also understood the play of natural light on the spaces that he was creating, and I think that Aalto did, of course, in another way. But there is no one way, and I think that one learns, not only from the immediate past, but, as I mentioned earlier, from Borromini as well. Certainly the way in which his spaces are made through the use of natural light is a very important lesson to all architects.

Diamonstein But aren't you very often responsible, particularly in houses, for the interior design?

Meier Quite honestly, I don't think I would do another house where I did not have complete control of the interior design.

Audience What do you think of all the new construction going on in midtown Manhattan, on Madison Avenue?

Meier The five new buildings that I've observed, one on the corner of Fifty-seventh Street, one on the corner of Fifty-sixth Street, and one on the corner of Fifty-third Street, the one midblock on Fifty-third Street, and the one on Fifth Avenue and Fifty-sixth Street, are all hopelessly irresponsibly designed, in terms of the form of the city. I think each one attempts to say, my block is more important than your block, and therefore, I'm going to flex my muscles in a different way than you're flexing your muscles. Each one is a kind of singular statement. One of the things which I had thought had happened in the seventies was that there was a new awareness of the kind of conceptual responsibility of the architect, a responsibility to try to relate for better or worse to what was there, and to indicate a way in which a neighbor might live happily, but without feeling that his rights were infringed upon. I think each of those buildings infringed upon the public—for instance, the corner of Fifty-seventh Street. Here we have a city whose buildings are basically at right angles to one another in every situation. All of a sudden at the corner of Fifty-seventh and Madison, we have a building that says, I'm not going to respect the form of the city any longer. I'm going to turn my building into the corner, into the intersection. But no one is in the intersection. An intersection is where the cars are crossing one another. All of a sudden we add forty five degrees to a basically orthogonal organization which is the rest of the city—it's part of the quality of New York City. I feel that, you know, one has to look at the site of one's building, and build there respectfully, and my argument is that these are not respectful designs.

Diamonstein How do you think that came about? There are so many buildings, each of them so individual.

Meier By the way, I've been criticized for the very thing I'm criticizing others for, but I always do a building that's a singular situation in an open landscape where there is nothing to relate to. When you're dealing in an urban environment, it's quite a different matter, you see, than when you're working out on a garbage dump in the middle of nowhere. I think there are different ways of giving originality. I have no argument with originality, but I think that it has to be respectful, not assertive originality, especially when you're building in the city. My definition of success is just having enough work to do what you want to do. That may mean one building project every five years, or whatever, but just having enough work to keep you vital and active. I've been fortunate; I have had that up until now. I've had things which occupy my time and energy all of the time. I have a very small practice. We're fewer than twenty people in my office. There is no formal structure whatsoever. I do what I think is the most important thing to do.

CHARLES MOORE

Charles W. Moore
Born Benton Harbor, Mich., 1925
B. Arch. University of Michigan, 1947
M.F.A. Princeton University, 1956
Ph.D. Princeton University, 1957

Diamonstein Charles Moore is famous for his whimsy, his exuberance, his work's lively color. His houses and public buildings have been described as among the most important small-scale architectural work of the last decade. Charles Moore's schedule is as enterprising as is his architecture. A frequent commuter between coasts, not to speak of continents, he practices with his former firm in Connecticut, and with the Urban Innovations Group in Los Angeles. A former dean of the Yale School of Architecture, he is currently the head of the architecture and design program at UCLA, and a visiting professor at Yale this semester. In addition to all that, he is the author of several books, including *The Place of Houses* and *Body, Memory and Architecture.*

You've been crusading for quite some time now against so-called orthodox modern architecture. For years, you have told both students and colleagues that the Puritan revolution is over, that they should design for popular taste, in harmony with the dreams and hopes of the people, not their own elitist visions of perfect form. What do you think about the fact that these days almost everyone seems to agree with you?

Moore I am not sure that everybody agrees—maybe it is because I am moving farther and farther toward what I regard as better ways of getting people's visions into the work that we produce together. I am excited these days about participatory buildings. We are doing a church and have lately done a park in which the parish, in the case of the church, and the community in the case of the park have designed the projects with us in a series of workshops. I am very proud because in each case, I have been told that they have never run up against an architect who inserted his own images so little, and who so much welcomed theirs.

Diamonstein You are referring to the St. Matthew's Episcopal Church in Pacific Palisades where groups of parishioners were involved in the decision-making.

Moore The whole parish.

Diamonstein It's contrary to the familiar old saw that nothing was ever created by committee. Did you have an experience to the contrary? How did the parish react to this group process?

Moore Let me back up. We were hired partly because we were among the few architects they could find who were willing to accept in our contract the requirement that two-thirds of the parish would have to vote in favor of the design. This very elegant Episcopal parish in Pacific Palisades had never been known to agree on anything. And they had just finished having a difficult time agreeing on a new rector after the one of thirty years had retired. And so we expected trouble. What happened was that we started working in a series of workshops. It wasn't like a committee telling the architect what to do, but rather a series of people, with us helping in an avuncular manner. We helped them arrive at the images that they had about the church, which turned out to be very strong, and in remarkable agreement. Finally, a month or so ago, we got an eighty-three percent vote in favor of the church that we had all been designing together. People would sit around tables in groups of ten to fifteen, and make a scheme. They would come up with maybe seven or eight of those schemes, and it would turn out each time, to our astonishment, all very much the same. I am not sure it would always happen like that, but there, the church we got was the church that was on the minds of most of the people involved. There were a few that didn't like it.

Diamonstein How close was it to the minds of the architectural firm involved?

Moore We have no mind.

Diamonstein Never mind.

Moore No. It makes no never mind. One of the things I think that's urgent about operating in that way is that the architect can't make up his mind about what the thing is going to be like before it is started. Otherwise, he is just going to be in constant conflict with the people who are forming their own minds. I care a lot about the church and have been doing all sorts of things to it as an architect in the month since the scheme was arrived at. The rector congratulated me after a particularly hot and heavy evening, when a lady of some years had been trying to tear me to pieces. I had been smiling and thinking, "How lovely, this nice old lady is tearing me to pieces," and he expressed amazement that I never seem to get defensive. I think that the secret of making all that work is just not to be committed beforehand to some scheme that you feel obliged to defend. I don't get defensive about anything until what the people want comes out. Then, I guess it's a manifestation of my own immense ego; but I think I can make a nice building out of anything that they come up with. This process is a great deal different from the advocacy planning of the sixties, in which young architects, and a few old ones, went in among the people to act as midwives for the people's visions. All that seemed to involve depended entirely on the shapes that people wanted, you know, making things the way they saw them. In many cases, those shapes turned out not to be definite enough to produce buildings. So that advocacy process very often just didn't produce stuff. Now, we are still acting as designers, doing things that we have been trained for, that we can presumably do more efficiently and better than people who haven't been trained. So making the shapes is up to us, but they are the shapes that people tell us they want. Refining the shapes is up to us.

Diamonstein And they define them?

Moore They define them and we refine them. We did a Rorschach test with slides, and the parish in Pacific Palisades, for instance, voted on a series of a hundred slides. The most votes for what they would like to see for St. Matthew's, went to Alvar Aalto's church at Imatra. The church they would least like to see was St. Peter's in Rome.

Diamonstein You have referred to sixties architecture as advocacy architecture.

Moore Some of it.

Diamonstein Some of the new architecture has been called everything from pop to post-modernist, from conceptual to post-functionalist. How would you describe it?

Moore I can't think of anything suitably bizarre to say. I am fond of the people who have made up the post-modern appellation, so I don't like to be sour about it. But it seems to me that the term covers so many different attitudes, from the very architectonic ones of Michael Graves or Richard Meier to the populist ones of people like me, that it's very hard to derive much meaning. Except that we are all interested in trying to make architecture more interesting by attaching to it images from people's pasts, from people's memories, that make it mean more than the pure forms of the last fifty, sixty years. I keep saying that I would rather be pre-something that post-anything. And I wish they would find another term.

Diamonstein How about neo-?

Moore I'd rather be paleo-. Actually, I'd rather be proto-. I'd rather be proto-whatever it is we are going to do next.

Diamonstein And just what is that going to be? This movement away from the glass box—is it taking a form that you are comfortable with, or do you think it's going in the wrong direction?

Moore Well, it's going in so many directions that it's very hard to say. It's very difficult to figure out what any chief direction is. Someone pointed out to me the other day something I had never realized, that Sigfried Giedion's *Space, Time and Architecture,* which served as a bible for my whole generation when we were going to school, which covers some five hundred years, contains some thirty-three examples of all periods that we were all supposed to agree on—arbitrarily selected buildings that were a very few out of millions that people were building. So we have been brought up on what a colleague of mine calls mainstreaming, in which the historian figures out what the mainstream is. It might include the front of some building but not its back. You know, the architect was in the mainstream when he did the front, so it's important. But when he did the back, the door had to be off-center, so he wasn't in the mainstream anymore. This is nuts. It doesn't lean toward helping us figure out what to do next, certainly. What I hope is happening is that the bonds are loosening a little bit. We are being given a chance to draw on many, many images from many, many places, and to do them with the agreement, rather than the passive submission, of the people who are going to live in the places. This is doubtless helpful. It produces some terrible-looking buildings, I have to say, but I don't think that renders it invalid.

Diamonstein You have been described very often as being concerned not so much with any structure's appearance and beauty, in an intellectual way, but rather with its comfort and pleasure, in a sensuous or physical way. Many of your buildings are known for looking more expensive than they really are. The other day, I read a quotation by Ambrose Bierce, who once defined an architect as one who drafts the plan of your house and plans the draft of your money—a very contrary procedure to yours. I'd like you to comment on the relationship in your work between costliness and the appearance of costliness.

Is that an attempt on your part to deflate pomposity?

Moore The relationship is complex. I had a friend, William Wilson Wurster, who was the dean at Berkeley when I went there long ago. His wife said of his work, which was very, very elegant but very understated—Bay Region and shanty—"No matter how much it costs, it will never show." I admire that way around as much as the one you were describing, although I haven't had very much chance to do the "However much it costs it will never show." I have felt a kind of professional requirement not to spend too much of people's money. I know that there are architects who give people pleasure. The board of directors of a bank comes and says, "Mr. Architect, we have a cunning little two-million-dollar bank," and the architect says, "You creep, how come you have a two-million-dollar bank, when you should be spending at least twelve million?" And they say

"Yes, sir, yes, sir. If we spend twelve, will it be wonderful?" And he says, "Yes." And they all live happily ever after. That gives me the creeps. I have tried very hard to make things that didn't cost more than the clients seemed to think they wanted to spend. But, I've missed a number of times with that premise. There are people who have been very disappointed that they got a cheap house after they asked for a cheap house.

Diamonstein You are also well-known for the humor in your work. You are one of the chief exponents of the building-as-sight-gag school. I have often wondered who the humor is for. Is it for architects, for fans of architecture? Is it for the public at large?

Moore I used to describe it in terms of buildings speaking; that there are many voices with which buildings can speak. Of course the words are put there by the designers and their inhabitants, and everybody involved with them. It seems to me that during the last half-century the language open to buildings has been drastically and catastrophically reduced, so that they can only look like the savings and loan, which is regarded as the most dignified way for something to look. I am against that. I think that buildings can and should talk in different voices for different occasions and with different special circumstances. There is no reason why they should, in their desperate attempt to achieve dignity, be robbed of that chance. That doesn't mean that I am for the one-liner I think an awful lot of post-modern buildings that I object to are. You know, you spend fifty million bucks and you build something and everybody says, "Whoopee, it looks like a fish." And then that's that. Everybody knows it looks like a fish and nobody cares again. Whatever set of moods any building is trying to create, it has to have in it lots of emotional colors, so that it means different things at different times to people. I think the overall require-ment of anything that people are going to spend money on is that it should be a pleasant place to be. It should be nice when the sun comes up in the morning and shines in the breakfast room, or nice for the view out over the water, or whatever. And I think that the gag is really not very funny in architecture. The building built to allow some writer for the architectural press to say something cute is not worth the trouble.

Diamonstein I'd like to talk about another innovation of yours. For hundreds of years, until the modern movement banished them, architecture used classical ornament systems, called orders, such as the Doric order, the Ionic order and the Corinthian order. With wonderful playfulness, you have added something to the Vitruvian canon by introducing a new order. You in-vented the Delicatessen order for the Piazza d'Italia in New Orleans.

Moore We thought we were going to have a delicatessen in it, which is why it got called that. But it's going to be an elegant Italian restaurant instead.

Diamonstein That's another spoof.

Moore Well, spoof. I didn't do that first. Early twentieth century architects and American architects, since there have been any, have been busy inventing column capitals with corn and wheat, and I suppose barley and oats, and Indian spears, and anything else we could think of that would be interest-ing to people. We wanted to put something people could relate to onto their buildings, and also to cope with that difficult place where a vertical support meets the horizontal that it's supporting. We had this delicatessen, we thought, because it was at the top of the map of Italy and therefore it would be in some vague way Germanic, with sausages in the window.

Diamonstein But not germane . . . Your Piazza d'Italia Fountain in New Orleans was commissioned, as I recall, as a celebratory space for the local Italian community. And you produced what has been called a razzmatazz design and one that caused considerable controversy, as actually one might have expected when designing any public square that in a way resembles a stage-set, with a fountain, a map of Italy in the pavement, and classical Corinthian columns, painted yellow and decorated in neon. Perhaps you might tell us how this design evolved, and what it was that you were trying to do.

Moore It is a celebratory space, so it seemed important to make it not like a savings and loan. In New Orleans for the last several years the local ethnic groups have gotten together and supported spaces, most of them really quite minimal. There's the Place de France, which is about five feet wide, with the inevitable Joan of Arc, in the middle of the highway. And there is the Plaza de España, much bigger with a lot of tiles and a fountain. And I think there is or is about to be Ein Deutscher Platz. God knows what else. The Italian community in New Orleans is very well organized, with a bunch of very influential civic leaders. And one of them gave the city an L-shaped piece of land at the bottom of a 23-story building in a field as a trade for some other land where the city closed a street. So that was the site, with some beautiful old warehouses on it. Then they had a limited competition, in which we participated, which was won by a local firm, August Perez. I ended up as the fountain consultant and second-place winner. My scheme had been a big elliptical swirl, of dark and light stripes that crunched up into a fountain, to continue the vertical stripes of the building, so as not to contrast with it or show it up too much. It is a very simple, modern building. We were meant to make something Italian. We used a considerable amount of sophistry to announce that it reminded us of the Piazza San Marco's Campanile, because it's tall. The scheme, the winning scheme, had a round piazza, which was kept. The idea was to have a big fountain that could serve as an altar on St. Joseph's Day, the day of the patron saint of the Italian community in New Orleans. Food is put on altars and then at noontime is given to poor people. Children dressed as Jesus and Joseph and Mary march around and give the food away and say things suitable to the occasion. So that was why we needed a big fountain. We said, "What shape should the fountain be in?" What was the most Italian shape we could think of? Well, Italy. And, then we said, "We can run the water down the Po and the Arno and the Tiber."

Diamonstein Those are the three fountains that represent the three rivers.

Moore The three rivers. Then we could have it run into the Tyrrhenian and Adriatic seas, where people could splash. And then I said, "Hooray, we can also have tiki torches on Vesuvius and Etna." And they said, "No, we cannot do that, for that is tacky."

Diamonstein And besides, it's Sicily.

Moore It turns out that, ninety-five percent of the Italian community in New Orleans comes from Sicily. Sicily had to be the middle of this thing—as for example, a podium for speaking—and people could sit on Sardinia to listen to the Sicilians talk. So it would not have been suitable to have had a tiki torch under these speakers. Or at least so they said. Then we all sat around and said, "We have to have more water than this; this is no fountain." I am told I didn't think of Italy, but I did think of the orders. The way we operated, it was impossible to know who thought up what twenty minutes later. Then we invented some schemes for marching the orders across the piazza, and it hid Italy. Then we found a way of pushing them back around so they wouldn't be in the way. We spent weeks thinking up ways that orders could be made out of water, with the acanthus leaves made by crunching a spoon around so that the water forms the leaves. And water rolling around in the volutes of the Ionic capital, and a little water up in the metopes—that got to be called wetopes. There got to be a lot of stainless steel in it. Water rolling down stainless steel walls seemed wonderful to us. I had a special place that I was very proud of, where the water on the Doric fall, running down the stainless steel, was going to be intercepted above the arches by huge truck windshield wipers.

Diamonstein There must be another place that you are very proud of as well. On one of the walls there are a pair of heads that spout water. And those heads, whoopee, look like Charles Moore! How did that come about?

Moore Well, my colleagues, desirous a) of not having those truck windshield wipers, which they thought were tacky, and b) of doing something funny, did all that. They managed to keep it a secret from me. The two designers in the Paris office did this bizarre thing. I immediately shaved off my whiskers so as to avoid recognition.

Diamonstein Paul Goldberger [architecture critic of the *New York Times*] has called it the most significant public plaza that any American city has erected in many years. At the same time he said that it was an expression of a wild imagination, as if the Roman Forum were reerected in Las Vegas. Is that what you learned from Las Vegas?

Moore I never learned anything from Las Vegas. I am sure I should have. But each of us has a threshold of tackiness—

Diamonstein Beyond which we cannot go?

Moore Beyond which we cannot go, yes.

Diamonstein Your houses do not fit into any easily classifiable style. Often, they remind one of collage, an assemblage of elements, that are not visibly related to one another, except in their ability to please the client, and, I guess, the architect. The point is that one cannot say "Moore," when given a picture of something, quite so easily as one might say "Meier" or "Gehry." Is this deliberate?

Moore Yes. I think that's a straight answer. How is it for the people who inhabit them? I get much more pleasure out of trying to figure out what would turn them on, what dreams and visions and images they are hanging onto in their heads. Then I try to make those happen in some way that's full of a choreography of elements that interest people. I get much more pleasure out of that than I would out of making my own set. I've made six houses for myself, and that really is plenty to try out my own images. But I realize that my hand is evident in things I do; I guess it couldn't help but be. I feel very proud when people say that I did not push them, but helped them to get what they want.

Diamonstein What would you call your style, if you have to give it a name?

Moore There are a couple of writers who call it free-style, which I think is a good way of getting at some of the qualities. Many architects find it very helpful to make a set of rules and then work within them. There have been lots of distinguished examples in all the arts in this century. Stravinsky's *Poetics of Music* does a beautiful job of describing that point of view, of saying the artist should limit and hone and squeeze to get the grounds for producing a great piece of art. I think that's very impressive; I don't quarrel with that. It's something that some artists and some architects can and should do. But I get a lot more pleasure out of the elusive attempt to put together everything that comes to the project—the client's visions, the stinking little budget, the whole business.

Diamonstein Some architects love empty spaces, but you fill them up, celebrating clutter and the idea that we surround ourselves with objects that we love and know the best. Among your best-known buildings are your own six houses. I am thinking particularly of the houses in Orinda, California, and in New Haven. Perhaps you could describe the environment and some of the innovations you have created for yourself. What's a pyramid doing in a bedroom in Connecticut?

Moore It's a compositional device, with a message, which is what anything ought to be, I guess.

Diamonstein The message is?

Moore Charles Jencks calls these things double-coded. The main room in my little house in Essex, Connecticut had been a lawyer's office. It was dark wood and big and located under the eaves, so the edges sloped toward the top. I'm not neat by nature. It was both a living room and a sleeping room, and I needed something to hide the bed. It seemed to me that it would be more interesting to have an object to hide the bed rather than just to have some grungy little thin wall doing that. Also, that would let me have a closet, which was useful, since there were no other closets in the house. It came over me one day, when I was looking at one of my last remaining dollar bills—that it would be a kind of endearment if I could hang on to that concept.

Diamonstein The dollar bill—not Egypt—inspired you.

Moore Oh, yeah, because the dollar bill has that wonderful Masonic eye over it, which was the thing I was really trying to get. I never made the eye right. It should have glowed, or something. Once I had a pyramid, Olivetti sent me a calendar that had a nice Egyptian pyramid, with those little ant-farm burrows in it, that took you down to the pharaoh's tomb. I thought that would be nice to put some of my numerous objects in. And then we mixed up the green for the pyramid which was supposed to be dollar-bill green, and somebody said, "This is not the green of the dollar bill, this is the green of a watermelon." And we all said, "Whoopee. We will now make the inside pink." A watermelon is much more interesting on the inside than a dollar bill is, when you get right down to it.

Diamonstein Your work is known for its color, and its supergraphics. In Connecticut there is a boldness of graphic material. Would you describe that environment?

Moore The room was too dark, but the dark-beaded boards were beautiful. So we thought, we have to paint some of this room white and leave some of it with the pretty dark-beaded boards. What can we do? We already had the dollar-bill pyramid, and so it was natural enough to think of all the things that dollar bills say on them. That caused quite a lot of ruckus, because it's very hard to paint lettering on a ceiling if you haven't done it before.

Diamonstein Especially in a circle.

Moore Especially in a circle. A real pain.

We had been very much involved in supergraphics in the sixties. I guess it's not wrong this much later to call it a revolutionary gesture, at a time when there was an attempt to change everything super fast, and in our case, anyway, without spending much money.

Diamonstein What was the purpose of that device?

Moore The purpose of the supergraphics was to attack reality. Supergraphics of the sixties, with their bright colors, reflected the mood of the period. They were meant to change your impression of a building or a wall, or whatever the supergraphics are painted on. Unless it does that, it isn't, in my limited definition, supergraphics of the sort that we were interested in. Genuine supergraphics mean shapes that are much bigger than the space that you are in, so that you feel as though you're in the bottom of some room infinitely larger than the one you are actually in. They were very interesting for us in the sixties. They have let us do some cheap remodeling on places where we didn't have the money, or where nobody wanted to deal with more permanent materials. They let us put some excitement on things like very low-budget public housing, things like that, that would benefit from the cheer that supergraphics would give. But we don't need or want to do it anymore, now that it's the eighties, or even while it was the seventies. Everyone's desire to change everything drastically has, I think, passed away in favor of the expectation that if things are to be changed, it will be much more effective if they are changed slowly and carefully, and if they are based, at least in part, on traditions we have. I'm fond of saying that I think architecture is most usefully seen not as a composition of shapes, but as a choreography of the familiar and the unfamiliar. You need the familiar to get people involved, to make people feel it's theirs. And you need to have the surprise of the unfamiliar even to make the familiar evident, because people get bored with the familiar and need the excitement of surprise sometimes. But if you just blast them with surprise alone it's not illuminating, not useful.

Diamonstein Your interest in the participatory nature of the exchange between the architect and the client, and what you have called your own populist approach, is particularly manifest in the use of videotape to interest people in urban design. How and where and to what effect have you used that device?

Moore It's actually not videotapes but live TV, in which—and we're in our fifth city now—we roll into town for a period of months. People from our office open a store-front office to encourage people to come in and tell us about what they are interested in and the problem at hand. In Dayton, Ohio, it was the riverfront. In Roanoke, Virginia, it was a downtown urban renewal space that was mostly torn down. In Watkins Glen, New York, we're now doing a lakefront scheme, in a little town that has railroad tracks along the shore, at present.

But it's worthless, we think, for a team of architects to roll into a town and tell the town what to do. Until they've been asked, they can't be anything but suspicious and generally angry. So we ask. Dayton was the first one. Mostly we were trying to think of some way to get the job away from Larry Halprin and RTKL, who were also trying to get that job. We figured they would think of most other things but they'd never think of TV! And then we got hooked on it. A couple of people in our office in Connecticut, Chad Floyd especially, now spend most of their time organizing television programs. There are usually a series of programs. We usually have a bank of six telephones, lots of notices in the newspapers and on the radio beforehand to encourage people to listen and then to call in with their ideas. We deal with the subject progressively—from introducing the idea of what the area is like there for people who haven't looked at it much, to preliminary models, to more refined models. The programs give us a chance to act like architectural short-order cooks, moving models around, and making pictures of what people call in and say they would like.

Diamonstein Do you often get eighty percent agreement, as you did in Pacific Palisades, California?

Moore We get an enormous amount of consensus. I think that there is much less conflict about what people want in a city, or in a little town, or in any situation, than architects have always chosen to believe. People aren't sitting lost in a miasma of self-doubt and confusion, waiting to be saved by some heroic architect. They are pretty close to getting it together, but somebody has to help give it shape. The shapes are inevitably complicated.

Diamonstein Are you pleased with the results?

Moore In Roanoke, they have raised, by one means or another, including some public bonding, something like thirty-three million bucks since we did our television thing several months ago. They are building most of the things that they said they wanted to build during our programs.

Diamonstein How closely did their requests match your forethought?

Moore We didn't have any forethought. We didn't know what they needed. We were from out of town.

Diamonstein Well, if that's the case, why shouldn't a local architect be designing and planning for them?

Moore This wasn't true in Roanoke, but in some cases we have been called in because there was a groundswell of resentment against local architects. They seemed to be doing stuff secretly. People thought that in some way they were being had. Even quite beautiful things designed by local architects were not seen as meeting the needs of the people. And so we were asked, I think, not for whatever previously organized images we might have had, but for our capacity to find out what people had on their minds.

Diamonstein You have been rolling into a lot of towns and a lot of cities and a lot of countries for quite some time. How important is it for an architect to travel? How important is it for an architect to collect memories and learn his history firsthand?

Moore I don't suppose I should make any across-the-board pronouncements about it. But this planet is full of wonderful buildings and cities, parks

Live TV, Watkins Glen, N.Y.
Picture credit: Marcia E. Kelley

Piazza d'Italia, New Orleans, La.
Picture credit: Norman McGrath

New Haven House, interior,
New Haven, Conn.
Picture credit: Norman McGrath

New Haven House, interior,
New Haven, Conn.
Picture credit: Norman McGrath

and trees, and various places. For my increasing conservatism as I was describing earlier—the choreography of the familiar and the surprising—I think getting familiar with a lot is helpful, and for me absolutely necessary. I can't imagine not running off to see something as soon as I've heard about it. But I am sure there are people who have much better meal schedules and all, by staying put. I don't think I would like to recommend that everybody take off this very minute and roll around the world. But I would certainly like it if I could take my history classes to the things in question, rather than just showing those everlasting slides.

Diamonstein What, if any, historical precedents impress you? What precedents do you use as models for your own approach to architecture?

Moore My favorites these days, subject to change always, are a trio of early nineteenth century architects who are no surprise to anybody: John Soane in London, Karl Friedrich Schinkel in Berlin, and Thomas Jefferson on these shores. I find them very exciting because they were at once at the dawn of a new era, the Industrial Revolution, and yet so involved in the past. Schinkel, who was investing heavily in iron works, and Jefferson, starting a whole new country . . .

Diamonstein And Soane investing heavily in acquisitions . . .

Moore Lumpy rocks. But still, they were nice lumpy rocks.

I think Soane is in some ways my favorite of the lot. But these guys were all on the threshold of a whole new era, doing something exciting, but expecting that the past that they had inherited and loved would be helpful to them in facing the new era. They had all had their grand tours, Schinkel and Soane to Italy, and Jefferson to France. They had picked up on things they thought were wonderful and that they could bring back and use with dazzling freedom. A Soane column capital has about as much relation to an Italian column capital as Richard Meier has to those Belgian architects. All of them could get the essence of the classical past in one incision, and still not leave out the thin incision and just go blank, the way some of our more immediate predecessors seem to have done. For me, they are a very exciting trio.

Diamonstein Your work habits are legendary, as well. We have seen examples of ink sketches on cocktail napkins that you have been drawn on airplanes. Those sketches seem entirely compatible with your now legendary peripatetic existence. How and where do you work?

Moore Less in airplanes now, because all the cocktail napkins are really crummy. They have little patterns on them. They are very hard to draw on.

Diamonstein May I remind you of the work you did while you were seated here this evening: a splendid Charles Moore drawing for a work in progress, that I guess the rest of us will have the opportunity to see about a year from now. This work in progress is yours together with that of an artist. Would you comment on and evaluate the general nature and quality of collaboration that has existed, as you see it, between architects and artists from 1945 to the present?

Moore Well, that will be fast. While both architecture and art, including sculpture, were apparently scared of content, scared of saying something specific, the opportunities for the artist and the architect to collaborate were just about nil. So the typical thing was the Mies van der Rohe creation of an absolutely neutral grid, in which some wiggly thing by an artist could be placed, set off, contrasted. In the past, before 1945, and perhaps best in the seventeenth century, there were so many things to talk about and to do with buildings and sculpture and painting that they were natural cohabitors of the same space. You had a batch of saints or devils or whatever, rolling around in the building. I think especially of something like Bernini's San Andrea al Quinnale, where there is a crowd of good-looking young saints—full size, plus cherubs. It adds considerable conviviality to the elliptical church. My hope is that it will revive in the years just ahead, starting tomorrow afternoon; that content will return—and I hear both painters and sculptors, and architects, as well, announcing that it will. It's happening already. I am looking desperately for the return of figures to the cornices of buildings and—all over the place.

Diamonstein If we have the return of the classical order, the column to contemporary architecture, can figures be far behind?

Moore Well, the trouble is not very many people know how to do them. At some cost, you can whop column capitals together. We suggested to the people in New Orleans, for whom we are doing a scheme for a Federation Hall for the Italian community on the piazza, that the best that we could think of for figures was to get some of the young people of the community to yank their clothes off and be cast. And they were offended by this concept . . .

Diamonstein Any volunteers?

Moore Not a one. No, their elders headed it off before it got anywhere, and we were seen as extremely dirty middle-aged persons. So more subtle approaches will obviously have to be devised.

Diamonstein Do you enjoy working with artists? Are you helped or hindered by such a collaboration?

Moore I haven't worked with very many.

Diamonstein Why?

Moore Well, to begin with, most of the things we do are sufficiently cheap so that there aren't any dollars left over for the fees. Or for the works. But I teach with sculptors and painters, but sculptors especially, and I enjoy that.

Diamonstein Is there a natural alliance between architects and artists?

Moore I don't think there has been, for the reasons I have described. But I think there should be, and I suspect will be.

Diamonstein Would you ever like to design a museum?

Moore I'd love to. We're adding on to one at Williams College at the moment, which is very tiny. Williams College has a museum, which is getting expanded. It has a beautiful octagonal building from the 1820s, done by some person who was twenty-five years old at the time. And we are adding on to it, which is great fun.

Diamonstein What are your primary concerns in the design of that museum space? Is it light, is it space, is it flow?

Moore I bring two preconceptions to it—after having said that I wouldn't do that to buildings. First, it seems to me, from the museums I have been in, and God knows I have been in plenty, that rooms are nicer than flowing spaces, that I would rather be in a museum with a series of definable rooms in a definable order than in the kind of limitless space that was popular thirty years ago, and has been since. I also feel strongly in favor of the complexity of natural light. The whole issue that architects like

Alvar Aalto did so much with, admitting natural light to museum spaces without letting sunshine damage things on the walls, fascinates me. Also, I hate to be in museums where I don't know whether I am ever going to get out.

Diamonstein There is a maximum viewing time, don't you think? And, I suspect it's about forty-five minutes.

Moore The nicest thing in the big museum in Philadelphia, in my opinion, are the windows that look out over the river—you know, a lot of air after you've seen lots of wonderful stuff. But you can stand just so much wonderful stuff. That place is too big.

Diamonstein You have the opportunity to practice both on the East and the West Coasts. I wonder if you find any regional differences in those practices.

Moore I don't think there is as much as people seem to believe. I think people used to lead more carefree lives in California. But then we got that governor and various other phenomena, and now casual living is heavily restricted. I have always found that the young architect has, I think, a better chance to get jobs and get ahead in the East than in California, which has always been more strictly in the hands of the establishment than the East Coast—which is the opposite of people's conceptions. Because of the accelerating difficulty of building anything in California, it's probably easier to do something that you and the clients want to do here than it is there. It certainly is cheaper.

Diamonstein There is an alternative establishment in California that you have written on. I guess you were one of the first in a 1965 article in *Perspecta,* to comment seriously and persuasively on the architectural influence of Disneyland. How did that all turn out for you?

Moore Well, badly, I suppose. I still believe it. I go there a lot, and I think that that version of reality, though it's got obvious restrictions and limits and doesn't carry political freedoms and the like, is certainly more encompassing and more interesting, than most of the standard professional visions of a public realm that have otherwise been built. Obviously people of enormous skill put together Disneyland in California and Disney World in Florida. They went to make a community, which Paul Goldberger and Peter Blake wrote about years ago—and everybody had extremely high hopes that all the excitement and the functionalism of Disney World would be in this community. It's really discouraging to see how pedestrian and, I think, dreary it turned out to be when those same incredibly talented people faced what they see as the real world. I think if we could turn it around so that the rest of us saw ourselves as facing our own little Disneyland, that we would all get much more out of it.

Diamonstein Your notion is that the fundamental principle of architecture is territorial. I wonder, while we are still in California, if you would say a few words about Sea Ranch, a very influential community whose nucleus you helped design on the coast. I wonder if the early planning decisions there have been vindicated by the way Sea Ranch has developed. Are you pleased by what you have helped wrought?

Moore Yes and no. I have a house there still, which I love, and it's home. I go there every chance I get, and am delighted when I do and feel better there than anywhere. And yet the whole place is full of really egregious examples of human greed and avarice and ineptitude and disgusting points of view and lousy architects. It's a mess.

Diamonstein How did that happen?

Moore Well, human greed and avarice and sloth. It was put together on a kind of fluke, I think. In the early middle sixties, there was a client, a vice president of the development firm, who wanted all the right things. There was also a president of the firm who was a marvelously benign man who wanted the right things, too. And soon after the first part was finished, the president was retired. The vice president quit. We were all fired. And so they have been going on on their own ever since. Just in the last few years, they've gone right up against California's Coastal Commission, which they respond to in the spirit of Louis, probably the XIII. I don't think they show his successor's breadth of vision. So this ridiculous fight goes on, and many, many pieces of paper are sent to all of us who have property there, describing the tearings and clawings of the extreme left in the Coastal Commission versus the extreme right of the property owners. As a simple liberal, I am disgusted with them all. So it has not fulfilled its promise, in any way, to the letter. But it's at least sufficiently confused so that the really gorgeous country is still there and is only very slowly being destroyed. If anybody were efficient, then that would be curtains. But since all they do is fight with each other and not build anything, we are okay for a while.

Diamonstein When we talked about museums, you referred to looking out the window and seeing water. It seems to be a recurring theme in your life. As I recall, your 1957 Ph.D. thesis talks about water and architecture, and a book that you are now preparing is called, *Water in Architecture*. How important *is* water to architecture and to you?

Moore Actually, the book keeps getting its title changed. It's now *Designs for the Water Planet*. I picked that topic for my Ph.D. dissertation some twenty years ago when the whole freedom to have content, to let buildings speak was much more restricted. It seemed to me that to deal with something that clearly had a great deal of meaning for people would be a way of getting at more general issues that interested me. They continue to. Water is a fascinating medium, because, in addition to its physical qualities, it's got all those associations, from biblical ones to poetic ones, to ones that come automatically to people. It's everything, from wondering where it goes after it goes into the ocean and where the clouds come from, to the biblical parallels between water and blood. It's a fascinating material, and its been dealt with very little in our time. You know, those horrid little squirts that happen in shopping centers are about the size of it. So while I am doing my dance to return figure sculpture to the world, I would like to get a lot of water shooting around, too. One nice thing about water is that it's festive. That is one of the things about the Piazza d'Italia that has caused me to argue with lots of people. A fountain is not going to solve the physical problems of the world. It is not going to feed the hungry or succor the needy. It's going to make something pretty and pleasant for people to enjoy, and to cause people to get together where it's happening, like they do at the Piazza.

Diamonstein Your book, *The Place of Houses,* was a testament to the imaginative design of one's own living places. You said in that book, "The design of a house is the search for the habitable, both the physically habitable, where we can be comfortable and live our lives, and the metaphorically habitable, where we can go beyond where we actually are to wherever our imaginations will transport us." "A good house," you go on to say, "speaks not just for the material from which it is made, but of the intangible rhythms, spirit and dreams of people's lives. Its slice is only a tiny piece of the real world, yet this place is made to seem like an entire world."

Is that the definition of an ideal house?

Moore Just that. I don't know how better to say it. That was said by Gerald Allen and Don Lyndon and me, after about forty-three nights of heavy argument about how to make that sentence.

Diamonstein Let's talk about one of the most unusual commissions that you or any other architect has ever had. You often talk about making a sense of place instead of the traditional modernist space. And part of making places seems to have to do with kinesthetic values. From this point of view one of your most important buildings would be your design for a house for a blind client and his family. Can you describe the house and how you developed it?

Moore It's a very big house for a really amazing man, who went blind in his early thirties—with a disease called retinitis pigmentosa. He leads an extraordinarily active life. He has a house in Aspen and skis, fast, following some guy doing a Swiss yodel, I guess. He has walked all over that farm that the house is on. He walked over it before he went blind, and he continues to walk over it, at high speed. And so our fascinating chance was to make something for him. Also, we wanted the house to look nice, because he remembered what his paintings looked like for instance, and he had a sighted family. But the house is also meant to work so that he knows where he is at any point, so that he can, without the help of sight, be oriented, centered, and feel that he is in clear charge of where he is. He wanted a house with lots of discrete rooms which freaks out modern architects. No flowing space. We managed to get some flowing space in the middle, in an orangerie and jungle garden, with a pool in it. When it's working the pool makes carefully tuned splashes so that he knows where it is, and therefore where he is. But that flowing space has in it a rail that he can trail unobtrusively with his fingers, so that he knows, as he goes through this rather serpentine place, where he is and which way he is facing all the time. The really awful part for him was when they were moving in, and he had no way, of course, of knowing where the stuff was or who had put anything where. It was really awful for about three weeks. But then it all got put together, and he got on top of it. I don't know whether I can generalize from it, because he's a genius. There are few like him and his amazing capacity to overcome his problem is staggering.

Diamonstein Can you derive anything from that house that applies to the sighted community?

Moore I think so. I have taught at Yale for almost fifteen years now, with a sculptor named Kent Bloomer, with whom I wrote the *Body, Memory and Architecture.* In that book, we emphasized over and over that there is more to inhabiting a building than just seeing it. That's why slides are so confusing. What you do in a building is feel it and inhabit it by moving in it, by touching it, by sensing it. What doing a house for a remarkably gifted blind man did for us was to let us and him, very carefully over a long period, deal with those non-visual things that are a very important part of the built world.

Audience On the Best Products store facade that was in the Museum of Modern Art show, where did the elephants come from, and why did you choose to use silver?

Moore The elephants came from the Elephant Tower at the 1939 San Francisco Fair, which influenced me heavily when I was fourteen years old. I had sort of lost track of them, which I regarded as a desperate loss. But some few years ago, I was doing an article for the *Architectural Record* about building-type studies, and there they were, the most wonderful building-type study I had ever seen. And I thought then that the Elephant Towers had to be brought back at all cost. In England, if you go to lecture, the students take you around to see Edwardian things, which they are heavily tuned into. There were a couple of architects of the early twentieth century who made really astonishingly good things with elephants. That confirmed my belief that elephants were probably central to our future.

Diamonstein Does that mean we can expect to see more of them from you?

Moore Yes. Any chance I get. The thing is that most people don't have elephants on their minds so when you're doing a participatory piece of work the likelihood of elephants resulting from it is zilch.

Diamonstein It depends upon with whom you are participating.

Moore That's true. And if you're doing something with yourself or for some eleemosynary institution, the chances of having elephants are very, very good. There is silver in the suburban store-front because I would have liked mirrors. But I have a negative image of young vandals in suburban shopping-centers breaking mirrors and causing me pain and stress. And so I thought that maybe a simple shiny porcelain enamel gray would do something like the same thing. I am also getting very excited about old galvanized iron, which I am nailing onto the inside walls of my house in L.A. It's wonderful stuff. It's extremely subtle. And kind of sharp at the edges. I think I may find myself setting up practice to do galvanized iron elephants, too. I think they are an important part of the future . . .

I. M. PEI

I.M. Pei (Ieoh Ming Pei)
Born Canton, China 1917
B. Arch. Massachusetts Institute of Technology, 1940
M. Arch. Harvard University, 1946

Diamonstein One of the country's most renowned architects, I. M. Pei was the 1979 winner of the American Institute of Architects' highest award, the Gold Medal. Based in New York, I. M. Pei and Partners have a large practice, that has always sought to merge aesthetic concerns with economic ones and has ended up being ranked both with serious high-design offices and with commercial ones. Born in China, Mr. Pei came to the United States forty-five years ago to study, and has been here ever since. Among the many outstanding buildings he has designed recently, for which he has achieved considerable popular and critical acclaim, are the JFK Library complex in Dorchester, Massachusetts and the East Building of the National Gallery of Art in Washington, D.C.

Why don't we begin with some of your recent words? You have said, "The talk about modernism versus post-modernism is unimportant. It's a side issue. An individual building, the style in which it is going to be designed and built, is not that important. The important thing, really, is the community. How does it affect life?" And then you go on to say: "To capture the spirit is more important than to satisfy the function. We tend to put too much emphasis on function, on how a building works, rather than how does it affect." Is that an accurate description of your design philosophy?

Pei I think so. When you look through history, you will find that the Greeks had their agoras and the Romans had their Forum and other peoples have great squares and piazzas. That's where the life is. Architecture has to perform its function in the theater of life. I think that search is the great challenge to architects and architecture.

Diamonstein Shall we join the issue of post-modernism now? Was it ever an issue for you?

Pei Not really. About a year ago, this was a very hot issue among American architects. But to tell you the truth, when I travel around the world talking to architectural schools in different parts of the world, I find it is not an issue at all. I think it's a peculiarly American phenomenon to talk about post-modernism, when we are still in the midst of a continuous development of what we know as modern architecture.

Diamonstein How would you describe this period?

Pei Modern architecture, which began only fifty years ago, is still very much alive today. I don't think it's that easy to say that it's finished although I do agree with some of the premises set forth by many young architects today.

Diamonstein What are those premises?

Pei I don't believe in the idea that modern architecture has generally run out of steam and that we should look back to other sources of inspiration in order to be more relevant. I think that we are in the middle of a very vigorous period. I think the continuity is there. There are other issues far more important than stylistic ones.

Diamonstein And what are those issues of contemporary concern?

Pei Life is the issue. We are talking about architecture. We are talking about whether this style or that style is better. We are talking about looking back into history for inspiration. All these things are fine, but are we really solving the most serious problem of all? If you look at our cities today, in New York, in Philadelphia, Paris, London, what have we got?

We are not really building a civilized society. Our cities look terrible and they are looking worse and worse. Individual buildings may be interesting, one maybe more so than another, but we are not really building a civilized setting for life.

Diamonstein When did we last do that?

Pei Let's see. A long time ago. I think the nineteenth century, in France. Napoleon III for instance, had a very authoritarian way of getting things done, but at least he left something that today we can look back to with pleasure. The Georgian period in England also interests me greatly. Architects developed a consensus then. The style was accepted. The classical revival under Christopher Wren and Inigo Jones was a great and exciting period in civic architecture which extended from the seventeenth century almost to the nineteen hundreds.

Diamonstein Well, what are we to do, given that appraisal? The last time we tried to level American cities we ended up with the disaster of 1950s' urban renewal. How are we to improve not only the look but the life of American cities?

Pei Architects will have to begin to look at the larger picture, not just the individual building. A building has to relate to other buildings, and buildings have to relate to streets and streets to squares. If we begin to look at how the individual building fits into its setting, we can begin to develop a unified civic architecture that we lack today. The other day someone called my attention to the fact that Brunelleschi designed a building called the Foundling Hospital in Florence, in the fifteenth century. About eighty-nine years later, another architect, named Michelozzo, designed an almost identical building across the square from the Foundling Hospital. Now, that's civilized. That is very civilized.

Diamonstein Self-effacing, too . . .

Pei Well, there is the larger problem. Michelozzo was a very fine architect. But can you imagine that I would do a building just like Philip Johnson's across the street?

Diamonstein Or vice versa. Maybe part of the problem is the whole nature of architectural education. That's a continuing concern of yours. In what terms are younger architects being trained to think?

Pei I know that I wasn't trained to think that way when I was in school. But that was a long while back. I hope they are being educated that way because that's the hope of the future. Architecture is really the mirror of life itself. We have to agree on what is important in life. What's lacking today is a cultural consensus. I think we should have that. And once we have that, I believe architects will begin to become less frenetic in search of something new, but rather search for what is good and relates well to the larger environment.

Diamonstein Do you know any architecture school where that is taking place currently? I know you are deeply involved with the school you attended, MIT.

Pei No, it's not happening there, unfortunately. I try my best, but I think I am a bit out of date when I speak to them that way. The young architects and teachers feel that their concerns are very different from mine. But I continue to talk about it because I don't think they are right. I think they are wrong. The major concern architects will have to face is the building of a coherent architectural environment.

Diamonstein You have designed everything from complexes that transform entire cities to small, isolated museums. By now, your firm has designed more than fifty projects and many of them have been for the celebration of the arts; for instance, the Everson Museum of Art at Syracuse in 1968, the Mellon Art Center at Choate School in 1972, the Herbert F. Johnson Museum of Art at Cornell in 1973, and the East Building of the National Gallery in 1978. And upcoming is the Indiana University Art Museum and the addition to the Museum of Fine Arts in Boston. In Boston they started out with a plan to install climate control, and by the time they were through talking to you, they ended up with a new wing. Are there any other museums that we don't know about yet?

Pei Yes. I think the latest one is probably the most interesting. We are doing a small museum for MIT. It's called the Arts and Media Technology Building. I find it an extremely exciting project.

Diamonstein You see it as some breakthrough in your museum designs . . .?

Pei It presents a different kind of challenge. It's no longer a place where you hang paintings and/or sculpture. There's some of that, but that's not the important thing. It's a laboratory for art. MIT is a very renowned school of science and engineering, and its resources in electronics, computer, photography, film and sound are incredible—some of the richest in the world. What MIT hopes to do in this small building is not unlike what the Centre Pompidou tries to do in its enormous establishment. I hope it will be an interesting building because it has an exciting program. The important thing is that the activity inside will have a great deal of resonance. I think wonderful things will happen there.

Diamonstein Probably more than almost all contemporary architects, other than Philip Johnson and Edward L. Barnes, you have been involved with museum design. Which if any, of your original thoughts have recurred, have been confirmed, have been altered in the course of the design of all these museums?

Pei First of all, I think art has to look well in a museum. That's a must. If not, then something is wrong with the design. Secondly, a museum should be a pleasant place to visit. You can't really look at art in a concentrated way for too long a period of time.

Diamonstein When does museum fatigue set in?

Pei Well, Carter Brown, the director of the National Gallery, has always said he thinks that 20,000 square feet of exhibition space is the maximum a person can absorb at one time.

Diamonstein Can you translate that into time for us?

Pei Well, time is hard to estimate. Someone may spend a day walking around 20,000 square feet. Another person may just rush through it in five minutes. But the problem is the intense effect that a work of art has on the interested viewer; it is such that you really cannot take too much of it at one time. Art is simply too rich. That's why a museum should also be a nice, pleasant place to be in because from time to time you will need to come up for air. You want the place to help you do that so that you can continue to look at more and more art.

Diamonstein Are you designing a new kind of museum for a new museum-going constituency? Are you dealing with different numbers or different populations?

Pei I suppose so. When I was a student, I used to go to museums to cram for exams. Why? Because it was so quiet there. And that's a nice place to be. But today it's just the opposite. All you have to do is to go to the Metropolitan Museum on a Sunday. It's impossible to get up those steps.

Diamonstein How do you plan for circulation, for crowd control, for the space given to book stores, to food facilities, to all the support systems that the museum now requires to sustain itself economically?

Pei Oh, I don't agree with that. I think that's not the right direction for the museum to grow. When I contribute to a museum, I'd hate to see that money go to gift shops. While they need some of that, too much emphasis on food service, on selling reproductions, and so on, is not my idea of what a museum should be.

Diamonstein Why don't we talk about your idea of what a museum should be, and your most publicly acclaimed demonstration of that idea. I am referring to the building that is now just about two years old, the East Building of the National Gallery in Washington. To begin with, downtown Washington itself is something of a monument. There is no other place in the United States that can match it, either in scope or in its history. However, it also had a penchant for monotony. That is, at least until the opening of the East Building. The National Gallery itself was founded in 1937 and at the time both the gallery site itself and its adjoining trapezoidal plot were put aside for future use by Mr. [Andrew] Mellon, the founder. That site, with that location and shape, obviously posed a number of challenges. How did you go about solving the problems? What was the source of the inspiration for that shape building?

Pei You have to look at the site in relationship to the other buildings already on the Mall. The most immediate neighbors are the West Building and the South Building. Most of the buildings are neoclassic in style with a very strong axis, whether it's east-west or north-south. Usually, you have axes in both directions. Since I believe that a building, particularly in a place as important as the Great Mall, should become part of a larger family of buildings, the first thing I wished to do was to recognize the east-west axis of the National Gallery West building. But the fact that the larger family happened to have a neoclassic face doesn't mean that our building has to have the same. Of course we can't do that. But what we have to take note of is that these are neoclassic buildings, that they have very strong symmetrical axes, and we will have to respond to these axes. Since our site is asymmetrical, it was difficult to respond to that east-west axis.

We finally solved that problem, really rather accidentally, I suppose, when I drew a line connecting two points in this truncated sort of asymmetrical triangle. Out of that we were able to develop an isosceles triangle and a right triangle—just the device we needed to accommodate that east-west axis. From that point on, everything followed that triangle. It became the leitmotif for the design of the entire building.

Diamonstein Can you tell us something about the soaring spaces, the monumentality of the building, the balconies and the bridges that often lead to mysterious destinations? How did you decide to build those museums within the museum?

Pei I mentioned earlier that a museum should be a fun place to be, a pleasant place for people to linger and return to look at more art and then come out and refresh themselves and go on and on. That's why the building is designed that way. You see, I think this museum in Washington is different from museums anywhere else. Across the Mall from us we have the Air and Space Museum. It's a very exciting place. I don't know whether you've been there or not. I'll tell you I recommend it. The East Wing had to compete with all that.

Diamonstein The Air and Space Museum is the most visited museum in the entire country.

Pei Not only do they have these modules that came back from the moon, but they have one of the greatest movies I have ever seen. It's a powerful draw. How can we compete with that at the National Gallery? By using architectural means, we tried to make the interior exciting. The bridges, the daylight, are all calculated to give the place a sense of vitality, so that families who come, particularly ones with children would say "Let's stay a little while longer."

Diamonstein You said earlier that you did not approve of giving too much space to gift shops or food services. But as I recall, there is a very extensive restaurant facility bridging the two buildings. What were the constraints placed upon you when you took that commission?

Pei To begin with, we had to eliminate an existing restaurant in the old building. Having eliminated the restaurant, we had to put something back. So we have concentrated, in one place, a larger restaurant than the original one to serve both the East and West Buildings. The number of seats that we finally decided to put in there was based on a real need. In Washington, D.C., unlike New York and many other cities, there are not many public eating places on the Mall. In terms of the number of seats, we planned this restaurant to serve not only the museum, but also to serve many other public places as well. So it's larger than I like, but it's always full. I would have preferred to devote that space to more exhibition space, but in this case, I am afraid that the large restaurant is necessary.

Diamonstein You raise an inevitable question for a famous building that is now nearly two years old—old enough for reaction to set in. You said you would like to have devoted more space to exhibition space. How do you feel about the recent criticism, especially over the amount of exhibition space that is available?

Pei I feel some responsibility for that.

Diamonstein I've heard so many figures. What *is* the amount of exhibition space? And is the public aware of the total amount of exbibition space there?

Pei I don't think they are aware of the total, simply because there are so many galleries that very few really have a chance to see all of them at once.

Diamonstein Are all the galleries open yet?

Pei One or two are often closed at certain times for installations. The East Building cannot stand alone as a museum. It's designed to complement the West Building, the original National Gallery. Now, that museum is a veritable storehouse of masterpieces—a small collection, compared with the Metropolitan's, but one of the greatest in the world. What they lack is a place to exhibit new shows coming from other parts of the world, large and small, all happening at once. So we have to look at the East Building in that context.

Diamonstein It also functions as a study center.

Pei Oh, yes. The East Building with 600,000 square feet is larger than the West Building, which has about 475,000 square feet. The museum occupies only one-third of the area. Another third goes to the study center. It's a place for research, for scholars to come to write, for administrators of the National Gallery to plan their programs, to send exhibits and works of art all over the country and all over the world. The other third supports not only the new building but also the old. It includes shops, laboratories, restaurants, storage, parking and service in general. It's like an iceberg—what's below ground is much larger than what you see above ground. So we only have one third of the total area devoted to "museum display space."

Diamonstein There is another criticism that I hope you will comment on, as well. It is said that the desire to create something monumental was so strong that it overwhelmed the gallery areas which some critics feel are leftover spaces, and that the museum was really designed as a public forum to serve official Washington, which indeed it does in some measure.

Pei I think that was in the program because the National Gallery is not only a place to display and store art, it's also a very important center for social and artistic life in Washington. When the President wants to greet someone from another country, like Deng Xiaou-ping, for instance, or maybe the French Minister of Culture, the National Gallery is often chosen as a site for such receptions. The West Building performed much of that kind of function already. The East Building will have to do more. The Garden Court is a very large space, no question about it. It has to be large to accommodate a very large number of people at once. If you go there at Easter time for example when the schools are out, that Garden Court is jam-packed with people. If you didn't have that space, it would become insufferable, spatially. So you need it. That space is not primarily for art, although we do have a Calder, a Miró tapestry, a Tony Caro sculpture, and a few things like that.

Diamonstein So it was meant as a public indoor piazza.

Pei That's right. It's an orientation space. It's a space for that kind of miscellaneous and very important activity. But then you go into the galleries—and there are many, many galleries of various dimensions for different types of exhibits. The art is completely in scale with the spaces that house it.

Diamonstein Together with Carter Brown, you traveled throughout the world, looking at other museums. Was any a particular inspiration?

Pei Yes. We both got carried away with a feeling that this museum should not really be a large museum but should be broken down into a series of small museums, sort of loosely joined together under one roof. We really have three small "house" museums in the East Building, and the Garden Court joins them together. The museum that really excited us the most was the Poldi–Pezzoli Museum in Milan. It's a three-story museum, connected by a very elegant stair. Altogether, it's very much like our "house" museums. It's perfect. It has as much space in it as one can take if you're really serious about art. We learned something from the Poldi—Pezzoli. One loses oneself in big museums. In spite of the Garden Court, I think, this museum has galleries of intimate scale.

Diamonstein It seems to me that the East Building was an architect's dream come true, a great site and a very great client. The entire cost estimated at 94.4 million dollars—and by way of contrast, the Hirschhorn Museum cost 16 million dollars—was paid by a private benefactor, Mr. [Paul] Mellon. So the question is whether there were restrictions or definitions or limitations placed upon you because of the nature of that assignment. Did the trustees, the benefactors, the fact that the National Gallery *is* a national gallery—and I guess we tend to forget that all but six employees are civil servants—restrict you in terms of design, materials?

Pei Yes. But not too much, fortunately. One restriction was that this building had to last forever. We had to build it out of marble, just like the West Building. It's very expensive.

Diamonstein How did you arrange to do that?

Pei Asked them for more money.

Diamonstein How did you match the marble?

Pei We had to go back to Tennessee to open up the old quarries.

Diamonstein The same ones from the original building?

Pei The same ones, yes. Not only that, we even found the man who was responsible for the marble work of the West Building, Malcolm Rice. He is now eighty-some years old. We took him out of retirement and put him in charge. He supervised the selection and matching of the marble from several quarries all over Knoxville, Tennessee. It was a very big effort, but we didn't do as well as Pope did. We could have done better. But I'll tell you, it's a remarkable feat that Mr. Rice did so well. John Russell Pope, who designed the West Building, had five shades of marble to choose from, ranging from off-white to brown. We only had three shades to choose from. And therefore the matching was much more difficult in our case than it was more than forty years ago.

Diamonstein You refer to the Miró, to the Calder, and a Tony Caro that are in what you have called the orientation space.

Pei And then Henry Moore, if you look out the window or the main door. And you see Dubuffet in the pool.

Diamonstein How does that work relate to the architectural design of the museum and how were those works selected? Were they specially commissioned? Who commissioned them?

Pei There was an accession committee for selection of works of art—I think it probably still exists today. That committee expanded its function to include commissioning. So at the very beginning, I mean soon after the building design was accepted, I believe it was I who called to this committee's attention that there might be a need for commissioning works of art of a certain scale in order to match the scale of the building. Carter Brown and I were then asked by the committee to make recommendations. Before the building was jelled—unfortunately, we should have started a lot sooner—we put a model of it in the West Building. Then we invited artists, many of whom finally accepted our conditions and eventually did works for us, to come and look at the model of the building.

Give and take took place between the artists and ourselves that resulted in the choice of pieces, the scale of each piece and the positioning of the piece. That relationship between artists and architects is not as ideal as in Renaissance times when the two disciplines were often combined in one man. But it's as close as we are able to get to it, considering the distances involved. Henry Moore works out of London, and we are in New York. We can only meet so many times before we can agree on what the piece should be. It's not a perfect collaboration, but it's a pretty good one.

Diamonstein You have worked a great deal with Henry Moore, in fact so much so that a Moore sculpture in front of some Pei buildings might even be called a trademark, so to speak. There's the Henry Moore in front of your work in Columbus, Indiana, another in front of the National Gallery in Washington, D.C. and now the recently dedicated Dallas City Hall. How does that relationship work and why has Henry Moore become such a recurring theme?

Pei First, we have to think of scale. Contemporary buildings have a very big scale, a scale that sculpture of Rodin's tradition can't satisfy. Take a sculpture like the *Burghers of Calais.* You can't blow it up to three or four times the size. It would look grotesque. There is a limit to the size of a human form. Even Michaelangelo's *David* looks ungainly, almost grotesque in the Piazza del Signoria in Florence. This situation cries for a new way of seeing. I think that's what Moore and Picasso have done. We're also responsible for the Picasso at New York University.

Diamonstein *Sylvette?*

Pei Yes, Picasso's head of *Sylvette.* It's the abstraction that makes the very large size possible. It's not the human figure anymore, although it might have been inspired by the human figure or by the skull of an elephant, as in Henry Moore's case. By the time it's finished, however, you no longer associate it with a human figure. That's why in 1958, when I first saw the *Sylvette* in Paris (it was only a tiny photograph of the maquette), I realized immediately that finally here was an artist able to do something that can become very large in scale. Because it's abstract. I wouldn't consider enlarging a Maillol or a Rodin. Because Moore's works are quite abstract, they can be expanded in size and scale to match the buildings, the space.

Diamonstein Who determines that expansion in scale, you or the artist?

Pei Together. Even with Picasso, we had to consult him. We sent Picasso a maquette of the three towers at New York University, and we gave him their scale. A sculptor friend of his took it to Vallauris and after he looked at it, said, "I think my piece should be this way," and that, believe it or not, turned out to be within ten percent of what we, as architects, thought it should be.

Diamonstein And whose determination prevailed?

Pei His.

Diamonstein That isn't often the case.

Pei I think we wanted it forty feet high and he wanted it thirty-two or thirty-five feet high. It's about a ten percent difference, and we chose his dimension.

Diamonstein You said most every artist accepted your commission for the National Gallery. Were there any who rejected it?

Pei I think Jean Dubuffet accepted the commission with reservation. After he completed the maquette the reservation was on the other side, on the part of the accession committee. Eventually that piece was not commissioned, although the maquette was exhibited on the pool in the National Gallery. That piece was intended to be where Henry Moore's is now, at the front door of these buildings. The piece was intended for the entrance. It's a group of figures in red, white and blue. Some people felt it was sinister, but I think it's very gay. He called it *The Welcome Parade,* which is apt. It is a bit like a circus beckoning one and all to come in. I liked it and really fought for it. But I lost. The committee felt that Washington is still very conservative and was concerned about the reaction of the congressmen and the senators.

Diamonstein Other than Philip Johnson, I know of no other architect as deeply involved with the visual arts and artists as you are. What do you see as the state of the collaboration between artists and architects and the future direction for that collaboration?

Pei I think that the days are gone when one man could be both artist and architect. The technological complexity of modern life alone would inhibit Renaissance man. I don't think that we will ever see that again.

Therefore, artist and architect must begin to understand each other. We have not perfected that. We are far, far away from it. Today, I think artists feel very much left out. They also feel that they have gone way beyond the architects and they are right. I was uneasy about the commissioning method at the National Gallery. Although we tried to do a little better, we haven't really reached the ideal. We are trying to improve on it in the Arts and Media Building at MIT. Before we even had an idea for a design, we decided to involve six artists. Four have already come in to see us at the very beginning. We emphasize that the artist's work will not be an individual work of art standing in space or hung on a wall. It will be part of the building, a permanent part of the environment. For instance, Ken Noland was rather dubious about the collaboration. But after we exchanged ideas about the joints between the metal grids in our design, and since the width of the joints have not been designed yet, he expressed interest in putting color in those joints. I understood what he was talking about, and since the width of the joints have not been designed yet, we have increased the widths and are now waiting for him to respond. The color of the joints will have an interesting effect on the surface of the building. Now, here is another example. Dan Flavin came in. Dan Flavin, the artist who works with fluorescent tubes in different colors, suggested using different colored tubes in our ceiling which is composed of unistruct grids. As long as he follows certain specifications, such as a maximum allowable wattage and a fairly uniform distribution of light, I was sure we could integrate his idea. He accepted those ground rules completely. Although we started without too much optimism on my part or their part, both Noland and Flavin left with a very exciting feeling that something could be done.

Diamonstein In the more than twenty-five years that I. M. Pei & Partners has existed, your firm has designed more than fifty projects and more than thirty-five have won awards. In fact, it's often said that the firm may be the very best fraternity of architects functioning in the United States today. Is that accurate? How does the firm function? There are two hundred employees,

New York Exposition and
Convention Center,
11th Avenue elevation,
New York, N.Y., rendered view

New York Exposition and
Convention Center,
11th Avenue elevation,
New York, N.Y.

New York Exposition and
Convention Center,
New York, N.Y., model
Picture credit: Nathaniel
Lieberman

John Fitzgerald Kennedy Library,
exterior, Dorchester, Mass.
Picture credit: Nathaniel
Liebermann

National Gallery of Art,
interior, Washington, D.C.
Picture credit: Ezra Stoller
© ESTO

one hundred thirty-five or forty architects. Who designs what, and under what circumstances?

Pei First of all, I am very proud of the fact that we have such talented people in the organization. I really am prouder of that than of the buildings even, because without that talent you cannot have good buildings. The reason we have been able to grow to this size is because we have the right people to staff the firm. Many of us started together.

Diamonstein Was this during the Zeckendorf era?

Pei We started together then, yes. We were all in the architectural department of Webb & Knapp. The average length of service among our senior people, meaning senior associates up to partners, is more than twenty years. The six partners have been together for twenty-five years and in some cases, thirty years. We have learned to work together. We can talk and design in shorthand. Even though we may make decisions separately, we are seldom in conflict. And I think when you reach that point you can expand up to a point without fear of losing quality. However, there is a limit to it. We have to grow because we want to keep the people who have been with us for twenty years or more. When I started in 1948, I was alone. I was alone for two years before we started to expand. All our senior people were then fresh out of the universities. Today most of them are in their fifties. They want responsibility. They are ready for it. And in order to give them responsibility, you have to let them take charge. Before you know it, you have a fairly large organization.

Diamonstein How do you train a younger person to take charge?

Pei I am very much interested in that problem because I am already looking ahead to a time when I will no longer be here. Twenty years from now I'd like this firm to remain a force. There are many architectural firms that have been very good for a period of time and then disappear from the scene. I think that's unfortunate. That's the reason why I have a very special interest in the young. I begin to delegate more and more with the large projects but I continue to take small projects to give young people a chance to take charge. Of course I have to be there. Therefore, I now am taking on a new role in the firm. I hope to be able to help train the next generation when my generation becomes less active.

Diamonstein I can't envision that possibility in your case. However, I think we should take a specific example of how this firm does run, an example that is of considerable interest throughout the country. After ten years and two sites and two designs, the largest and most important new building undertaken in New York in decades, the New York Exposition and Convention Center, will be built. The building will cost 375 million dollars and will be located between Eleventh and Twelfth Avenues and Thirty-third and Thirty-ninth Streets in Manhattan. It's the largest exposition center under one roof in the United States, over 750,000 square feet in an 18-acre building on a 22-acre site. I am citing all these statistics to give an idea of the scale, the monumentality of the project and your attempts to humanize it. Eventually the building will accommodate a population of up to eighty thousand people. It will add more than fifteen thousand people to the city's payroll. Why did you take on such a behemoth? Who is responsible for both the design and the implementation of a project that is beyond the capacity of any one person?

Pei First, I want to make it clear that the construction cost is 203 million in the budget of 375 million. It's still a lot of money. It's difficult to keep within that budget in these days of high inflation but we are going to do it.

Diamonstein What will the differential of 172 million cover?

Pei Administration costs, financing costs, fees, consultants, environmental impact studies, etc. There's a list of consultants that long. As far as we are concerned, we have a maximum limit that is 203 million. We have to do it within that sum. If we don't, we have to redesign, and redesign again, until we do. The budget and time constraints for this project are very strict.

Diamonstein When is the opening?

Pei We hope to open this project in the spring of 1984. And if Richard Kahan, the president of UDC, has his way, he would like to open it in 1983. If he does, I think many of us will have to take a rest somewhere!

Diamonstein How do you fill the demands of a convention center and still come up with a building of human scale and of visual interest?

Pei You have asked me a number of questions in that long list of yours. I don't know where to begin. Let's start with the design of such a building. This building was conceived within a month. It was refined and tested as workable within two or three months. We are now only six or seven months down the road. In the last of many interviews, Mr. Kahan and two others came to our office to discuss the project. I thought that it was my chance to present my view. I said, "The Convention Center is a major public building. Every citizen of New York City and New York State can claim a piece of it. So this is a very exciting thing." Although I have lived in New York for almost thirty years, I have only been to the Coliseum twice. This means that the Coliseum, an exposition and convention center, has relatively little meaning to me, a citizen of New York. I wouldn't want it to happen to this building. Mr. Kahan said, "Well, what do you propose to do?" I said, "I only ask one thing. If you will give us five percent, or about a hundred thousand square feet of this 2,000,000 square foot building and let us do what we wish with it, we will turn it into a really 'public' building."

Diamonstein Is that space the "Enchanted Lantern" that Governor Carey referred to—the "Crystal Palace" portion?

Pei The model which is now on exhibit in the Museum of Modern Art features that hundred thousand square feet.

Diamonstein Why don't you describe then the "Crystal Palace" portion, the central part that has lightly reflective glass and tear-colored latticework to reflect the city, literally and figuratively. Who conceived that design? Forgive me for making the questions multiple, but I want you to touch on many points that interest us. I hope that you can describe in some detail the solution that you and your partner, James Ingo Freed, have come up with. Would you also differentiate your roles?

Pei When we first tackled the design about six months ago, we were in the process of completing the Kennedy Library.

Diamonstein That opened ahead of schedule.

Pei Yes, I think so. I mention this because it has a large glass-enclosed space where one is comfortable, whether one is alone or with lots of people. We have a glass pavilion there, seventy feet by seventy feet by one hundred and ten feet, that has nothing in it, except a stone bench. Now what makes that pavilion work? It works because it has daylight. This is also true of the Garden Court in the National Gallery. When you bring daylight into a space, it comes alive. It changes with the moving clouds, with sunny days, summer, spring. So we learned that important lesson. In the Convention Center, we have an enormous space, bigger than any space now existing in New York. There is no way to make it human scale; you must bring in daylight and that's the beginning of the idea of the "Crystal Palace." We remembered great examples of the past, the Crystal Palace outside London, the Grand Palais in Paris. These are buildings that have a kind of mystery and excitement. We made our decision then and there. In this case, "we" included many others as well as Jim Freed and myself; we agreed there had to be daylight, that there would be a pile of crystals.

Diamonstein Whose concept was the Crystal Palace?

Pei It is not an original idea. Perhaps because I was so involved with the Kennedy Library, I might have suggested that we use a space frame. That we should try a pile of that crystal and not worry about the human scale; the important thing was to bring the natural element into the space. Credit should go to Jim Freed for turning the idea into architecture. Two out of our six partners are running this job: Jim Freed on design and Werner Wandelmaier on adminstration and management. Many other senior people are also involved. We have a very strong team for this project so that I do not need to be involved in the day-to-day running of this job. Wandelmaier and Freed often have to attend three or four meetings a day. As long as the concept is not going to be changed, the project moves. And frequently without me.

Diamonstein Does that reflect the change in architectural practice that by the time you are really sure of how to use tools, you are very far removed from them? I mean, when was the last time you held a T-square? How has architectural practice evolved? How little do projects of that scale take shape in conventional ways?

Pei No, I don't draw very much anymore. I certainly cannot speak for Michael Graves! Occasionally I do draw a diagram or two. But really, if you're not able to draw in your mind, you're not able to tackle these problems. They are too complex. You've got to train your mind to see space. When you have two lines, you have a plane; when you have three lines, you have space. You've got to see it. It's only the most complex space that you have to test with other means and those means are not drawings. No, drawing is no longer as important as it was in the Beaux-Arts days, at least not to me.

Diamonstein I assume research and development is. That's something that your firm gives a great deal of attention to and there are some tangible results. As I recall, a neoprene gasket was used on the marble and the facade of the National Gallery. Is that an I. M. Pei & Partners development?

Pei Yes, it is.

Diamonstein What is a neoprene gasket anyway? Have other firms adapted a use for it?

Pei We all learn, one from the other. The gasket has been in use for some time because even stones expand and contract. This is why joints crack and the caulking falls out. We were aware of that problem. Then we looked at Pope's building. There were no problems except the moat wall. There were two reasons for that. One is that the wall stone is very thick. It absorbs the temperature and that minimized the cycle of change. Reason number two is simply that old Beaux-Arts buildings have a reason for being the way they are. Classical buildings have columns and pilasters, which provide marvelous slip joints that permit the building to expand and contract. A modern building doesn't have that. They have unbroken surfaces that run for two or three hundred feet. And if you don't have the solution for that expansion and contraction, you are going to have endless trouble. So we decided to search for new methods, new technology and new materials. The neoprene gasket is a perfect solution. Every stone has a gasket, which means every stone allows a certain amount of movement. In that case, there is no accumulated stress.

Diamonstein What about the latticework frame that was used at the John F. Kennedy Library complex and will be the support structure for the Crystal Palace portion of the Convention Center?

Pei It's exactly the same.

Diamonstein And was that developed by your firm?

Pei No, it's a product that you can buy in the market.

Diamonstein In the Convention Center you are planning two large exposition halls. Besides exposition and commercial uses, what do you plan to do with those spaces?

Pei We have a Great Hall. Let's call it a Great Hall. I'd like to think of a better name, but for the time being . . .

Diamonstein It's pretty good.

Pei That hall is going to be big. It's a place for people to meet. I would prefer not to clutter it with conventional types of exhibits, although once the building leaves the architect's hands you never know what will happen. I am sure they are going to exhibit all kinds of things in it. But most importantly, it is a people's place. We have crisscrossing currents of escalators which will animate that space and make it come alive. The second space is called the Galleria which runs east-west to the Hudson River. You have to go up to the upper level and cross over. That is also under glass. That space is the activity space for the general public. We now have to find suitable activities for it.

Diamonstein Is that separate from the complex of riverfront restaurants?

Pei Yes. You have a complex of restaurants at the other end, overlooking the Hudson River. But that space in-between, the so-called Galleria space, is equivalent to two city blocks in length. At the moment we have many, exciting ideas for that area.

Diamonstein Can you tell us what some of them are?

Pei It's premature. We'd like to show what New York has and is. If people come from out of town and don't have too much time, they could come to this place and feel they can see some of the best of New York. Not only its wares, not only what it sells, but also, its wonderful activities—the art, the exhibitions, the museums, and the theaters. I am sure we will have to use the most advanced media technology to disseminate this information.

Diamonstein Is that going to be possible with all that daylight?

Pei Oh, yes. They can enter booths and little galleries similar to those in museums. You might visit all the art galleries of New York just by turning a knob. We ought to do this sort of thing. People can then go to a particular gallery and see what most interests them.

Diamonstein You said that airplanes will be exhibited there. Do you expect works of art or computer versions of works of art? Are you planning to commission any for that space, as well?

Pei No, I wouldn't dare to commission anything here. I hope that new art forms will use this space. Laser is one. Inflatable is another. I think people like you should begin to give some thought to using this space for art.

Diamonstein Do you see this assignment as one of the high points of your more than thirty years of work in New York?

Pei I would say it's the highest.

Diamonstein Why is this project so important to you?

Pei Not because it's big but because it's so public. It's more public than the National Gallery, than the Kennedy Library. It belongs to so many people. It will have a life of its own long after we leave the scene. It's the first great public building, for the city of New York and perhaps the state of New York. What more can I say?

Diamonstein That's a lot to have said. How did the son of a banker-economist ever become an architect?

Pei Well, to begin with, he didn't want to be a banker-economist.

Diamonstein He wanted to be an engineer?

Pei No, my father just wanted me to go to England, that's all. I came here to study engineering because I didn't know any better.

Diamonstein Some of your best friends are engineers.

Pei That's true. Except that I don't think I would be a very good engineer.

Diamonstein You have called yourself an American architect absolutely. You arrived in the United States at the age of nearly eighteen, and until recently you had not visited China for almost forty years. To what extent does your Chinese background shape your attitude toward your architecture and toward life, a central factor of your architecture?

Pei I really don't think it has that much affect on my work. That's my belief, although I have been contradicted. As for a philosophy of life which is related to architecture, I guess in that sense it might have some indirect effect. Coming from a tradition that believes strongly in relationships between people, not only within the family but within society, a one-to-one relationship is extremely important. Chinese culture may have given me sort of an advantage. I am, I like to think, concerned with buildings as they relate to people using them. That concern is very important to our work and certainly in my work. So in that sense maybe I have to give some recognition to my background. But beyond that, one really doesn't become educated until very much later in life. My educated life is all here. I am a Western-trained person. I am a Western man. In that sense, I think my architecture is Western, not Oriental.

Diamonstein Well, you are about to have the opportunity to be involved in what you have called a search for synthesis. You are designing a hotel in the Fragrant Hills suburb of Peking. To begin with, Peking is a one-story city, and the entire inner city is a landmark. How do you design a new hotel without adopting your Western methods or without adopting the old palace style?

Pei That is an interesting problem. The fact that I was born in China increases its interest. I realized that Chinese architecture is at a dead end. There is no direction for it to go. Chinese architects will agree. They cannot go back to the old ways. The architecture of the temples and the palaces is not only economically out of reach, but ideologically unacceptable. They've tried the Russian way and they hate those buildings. They are trying now to take the Western way. I am afraid that will be equally unacceptable. Western culture is much less digestible in China than it is in Japan. The fact that today Japanese architects outdo us in the newest styles does not surprise me. But I cannot imagine it happening in China. So Chinese architects are really in a dilemma. They really don't know which way to go.

Diamonstein What are you trying to do there?

Pei Well, I don't know. I would like, in a small way, to pay a debt to the culture from which I came, to try to help them search for a new way. That sounds pretentious, but I think it is a difficult but fascinating challenge.

Diamonstein What does the hotel look like?

Pei I can't describe it. You will have to go there.

Diamonstein I intend to.

Pei First of all, what is architecture? Architecture really is the need to synthesize the best out of life, out of history. Whatever is still valid, I do not care how old it is, use it. And what is not valid, abandon it. There are many elements in Chinese architecture that are still very valid.

Diamonstein Are you retaining any of those elements in your design?

Pei Yes.

Diamonstein For example?

Pei In Western architecture we speak about the importance between the indoor and the outdoor. Without that concept there is no Chinese architecture. The indoor and the outdoor is always one. A library for a scholar without a small garden in front is not a library. That's one important element, the relationship between the indoor and outdoor, the role played by extremely small outdoor spaces. Maximizing the effect of very small outdoor spaces is the key to Chinese architecture.

One needs to use traditional materials in new ways. The art is in how they're used and I'd like to make some contribution in that direction. When the building is finished, we hope it will not look "Chinese," yet not look Western, either. I think the Chinese people will be comfortable with the building—they may even like it.

Diamonstein Is that their reaction now?

Pei I don't know yet. They won't see it until two years from now when the building is finished.

Diamonstein What about those to whom you presented the plans?

Pei Yes, they understood and they accepted the whole approach even though we are not giving them the newest technology, in design and construction. Rather it will be something they can develop. That approach can be duplicated by architects all over the country in 101 ways. That's the only way to begin a new vernacular in architecture. This is how the Renaissance started.

Diamonstein Of all your buildings, the Hancock Building has been the most controversial. Some have attacked it, others have praised it, but there is hardly anyone who does not have a strong feeling about it. I guess the Hancock Building is also the most famous of all architectural liability cases, based on a problem that involves a relatively new technique, double-layered reflective glass. I wonder if you can tell us something about the realities of that problem. We have all heard so many stories. And here comes a multiple question again—did that building damage the future for other curtain-wall buildings and how do you think the future will deal with the John Hancock Building?

Pei I think the future is already here. It has recognized this to be a great office building. I am very proud of it because it was designed by my partner, Henry Cobb. The John Hancock Building is a very interesting case for architects. I have seen that architects are not very good at banding together. The American Institute of Architects could have taken a greater interest in the matter. But all these are things of the past. What I can tell you now with considerable satisfaction is that the cause of the glass breakage in the building is now known. It hasn't been tested yet in court, but we are almost certain it's going to be judged that way. That product is no longer on the market. You can't buy it anymore.

Diamonstein With all the research and development and expertise of a firm like yours, how was that possible? What was the cause?

Pei Mike Flynnn, one of our associate partners, is one of the best, if not the best, curtain-wall specialists in the country. But architects should only set forth performance specifications. The burden of proof should be on the manufacturers. They are the ones making money from it. I don't think architectural firms should be responsible for the testing of materials.

Diamonstein Is there any secret dream that you have for a specific building or a specific location for which you would like to create a design?

Pei Not at this moment. We have enough to do.

Diamonstein Well, you're a long-range planner.

Pei Oh, no. Now that we have an important building in New York, I think I am content. The important thing now is to build that building and have it turn out the way I hope it will.

Diamonstein For what would you most like to be remembered?

Pei I have answered that question several times before and always the same way. I'd like to be known, really, as an architect of my time. I am trying to do my best under that circumstance. That's all and nothing more.

CESAR PELLI

Cesar Pelli
Born Tucuman, Argentina, 1926
Diploma of Architecture, University of Tucuman, 1950

Diamonstein A native of Argentina, Cesar Pelli came to this country for nine months on a scholarship from the Institute of International Education. That was in 1952, and happily for us he has remained here ever since. For the next twenty-five years, he worked in Illinois and California. Then in 1977, he came East to assume the duties of the dean of the Yale School of Architecture and to open his own architectural office. Mr. Pelli has always sought to combine pragmatic and aesthetic concerns, and has tried to place his practice at that point of intersection. To backtrack to the beginning of his career for a moment: After earning a master of science degree in architecture in 1954 at the University of Illinois, he spent the next ten years working in the office of Eero Saarinen in Bloomfield Hills, Michigan, and in New Haven, Connecticut. Actually, Saarinen's independent professional life was a very short one. He opened an office separate from his distinguished father, Eliel, in 1950, and then died in 1961. For seven of those eleven short years, you were involved in a very close relationship with him.

Perhaps you would describe life in that office. Did you learn any kind of formal design system from him? Was he an important influence on your work?

Pelli Yes. He was a very important influence, probably the most important influence on my work—not in formal terms, but more in conditioning my understanding of architecture, my love of architecture. He helped me lose the fear that one sometimes has of making buildings. His office was a wonderful place to be, particularly because it was continuously changing the whole time I was there. When I joined the firm it was still a little atelier of about twenty-five persons. By the time Eero died, there were 120 persons in the firm, and it had become a very highly organized and efficient machine. The other important thing was, of course, that Eero was engaged in a continuous search. Some of us were able to participate. It was a search with no given end, open-ended. He was not selling a style or a personal philosophy. That allowed each one of us who collaborated with him to conduct our own private search at the same time—to follow our own ideas. In that way, it was an extraordinary place to serve one's apprenticeship.

Diamonstein You've compared that 1950's office to a 1970's office. What do you mean when you say that?

Pelli The office really was very much a 1970's office. I believe there was no design office at that time that was so efficiently run, the way most of us have become today. Eero had a tremendous sense of responsibility. It was the basis of his attitude towards architecture. He felt that he was engaged to perform a very important service, and the delivery of that service was preeminent in his mind. Most of us who worked with him acquired that same sense of primary responsibility in the delivery of a very important, difficult service.

Diamonstein All of the buildings which he considered important were built or finished after he died, except for the General Motors project. In the case of the CBS headquarters building, he died the week after the gray granite was selected. Who was responsible for the completion, and in some instances, the initiation of the projects?

Pelli Kevin Roche. For the last four or five years of Eero's life, Kevin had a very special position within the firm. He worked very closely with Eero on all projects. He understood Eero's intention clearly and completely and was well able to carry through and finish a design by Eero, as if Eero had been alive.

Diamonstein Among other responsibilities there, you were the project director for both the TWA terminal at JFK International Airport and the Vivian Beaumont Theater at Lincoln Center for the Performing Arts, two highly acclaimed and highly controversial buildings. Can you tell us something about those commissions, the evolution of the designs and your role in them?

Pelli Actually, on both of those projects, although I was project designer, I shared that position with two other designers in the firm. I got involved in both halfway through their development. I was put in charge of the TWA team after the basic *parti* had been established, but not the forms or the formal vocabulary. With the Vivian Beaumont Theater I got involved after the exterior had been designed but before the house was developed, so I developed the interior of the house. I ran a few other projects from beginning to end—that is I ran them for Eero. Eero was the architect. I was in charge of the two colleges for Yale University. I was involved with them for many years.

Diamonstein Did you work on the interior of the Vivian Beaumont with Jo Mielziner?

Pelli I used to work with Hugh Hardy, who was with Jo Mielziner.

Diamonstein Eero Saarinen tried to enrich the vocabulary of architecture. But he did it in a way that he knew would often bring criticism—for example, the bird-like shape for an airline terminal. What did you and the people within that office think of the evolution of that approach to design?

Pelli Eero's designs were criticized as much within the office as outside it. The criticism was rather free and open. Looking back, I think that was very healthy. Eero was always a man, a very good man, a very good architect that we all respected, but he was always a man. He was never a god.

Diamonstein What does that mean?

Pelli To those working with him he was no god or genius or guru. He was a man, a very good but fallible man. That was very healthy. That is one of the reasons why so many of the designers who worked with him have done so much on their own.

Diamonstein So many of them have become so well known. There were only twenty people in that office.

Pelli That is correct in a way. Throughout his life there must have been about twenty designers who worked closely with him, who were given design responsibility.

Diamonstein Who were some of them, besides yourself?

Pelli Kevin Roche, of course, Bob Venturi, Tony Lumsden, Paul Kennon, Gunnar Birkerts, Warren Plattner, Bruce Adams, and Chuck Basset. I'm probably forgetting some very obvious ones. They will be calling me on the phone afterwards.

Diamonstein Saarinen spoke often of decoration, which he thought was necessary and inevitable. And you mentioned the Stiles and Morse Colleges at Yale that you were so profoundly involved in. How well do you think the ornamentation there has stood up?

Pelli   Eero always felt that modern architecture in the International Style version was lacking something that today we would call semantic content, or the ability to communicate. He was a graduate of Yale, of course, and a very dedicated alumnus. For him, the preeminent responsibility was to give Yale the best he could, regardless of what this would do to his career as an architect. I mean he knew that in trying to do a building that would have a medieval character, or a building that would be reminiscent of buildings at Oxford or Cambridge, that he was courting criticism, which he indeed received. But he felt that this was the only way that he could fulfill his responsibility to those undergraduates at Yale.

Diamonstein   After the Saarinen experience, you practiced for some time in California, first with Daniel, Mann, Johnson and Mendenhall, and then with Gruen Associates. In quite a remarkable fashion, you managed to become one of the few architects in the country to make a major reputation on your own while associated with a large corporate firm. While you were at Gruen Associates, a number of notable buildings were completed under your direction. You have described the 1973 Commons and Courthouse Center—in that centerpiece for American architecture, Columbus, Indiana—by saying that it subverts the normal decision-making process of architects. What do you mean by that?

Pelli   Today, in the accepted decision-making process, the primary preoccupations are formal. The architect is assumed to be fully in control and primarily responsible for the formal outcome of the project. In Columbus, my primary responsibility was the function or role that this building would play. By function, I do not mean functionalism, but rather the purpose or intention of the whole building. Our client and patron, Irwin Miller, together with his wife and his sister, Mrs. Tangeman, had the project built and then donated it to the city of Columbus. Their intention was to provoke a change in the way that the city functioned, to bring people and life back into downtown Columbus. By the time we were engaged, many of the existing stores were being boarded up and people were fleeing to the suburbs. So the primary intention was to develop with architecture a condition that would effect social change. This was what was preeminent in our minds. In a town where the primary action takes place in the suburbs, the town fragments itself into ethnic and economic enclaves, which may be good—though I doubt it very much—for the most affluent. But it clearly diminishes the quality of life for the less affluent. If one can say that vertical cuts separate economic and ethnic groups, there are also horizontal cuts that separate age groups, teenagers from the old, and children. When these groups become segmented, our lives become poorer. A fully working downtown should be able to attract and provide a rich life for all these groups—not separately, but together. This is very difficult to do with architecture, because architecture is not a social mechanism, *per se*. Designing a building is like making an instrument. The instrument still has to be played. No violin produces music by itself, even if it's a Stradivarius. It still needs a good violinist. Now, in this project, the challenge was that we were building this attraction for a town of thirty thousand people. That is, none of the devices that you can use in a large city to create excitement— where you bring people out of their homes for something unusual—would work here, because you get very tired of unusual exciting things. What you need is something that will give you life and recharge you on a day-to-day basis.

Diamonstein How did you choose to solve that in this small town, in terms of the scale, in terms of a magnet for continuing interest, both outside and inside the center?

Pelli The important thing was to create an element that would allow people to enjoy the space alone, in small groups, in larger groups, or in very large groups, up to about 1400 people. We proposed not only a building, but a way of running it. We thought that if our project was successful they would have one event a month. If it was very good, they would have a few extra events for special festivities, maybe twenty events a year. For the last four or five years, they have been having 270 to 290 events every year. Most of these events are not promoted by the center. Some of them are started by preexisting groups, but primarily the groups are *ad hoc*. Nowadays, everything of a public nature that happens in Columbus takes place at The Commons. People go there to see a play, listen to a concert as well as to read the paper, to play chess, to meet friends, and to do business. The activities cover the whole spectrum of public social life.

Diamonstein Did you ever expect your design to unleash that?

Pelli We expected that it would work well. But we did not dare hope that it would work as well as it has. Now, the principle that we used is a very simple one. It was an accumulation of small moves. Whenever there was something else we could add that would improve the quality of life in that space, we added it even if we had to sacrifice some aesthetic aspects of the building. For example, the building was under construction when they told us that they had finally convinced a theater chain to put two movie-houses in the center, a plan we had given up earlier. This meant an intrusion in an already designed building that considerably distorted one of our elevations. But when I was told that they could have these two movie houses, I didn't hesitate for a second. I said, "Wonderful, we will make room for them."

Diamonstein So your primary concern was not aesthetic, but whether the building would work for Columbus.

Pelli We were concerned with aesthetics, and I think we have a very beautiful building that is part of the town. It has the scale of the town, but it looks radically different. You can see it's not one of the other commercial buildings. It's a very special building which belongs to everybody in town.

Diamonstein Particularly in that part of town.

Pelli I think the building is highly resolved aesthetically, but the aesthetic resolution yielded to the primary concerns. With The Commons, we were creating a new type. One problem I had with that building is that I cannot call it anything. It's not *a* something, because there is no other space like this anywhere. It is unique. It should be a prototype for other buildings because it works. Of the many interventions that have taken place in our cities, particularly in decaying urban centers, very few have succeeded. The record of intervention in decaying urban centers by planners and urban designers has been rather poor. This building is a fantastic success. And it really should be a prototype, but it has no generic name at this moment. So far, it's just The Commons of Columbus.

Diamonstein Can you imagine it being replicated or adapted elsewhere?

Pelli It could not be replicated exactly, because this building has been carefully tailored for Columbus. But the principles could be used elsewhere and the basic intentions, the basic ideas, are applicable to other cities.

Diamonstein When you talked about Saarinen you said that he was never a local architect, that he didn't feel tied to a specific locale or to a landscape or to a life, the way many other architects describe themselves. He was born in Finland, and you have said that he had the characteristics of other immigrants who come to this country—the openness to the American experience that makes them in some cases more American than native-born Americans. Your story of Columbus, Indiana brings that very much to mind. Would Saarinen's story be an accurate description of your own assimilation, as well?

Pelli Yes, yes. But somehow different, because Eero's Finnish roots were more important architecturally than my Argentinian roots. His father, Eliel, was a very good architect, with a successful practice in Finland before they moved to America. And of course, the fact that there were other important Finnish architects, like Alvar Aalto was very important to Eero. All cases are different. But basically, I think it is accurate, yes.

Diamonstein I am really thinking of your own identification.

Pelli In that case, yes. Sometimes I feel that I am more American than Americans are, yes.

Diamonstein You practiced for years on the West Coast, and then burst onto the East Coast architectural scene in a rather spectacular way, first by becoming dean of the Yale School of Architecture, and second by winning the commission to design the addition to the Museum of Modern Art. Before we discuss the specifics of those projects, can you say a word about the difference between East Coast and West Coast architectural practices?

Pelli The differences are in the cultural environment. In the years that I was practicing on the West Coast—I must say it has been changing rapidly in the last five years or so—an architect worked in a cultural vacuum, which for me was very good. It was very, very healthy. It was also what I wanted. For about two years, after I left the office of Eero Saarinen and was put in charge of the design department at DMJM, I didn't look at an architectural magazine or read an architectural book.

Diamonstein Was that a relief?

Pelli I needed to do that. I needed to be totally immersed in the act of making buildings. I felt I had to be free to make my own mistakes, which I did. On the East Coast it's impossible to proceed freely to make your own mistakes. Your mistakes are pointed out to you way ahead of time. The West Coast was very good for me, after having been with Eero Saarinen for ten years. But eventually there is a limit in what you can do working only with yourself. At that point, if you want to keep on sharpening your own perceptions and processes, the level of critical exchange has to be higher. Here, the pressures force you to hone your own thoughts, ideas and sensitivities to a much sharper edge. The change for me at this moment in my career has been very, very good. Perfect timing. I have been very fortunate, very lucky.

Diamonstein You are now dean of the Architecture School at Yale. You followed another West Coast architect, Charles Moore, who held that position. Has the East met the West in any significant way at Yale?

Pelli No, I'm not a West Coast architect. I was an architect practicing in California but not a Californian. I understand California; I love it. I think I could take the best that California could give me, and I hope to be able to keep on practicing there. I have a couple of projects that I hope will go ahead in Los Angeles. That would be very important to me. But I don't come to Yale as a Westerner.

Diamonstein Now that you have been at Yale several years, have you seen any marked changes in the students' work, and does what you see encourage you?

Pelli The students are absolutely wonderful. Right now I think they are the best I have seen. It is a very good moment for architecture and for architectural education.

Diamonstein How does that manifest itself and how do you explain it?

Pelli It manifests itself in the seriousness of their intentions, the intensity of their commitment, the quality of their work, the skills that they develop. They can draw beautifully. They design wonderful buildings, done very seriously. They are tremendously committed to architecture. And they work extremely hard. They work hard at their designs, they work hard at their ideas, they work hard at their skills. Teaching now—it's a marvelous experience. The changes are extraordinary. About three years ago, the students were very interested in post-modernism. Everybody talked about it. About two years ago, post-modernism had passed, and the main interest became the neorationalists. We know this because we have long meetings with large groups of students to see who are they interested in having as lecturers. That's how I get my primary feedback.

Diamonstein What's this year's verdict?

Pelli This past year, the students wanted only individuals who they thought were working with their own ideas in an original way. For this coming year—this is most interesting—I have a group of students who want to talk with architects who have built many large buildings.

Diamonstein What does that reflect? Is it a barometer of the students' work, or a reflection of the attitudes of their teachers, or of the architects to whose work they respond?

Pelli They are, as they should be, extraordinarily good weather vanes. They perceive the slightest change of wind in the intellectual or theoretical interests of the profession. And they can see at any moment where it points. But the students' present interest is in buildings, which is quite extraordinary. Elective courses that deal with putting buildings together, getting buildings built are highly subscribed. The students sense that what is at issue now is knowing how to get buildings built and to build them well.

Diamonstein Well, they are about to witness their dean take on one of the most hazardous tasks for an architect. I am referring to your current design for a residential tower and gallery expansion for the Museum of Modern Art, a project that is a response to complex and often contradictory demands. Why don't we deal with some of the problems that you faced with the museum? You might talk about light and shadow and density and aesthetics and demolition and neighborhood structures and community boards and architectural historians, and anything else you would like to add to that long litany.

Pelli Do we have ten hours?

Diamonstein Why don't you give us the capsule version.

Pelli Initially, the most difficult part of this project has been the fact that not only did we have to design this project in a glass bowl, but there were hundreds of people with hooks and nets and harpoons all around the glass bowl while the project developed. By the time we took our schematic design for approval, I realized that I had made about ninety casual presentations of the project, plus about forty formal, highly elaborate presentations. Normally a project of that magnitude will require two formal presentations, plus three or four casual ones, to reach that stage.

Diamonstein Who was the client that you, as the architect, had to serve on this job? Was it the museum, the city, the Trust for Cultural Resources, the public, the developer, the co-architects who were hired by the developer?

Pelli The museum. Clearly, this is a very important building for a very important institution. I have served the public also because the public has been truly concerned with the fate of this institution. Although the process has been difficult, and every time I came out of a community board meeting I was exhausted, I would say to myself and to my associates, "This is really a wonderful process."

Diamonstein That's why you were the ideal architect for the job. Among other things, you're resilient.

Pelli Maybe the process was exaggerated because of the tremendous interest. But this was true public participation. Members of the community board would stay incredibly long hours late at night, eating stale sandwiches and coffee for dinner. Some of them may not have agreed with me. But they did this with true dedication to a civic cause and without compensation. Our open hearings were crowded with interested parties, people who were very concerned about the museum or about New York. I cannot help but feel that this is tremendously positive. They may have made things very difficult for us, but I think that's a small price to pay for something so valuable.

Diamonstein I quite agree. But how responsive were you and the museum to some of the requests and suggestions from those outside forces?

Pelli The level of our responses will be judged differently, depending on your point of view. But we took every request very seriously. Some we felt were possible, made sense, and we incorporated them.

Diamonstein For example?

Pelli Oh, a great, great many having to do with how much we encroached on the garden or cast shadows or the design of the facades. We worked extremely hard to encroach the least possible on the garden and to keep the shadows to the barest minimum. We took all those suggestions very seriously. Some we could incorporate into our design; some we could not.

Diamonstein Well, why didn't you incorporate the Joseph Hunt facade, that was the bookstore, into the museum?

Pelli It was not possible. The first reason is that it was physically and economically unfeasible. The building was designed by Joseph Hunt (nephew of Richard Morris). The facade was built three to four feet inside the property line, while the tower, in order to make economic sense, had to be on the property line. Therefore, the main building would have had to cantilever around the facade or enclose it in some manner. The second problem was aesthetic—perhaps for me a more important aspect, a more basic one. We made models to try to preserve the whole facade, or parts of the facade. If we had kept the mansard, we would have had to go back fifteen feet from the property line, because the mansard sloped back that much. The mansard is an architectural device intended to be seen against the sky. To suddenly put it inside a building was wrong. It's not something that you do to buildings you love. It's not the proper way to preserve buildings. I think it would have been a very misguided effort.

Diamonstein In the Museum of Modern Art project, you have yet another constituency to deal with. On the Board of Trustees are four very distinguished architects, each of whom has designed a number of museums. One of them is responsible for one of the facades that you have done away with. Philip Johnson, Edward Larrabee Barnes, Gordon Bunshaft, and Wallace Harrison are all on the board, along with Ivan Chermayeff, the graphic designer, who certainly thinks like an architect and knows a great deal about architecture.

Pelli There is also Arthur Drexler, director of architecture and design.

Diamonstein How do you wend your way through this complex cast of characters? Is it worth it?

Pelli Oh, yes, it's clearly worth it. They have been wonderful, really; Philip in particular. I don't know how I would have reacted in his position, when we were forced to tear down and alter some of his structures. He has been extraordinarily supportive, patient, and good-humored. I am very impressed with how he was able to step back and look at this objectively. They all have been very supportive. We have had to make many presentations to them, and indeed I have listened to their suggestions with great care and given them serious consideration.

Diamonstein Did they make any notable suggestions that you incorporated?

Pelli No, we didn't.

Diamonstein Just a very good listener.

Pelli It's impossible to incorporate any notable things into this project because its determinants are rather unyielding. But, we were asked, for example, to study tearing down all the facades and making a single new facade. Some of the architects thought that an institution like this should have a single image, not a multiple one.

Diamonstein Why did you conclude that a multiple image was the successful solution?

Pelli Because this is the reality of this museum.

Diamonstein But isn't it only a partial reality if you have done away with the Johnson extension?

Pelli That was inescapable and never critical. It was built as a temporary building. Philip himself had planned earlier for a westward extension. Tearing it down was inevitable. But the building we kept, the 1938 Philip Goodwin and Edward Durrell Stone facade has become for many of us a symbol of the Museum of Modern Art. When I was living in Argentina and thought of the Museum of Modern Art, I always thought of that facade in one of the famous photographs of 1938. I can still see it in my mind's eye, that old photograph. This is very important and very real.

That facade remains in our design as the main symbol and the main entrance to the museum. That facade is being kept as the only discordant color element in the whole street. It is the only white element in a dark street. Back in 1938, if you built a modern museum for modern art, you built a building that was new and clean and white and sharply machined, and also one that stood in contrast to the older masonry on the street.

Diamonstein You raise a very important and interesting question. At this time, the ideological fervor that the museum had in the days when it was first opened, and its original building was erected, is gone. In fact, many people are questioning the purpose of a modern museum. Is it modern, or is it contemporary, in what some people call a post-modern period? Some even question whether putting a modern building there now is justifiable. How do you feel that you have solved that problem, if it has been a problem at all?

Pelli I don't agree with the concept that the modern movement is over. It isn't. Otherwise, there would be no terms like post-modernism. When you talk of postindustrialism, it doesn't mean that we're going back to a preindustrial society. When you say something is postrevolutionary, it doesn't mean that the revolution has been lost. It means the revolution has been won and its principles have been implemented. You can only have a postrevolutionary period if you've won the revolution. You can only have a postindustrial period if industry has become universal. In the same way, you can only have a post-modernism if the ideas of modernism are alive and well and universal. Now, "post-modernism" as a sect or school is another story. It's just a label for a group of people working in a particular way. But the larger meaning is very simple. It reinforces the validity of a main movement of which there is now an offshoot.

Diamonstein In this post-modern debate, some of which goes on with great animation on your campus, where on the spectrum is your voice?

Pelli Well, in school we are very open. We are living in a period when ideas are being exchanged, recast and reformulated. Our students want to be right there, where new ideas are being proposed and discussed. Therefore, we are very open to all those whom we feel have new ideas to contribute or old ideas to reexpress in coherent terms. The question is the validity, not the newness, of the ideas. So in that context, the school is pluralistic. I have no intention of imposing on the students or the school my particular vision or understanding of what architecture is or should be.

Diamonstein Let's come back to the Museum of Modern Art for a moment. There you are now faced with yet another complex decision that will have to be made soon after the extraordinary send-off that the museum is giving its former incarnation, in the form of the remarkable Picasso exhibition. Should the building close for two years, or should it remain open on a partial basis for a longer period?

Pelli Fortunately, that is not my responsibility. That is a difficult decision that the museum will have to make.

Diamonstein Obviously, neither solution is satisfactory for the museum, the architect or the public. Of the two, which would you prefer?

Pelli From a construction point of view, if you forget about all other issues, the simplest thing to do is to close it all. You build the structure and in two years you open again. But that is clearly unacceptable to the museum and

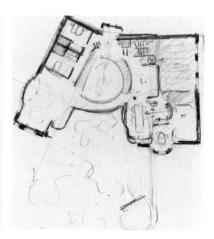

Gewirz House, Glen Echo, Md.
Drawing by Cesar Pelli

Gewirz House, Glen Echo, Md.
Drawing by Cesar Pelli

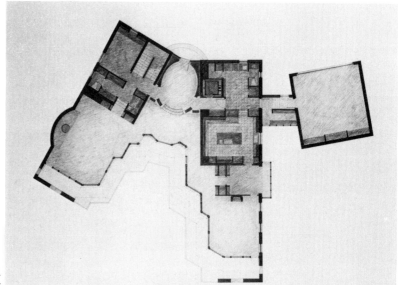

Gewirz House, Glen Echo, Md.
Drawing by Rob Charney

Hermann Park Towers,
Houston, Tex.
Drawing by Jon Pickard

The Museum of Modern Art, tower,
New York, N.Y., model
Picture credit: J. Severtson,
K. Champlin

Pacific Design Center, exterior,
Los Angeles, Calif.
Picture credit: Fred Clarke

to the people who love the museum. The museum is a part of New York. I don't think anybody imagines that the museum can close for two years.

Diamonstein What does that do to your projected September 1982 reopening date and your twenty-million-dollar budget?

Pelli The west wing should be finished by December 1981, and it should open soon thereafter. The west wing, the extension of the museum which I have designed, will double the size of the museum.

Diamonstein How many square feet are involved in the renovation?

Pelli There will be about 17,000 square feet of new museum construction.

Diamonstein What's the current status of the project? One hears that its design keeps on being refined. Are you up to working drawings? What are some of the recent changes?

Pelli Everything is happening at the same time. The design is being refined; working drawings are practically finished in some areas, and construction is moving quickly. Everything that affects the west wing is finished; the working drawings are sufficiently finished for construction to proceed. Meanwhile, we are refining the design of many interior spaces; we are designing the interiors of the new restaurants and the interiors of the bookstore.

Diamonstein How involved were the curators and heads of departments in planning the interior design and space for their areas, and does the Department of Architecture and Design have a special role in the design?

Pelli The galleries are being designed to suit the needs of the curators of the museum. We work closely with them on these areas. In the case of the Department of Architecture and Design, Arthur Drexler is designing his own space.

Diamonstein Have you often wished that you could just go off somewhere and design a simple building, free of some of these pressures and problems?

Pelli No, I do have some commissions where I design buildings free of these pressures. But I would not exchange these problems for anything. See, the Museum of Modern Art exemplifies in a very critical way the characteristics of buildings of our time, the kinds of decisions we have to make. Our world is not perfect. Ideal solutions are not possible. Actually, I believe that a search for ideal solutions does great harm to good solutions, because they divert our efforts from the possible to the impossible. The Museum of Modern Art is a project that brings those conflicts very clearly into focus. The most important decisions we make in life are about conflicting goals or ideals. Sometimes those decisions make the difference between a good life and a bad life. It's the same with buildings. Making the correct decisions, when you have conflicting goals, is what makes for a good building. I think the conflicts impart to this particular project a tremendous amount of vitality. The fact that there are apartments in the same site as a museum, that you don't have a pure, ideal site, that you don't have a very wealthy patron who will give untold amounts of money so that the perfect museum can be built—no, the museum is in a tight site in New York. Expanding it is very difficult. If you build a tower, it casts a shadow, and yet you have to build a building that will produce revenue to keep the museum solvent. I think it's part and parcel of life in our cities. In our cities, we mix commerce with culture with pleasure. That combination, that close affinity is what cities are all about. A person living in an apartment is not worth any less than a person looking at a painting. These are both legitimate manifestations of life and humanity, each manifestation has its own dignity.

Diamonstein You described the project earlier as designing in a glass bowl. That is certainly consonant with one of your longstanding interests, the use of glass. The aesthetic qualities of transparency have concerned you for some time. Some people call it literal transparency, but I believe you prefer perceptual transparency. Can you explain that term?

Pelli Well, my interest in the term arose because Colin Rowe and Bob Slutsky wrote a wonderful article on phenomenal transparency. They created a vocabulary, to describe this quality, and we have all learned much from it. But I did not agree with what they called literal transparency, and I felt they did not understand it. As I believed I did, I wrote my article on perceptual transparency. My interest is manifold. Glass is one of the materials we have to learn how to use. Architecture has been given shape, given form, given a theoretical background by stone construction for some five thousand years. All the traditional aesthetic theories of architecture are based on stone construction. Now, unless our society goes through a violent upheaval, the dominant role of stone construction is all over. There have been social changes that will make it impossible to go back to what we have known as stone construction. To build in stone, you need to have a large class of highly skilled people willing to work for almost no money. Today you'd have to pay highly skilled craftsmen fifty cents an hour in order to be able to construct buildings that would have all the qualities of traditional stone construction.

Diamonstein You're saying that arches and keystones and columns are really of quite another era.

Pelli They are gone, and the primary meaning of all these elements is also gone. The secondary meanings remain, and they will have life for a while, but they cannot ever again serve as a basis for any lasting transformation of architecture. A healthy architecture has to grow from the characteristics of its own time. The emergence of stone construction brought about a revolution over previous forms of architecture—nomadic constructions of sticks and grasses and skins, with totally different formal characteristics. The emergence of stone construction radically changed the theoretical basis for formal decisions in architecture. And the disappearance of stone construction will force us to change the basis for our development of a formal theory of architecture. It is still a very new condition. But we have to learn to deal with our materials and their qualities. If you look at the positive side, there are some wonderful things about it. I have to look at the positive side. I am an architect who builds, and therefore I am an optimist. Being an optimist is a prerequisite for anybody who wants to build, because construction is a matter of optimism; it's a matter of facing the future with confidence. I guess it's like needing a good voice if you want to be a singer, or good coordination if you want to be an athlete.

Glass is fragile. Now, fragility is a quality that Western architecture has ignored. Western architecture put its formal heart primarily in permanence, durability. This comes from our desire to build monuments to try to cheat death, to live beyond our own life. The only way to do this is with materials that are also dead so that they will remain. Stone will survive for some centuries. On the other hand, usually the most ephemeral and fragile things touch us most intimately—a flower in springtime, a sunset, the beauty of a person, which we know is going to change and fade. Those are the things that touch us the deepest. So an architecture that depends for its expressive qualities on fragility has the potential of being a richer architecture, more like our lives than an architecture that depends on permanence and the qualities of death. Now, fragility doesn't mean that something has to last for a very short time. All it means is that it requires a commitment on the part of the living to make it remain. The Temple of Ise in Japan is the best example. It's built of wood and grass, and has a very short life. It's a fragile architecture. Every twenty years it is taken down and a new, identical temple is built next to it. So, it has remained for close to 2,000 years, practically unchanged, but always new and always fragile. It's in better shape than any of Western architecture's 2,000-year-old stone monuments because of this continuous commitment. The moment the Japanese decide not to maintain the temple, it is going to decay, rot away and disappear. But while the commitment remains, that temple is new and fresh and alive. The same with a building made out of a lightweight steel structure and glass—if it isn't maintained, the glass will break away, the steel will rust, and the building will disappear. But while the commitment remains and the steel structure is repainted and maintained and the glass is replaced as it breaks, the building will also be new and fresh. I want first to contribute to *an* architecture and second, to *my* architecture. I see myself as working within a long time span. A century is behind me and a century is ahead of me—to make a contribution, I have to deal with the reality of my own time. I have to make architecture, make art with the materials I have, not with materials that do not have life anymore.

Diamonstein You have spent considerable time exploring the aesthetic possibilities of new surfaces. Your own best example is certainly your most critically acclaimed, and like all such buildings the most damned. It's the Pacific Design Center in Los Angeles, often referred to as the blue whale. It's much bigger than anything else around it, and I guess that's one of the reasons it has drawn that kind of attention. Can you tell us something about this building, and also about your ideas concerning context in general?

Pelli It's very difficult to talk about ideas of context in New York using the Pacific Design Center as an example, because it is built in an area that has no context.

Diamonstein How would you describe the Pacific Design Center? Why did you choose to build a glass building, which draws on the reflective qualities of its surroundings and its context, in an open space? You have done this on more than one occasion.

Pelli The Pacific Design Center is really a simple solution to a simple problem. It's a very large building, a warehouse for design showrooms that open into interior corridors. All over the country, such buildings are built as brick. Typically, they have no windows, because the back of the showroom is the exterior of the building. In California, it's a bad idea to build brick buildings because in an earthquake they shake and fall down. They impose a heavy load on your structure, and that makes it expensive.

Oddly enough, a building of glass works very nicely, because the glass just hangs there and shakes within its neoprene gaskets, and has hardly any effect on the structure. So glass appeared to be a very nice, simple solution, and we could do it in a wonderful color, deep blue.

Diamonstein Like the Pacific Ocean.

Pelli No, it was just my color. So it was really a very simple solution.

Diamonstein But you like glass in many things.

Pelli I have used glass. I like the qualities of glass. For one thing, during my practice with DMJM and with Gruen, many clients came to us not wanting architecture, just wanting a building. Therefore, they were only interested in spending the minimum amount of money. I learned to do architecture with no extra money, with only the absolute minimum budget available to build a building. And with glass you get a lot for your money. Just to give you an idea of the cost of the Pacific Design Center, it is roughly the same length as Beaubourg, the same width, the same height, the same number of floors, the same square footage, and it was built at about the same time. Beaubourg cost somewhere between 80 and 150 million dollars. Ours cost 18.

Diamonstein But that includes interior costs as well, doesn't it?

Pelli The 150 million includes interiors. I believe the 80 does not, which means the 80 million should be compared to our 18.

Diamonstein Well, it's still a very dramatic difference.

Pelli In general, those are the kinds of numbers we were working with: very, very minimal costs. Glass is one of those materials that I discovered you can do wonderful things with for very little money. And that's how I learned to love glass. I also like glass because it has some qualities that I find quite extraordinary. It is reflective. It's fragile and impermanent, and the qualities of fragility and impermanence are apparent in the quality of the glass itself. It's like the wings of a butterfly. They not only are fragile, but they look fragile, and their aesthetic qualities are part and parcel of that fragility. The same with glass. It has ephemeral qualities; the images change, the reflections change, the color of the building changes with the color of the day. The Pacific Design Center is bright blue. But towards dusk it becomes flaming red with the sunset. You can see the building go from blue to red to black. I do not control the final aesthetic qualities of my buildings, and I don't believe I should. The aesthetic qualities of a glass building only become what they are after the building is built. A model is a vague approximation, and a drawing is almost no approximation at all. Things that we love the most are like that, you know, like our children. If you really love them, you will help them be better themselves. If you like gardening, a plant that you really love should be what it wants to be. You can help it but you cannot change it. And so not being able to completely control the final quality of a building is not important to me.

Diamonstein Don't you make models for your buildings?

Pelli We build many models, so we can study other issues.

Diamonstein So you really work with drawings?

Pelli Yes, we also work with drawings, but they are secondary, because I cannot make drawings that will reproduce the important qualities of a building. I depend upon my experience, primarily. I guess at what the building will do. I never know exactly what it will do. I do not know how the Museum of Modern Art will look, exactly. Drawings and models are used to study other issues: proportions, entrances, relationship of parts, form, color, but not the perceptual qualities of the building. For example, from Fifth Avenue, the museum building will be reflecting CBS on one side; on the other side, it will reflect Canada House. If you approach it from Sixth Avenue, it will have a totally different quality, because it will reflect the 666 building. And on the other side it will reflect ABC. And if you turn a little, it will reflect the Dorset Hotel or the Warwick Hotel. So it will reflect either dark gray or the rich dark brown of the Dorset, or it will reflect white aluminum. Those reflections are going to change the colors we have placed on the building. They will intermix with the colors, and there will be a new reality that I can only guess at. Now, I am very good at guessing, because I have done enough of these buildings, and I spend endless number of hours looking and thinking about this issue. I can guess very well. But I can only guess. I cannot predict exactly what will happen.

Diamonstein Well, that guess is a very tutored one that reflects your views on what architecture should represent today.

Pelli It's all anybody can do.

Diamonstein It also reflects your ongoing philosophy. You have said that there is no high technology in architecture; there is only an expression of technology. The technology of today is industrial, but not all that industrialized. To sum up that particular view, you said, "I personally feel that the only safe ground is the middle ground." Is that a statement that you think has wider implications?

Pelli No, I meant it only in that context. You see, I am not advocating safety. I like to take my chances, too. But clearly, there are two things happening. One is exploration, and the other one is the construction of actual buildings, where we assume very specific responsibilities.

Diamonstein What is the question underlying the architect's responsibility?

Pelli When a contract is signed, the architect accepts a substantial responsibility towards the society that engages him or her for handling very large resources. These are the savings of our social body. The average cost of a building today, judging by my commissions, is about thirty million dollars. That's a lot of money for any social group now. The architect has the responsibility to judiciously spend thirty million dollars to provide a social good. Somebody else was entrusted with that money. Somebody, maybe the head of a commission, or somebody who has earned or borrowed the money—but somehow society has entrusted somebody with that money, with the special role, therefore, of a client. And the architect has to use those resources in an intelligent way. When you build a speculative office building, although the motivation may be to invest money, the purpose is to provide working space for a number of members of our society. That's the real intention, the real purpose. So even when you do speculative office building, you have a social responsibility to discharge. That's basic. Architects have always done so. And at the same time, today particularly, you have the critical responsibility to use our resources intelligently. Physical, nonreplenishable resources, as well as energy. Of course, very rarely does the architect assume any such responsibilities alone. Whenever a large building is built, the architect becomes a member of a team. One collaborates with the people who put up the money.

One collaborates with the people who will lease the building or operate it or run it. One collaborates with the people who are going to build it, not to mention of all the public bodies that have to support the building and provide it with electricity, water, sewage, etcetera. So one enters into a very complex collaboration, and one has to discharge one's part of that collaboration. That's very, very important to me. I feel that indeed, one has—and I have said this before—the privileges of an artist. But I can only exercise those privileges after I have discharged my responsibility as an architect. Only after I have discharged my responsibility have I earned the right to do art.

Diamonstein The potential collaboration between architects and artists is a question of increasing concern to many of us. Is that something you have ever done?

Pelli Yes, a few times. The most successful one was again in The Commons of Columbus. We worked with Jean Tinguely, who designed the sculpture for the space. Tinguely had come from France, and we first met at the Indianapolis 500, which is a wonderful place to meet.

Diamonstein What were *you* doing there?

Pelli Well, we were going to meet on Memorial Day, and the Indianapolis 500 is very close to Columbus. So our clients suggested going, and we said, sure, why not? For Tinguely, the race became an annual ritual. After that I gave him a program for the sculpture. I told him it should be about this size and this color range, and it should move slowly and it should have this formal quality. At first, he reacted badly. I thought he was going to walk away, because of course sculptors never get a program. But after a while he realized that I was not going to be on his back all the time. I never gave him directions afterwards. He was totally free to interpret the program and to develop his sculpture. We had many good discussions and meetings, so the sculpture and the building have been designed for each other. They go together. His sculpture—he calls it *Chaos Number 1*—activates the building, gives it life, and the building shelters the sculpture and gives it form. This is a very old device. The space comes alive by means of the reality of a positive element. The sculpture brings the space to life, not only in a spiritual sense, but also in a physical sense, because Tinguely's sculpture is delightfully alive.

Diamonstein When do you think collaboration is most feasible or desirable?

Pelli I am not sure I know. I guess when the architect and the artist have respect for each other and for each other's work. I don't believe it's possible otherwise. In the Middle Ages it was easy. You just hired the artist or the sculptor and paid him by the yard. But today architects and artists have to come together as equals.

Audience How do you determine which artist should work in a building that you have designed? Does the client have a voice in the decision?

Pelli I don't have a method for selecting an artist. In the case of The Commons, what I thought the space needed was a piece of sculpture that would be lively and have a sense of humor. The only artist I could think of who could do a serious piece of art with humor was Jean Tinguely. I had never met him, and so we corresponded until he agreed to do the work there. Then I presented our clients with the idea of his doing the work, and showed them many examples of Tinguely's work. I must say, the Millers were a bit uneasy at the beginning because they saw all this rusted steel on self-destruct pieces of sculpture. But I asked them to see *Eureka,* a very beautiful piece that he did for the Lausanne Fair and that is now in Zurich. And they shared my feelings at the time and we went ahead in engaging Jean Tinguely.

Audience Have you built anything in Argentina?

Diamonstein And if not, was the reason in any way related to the political situation.?

Pelli No. I have never had a commission in Argentina. I would love to have one. I'd love to build a building in Argentina.

Audience If we cannot afford an architecture of stone, will our cities become ephemeral, and more glassy?

Pelli No, I was not clear, I realize. I like glass, but glass is not the only material. Actually, we can use stone, but we have to use it as we use glass, as cladding. If stone is cut mechanically in thin sheets and hung like a curtain wall, it is competitive with glass in many cases. So are a number of other materials. When I talk about stone construction I talk about masonry construction where stone is a bearing material and where the richness of forms comes from from the carving of the stone. This is the architecture of the past, the construction system that gave form to Western architecture—capitals used as a transition between a heavy weight coming down onto a vertical member, arches as a way of opening up this very heavy mass. You know, all the elements we know in Western architexture that are charged with secondary meanings have their primary meaning. The primary meaning of an arch is to distribute the enormous weight of the wall sideways to make an opening. Secondary meanings are to convey importance to an entrance, et cetera. Now, stone will remain, but it will have to be used in a very different manner. Right now, we are designing buildings that are lightweight enclosures in brick, in stone, in glass, in metal panels, in ceramic tile. We are just finishing a building in Korea which is all ceramic tile, and it looks beautiful. But it is not ceramic tile used to cover heavy masonry construction, but ceramic tile used as a lightweight enclosure. The change is in the system of construction more than in the materials.

Audience You have used the word architect and artist. Today, by artist we mean painter or sculptor. Wouldn't it be more discreet to call them painters or sculptors?

Pelli I agree completely. Actually, I think only in English is the name artist reserved for painters and sculptors. It certainly is not so in my native Spanish. Artist would also include poets and writers and architects and musicians. But for some reason in English the word artist—and I was using it within that context—is understood to mean painter or sculptor.

Diamonstein What's the most important thing that we should know about your work?

Pelli I love to build buildings!

JAMES STEWART POLSHEK

James Stewart Polshek
Born Akron, Ohio, 1930
B.S. Western Reserve University, 1951
M. Arch. Yale University, 1955

Diamonstein James Stewart Polshek, a leading architect and educator, is dean of the Graduate School of Architecture and Planning at Columbia University. He is involved in the world of New York's public works design as a consultant and adviser to many groups. He has also helped enhance the reputation of his school, by encouraging the university administration to hire more top-quality architects. In the Polshek years at Columbia, Romaldo Giurgola, Robert Stern, Alexander Kouzanoff, Gwathmey Siegel, and others have designed works on campus, reversing a trend toward mediocre structures built by commercial architects. In addition, Polshek has an active private architectural practice. Among his best-known works are the Quinco Mental Health Center in Columbus, Indiana; the Friends Meeting House Brotherhood Synagogue on Gramercy Park in New York; Twin Parks Housing in the Bronx; Rosemary Hall-The Choate School in Wallingford, Connecticut; and the Teijin Central Research Institute in Tokyo.

For the past eight years you have been the dean of Columbia's School of Architecture. How did you first become interested in architectural education?

Polshek I wasn't. A very dear friend, Max Bond, who is one of our new planning commissioners and the new chairman, starting next fall, of Columbia's Department of Architecture, called me one rainy day and said, "Why don't you come up here? We're on the search committee and we're getting nowhere." And I said, "I have no interest in it." I discussed it with my wife and we thought it would be worth a ride uptown, on the theory that whenever you are asked to be interviewed for anything, do it, even if you think you are not interested. So I did go up. One thing led to another, and I became the dean. It was just about as simple as that. And I became increasingly interested in architectural education.

Diamonstein As I mentioned, you've helped to raise the level of architecture on the Columbia campus. How has the process of selecting architects changed?

Polshek For many, many years the selection of architects for major research universities, meaning well-endowed private universities, has meant that if you have a president who is interested in architecture or the quality of physical life, such as Whitney Griswold at Yale, then the university takes a deep interest in that. At Columbia that was not the case before McGill became president. Like anything in New York, selection of architects seemed to dwell on power and the sources of power in a kind of old-boy network. Before I accepted the Columbia position I asked that the president put into writing the fact that I would be his special adviser on all planning and design. We had an informal agreement that I would reform the process and have essentially the final sign-off on the selection of any architect for all buildings.

Diamonstein So you fill two roles at Columbia, both dean of the School of Architecture and special consultant to the president. I guess the way you get things done is by that special relationship with the president.

Polshek Yes, you kind of leverage one against the other. One is paid and the other is unpaid. But that has worked very well. As a matter of fact, it's worked remarkably well. And many important architects are doing their first buildings in New York City as a result and I'm very proud of that.

Diamonstein You have cause to be. Who are they?

Polshek The first major building, the Fairchild Life Science Building, was done by Mitchell/Giurgola. The next big building, just being completed by Gwathmey Siegel, is a twenty-three-million-dollar dormitory and student center. The third big building, a new chemistry building, is just being designed by James Stirling and Partners. Along the way there have been other things. Richard Datner's doing Baker Field over. Prentice and Chan are doing the East Asian Library, and Robert Stern did a law student commons complex. And there have been a number of other planning studies. Younger members of the faculty are doing work for various deans in other schools. It's a very active place.

Diamonstein What would you say is the prognosis for future quality design on the Columbia campus?

Polshek It's good.

Diamonstein Even if you weren't there?

Polshek I think a pattern's been set. I don't think the faculty would settle for the situation that existed before, when the president would go out and hire bad or mediocre architects, and really flaunt that in the face of the school. I mean it simply would be unconscionable.

Diamonstein Has this responsibility had any significant effect on your own work?

Polshek It's taken a lot of time, that's all. I mean I feel responsible to the profession. That's why I do it. I also feel responsible for good buildings. And most importantly, I am appalled by ugly buildings and there were a lot built.

Diamonstein Does your profound involvement in the School of Architecture, both with your peers and with students, have some effect on your work?

Polshek The students, yes. My peers, I don't know. The peer that I respect most is Stirling, so I hope he doesn't fall on his face with this building. But the students have had a very great effect on my work, in combination with the young people in the office. I can't really separate the two. They make you think constantly about what you're doing, and keep you from falling into patterns that might be more profitable, but nevertheless deadening in the end. So they've been quite significant.

Diamonstein Stirling is perhaps best known for his other university building at Leicester. Will this building be reminiscent, either in inspiration or execution, of that one?

Polshek I don't think so, because Stirling is changing all the time. Also the context is very different. I've seen doodles, but I wouldn't want to talk about it.

Diamonstein What building is his responsibility at Columbia?

Polshek Chemistry. The other was an engineering building. He's a very great architect, and I don't know what he's going to come up with. But I have a hunch.

Diamonstein Do you want to tell the class?

Polshek No. No sneak-previews.

Diamonstein You spent an early part of your practice in Japan, and are still very well-connected to the Japanese architectural establishment. How and when did that Cinderella kind of involvement begin?

Polshek My first commission was with a fellow student, a woman named Vica Schniewind a few years after we got out of school. I was still working for another architect. It was a little house in the country.

Diamonstein Twelve hundred and fifty square feet.

Polshek How did you know that?

Diamonstein Eighteen thousand dollars.

Polshek How do you know that? Eighteen thousand. That's right. And because I wanted to keep the building close to the ground, the heating system was in the ceiling, which didn't work too well. But the clients are still friends. And then they commissioned me to do another house, a town-house right over here on Eleventh Street. The first house was published. I didn't know how you got published, so I walked in to Elizabeth Sverbeyeff, who was at the *New York Times* then, doing the Sunday magazine. And I said, "I have some slides here. I think it's a nice house." And she published it, which was very nice. Then I did the second house. These people were very eminent scientists and one night they were entertaining a Japanese mogul.

Diamonstein You were then about twenty-nine years old.

Polshek Yes, I was about twenty-nine. I can't remember all the events, exactly. But I went over one morning to check out something in the house that wasn't working. I think that the Japanese industrialist and his wife were there. Both of them are extremely powerful figures in Japan. We went to dinner there, I think, my wife, Ellyn, and I, and in the course of dinner Mr. Ohya, the industrialist said, "Would you like to come to Japan and design a building?" And I said, "Okay," you know, thinking "this is not going to happen."

Diamonstein Had you ever been to Japan before?

Polshek No. No. My God, no. I was scared to death of airplanes besides, so I was kind of hoping it wouldn't happen. But three months later I was working for an office here in New York and the receptionist came in and said, "There are seven Japanese gentlemen to see you." I mean it was very weird. I remember I was working on the Juilliard School at Lincoln Center at the time. I went out to see them, and they said that they wanted to talk to me and wanted me to come to Japan to negotiate the contract, or whatever. The Japanese don't negotiate contracts in the way we do. I mean they'll sign something. So I said, "I am going to Japan," and my friends all took me to the airport a week or two later, and literally poured me onto a plane. I came back with a commission. I packed up the whole thing at Lincoln Center, and we left and we lived over there for a year and a half, or thereabouts. And while I was there the industrialist said, "We want another building."

Diamonstein Why don't you tell us about the first building which led to the second?

Polshek Well, it was a huge basic-research laboratory that today would be a twenty or twenty-five-million-dollar building—very complicated in program. I picked two or three people to assist me from a Japanese construction company. A couple of them spoke English. We isolated ourselves, and I was scared to death. I flew by the seat of my pants. I mean I went from a brownstone to a building like that. The building was a sort of vertical slab, not entirely successful in every way, but I won't talk about that now. The low administration wing was not really integrated with the tower. And then I got a second building to do, which was an applied research building for dyers and weavers and spinners in the textile industry. It's on an open industrial plan just outside Kyoto. That was much more interesting to me—about the same size as the first one, actually, but a very different program. And I did that one, too.

Diamonstein You did those in sequence?

Polshek Yes. Actually, one hadn't quite ended. It was a total Cinderella story. They didn't have contract furniture outlets in Japan at the time, so I would get old interiors magazines. I thought, and still do think, Ward Bennett is one of the few really wonderful designers around. I would get pictures of his furniture that he was doing then for Lehigh, I think. And I would say, "I want that chair" to the Japanese, and they'd come back with shop-drawings, and I would adjust the proportions a little bit and they'd make it.

Diamonstein Where are we now, 1960?

Polshek Sixty-two, sixty-three. Anything I wanted, I got. There were arguments, of course, but not knowing the language works two ways.

Diamonstein When you returned to this country, with which firm did you work?

Polshek I didn't. I never worked for anybody again. I worked for Pei when I got out of Yale. Then I went to Europe on a Fulbright, and when I got back I worked for about three years for Ulrich Franzen, who had just left Pei's office. Then I got fired by a series of architects, mostly for insubordination. And then I went to Japan.

Diamonstein And when you came back you started your own practice.

Polshek Yes. That was '63, because I remember I was working on my drafting table at home when John Kennedy was assassinated. You always remember where you were at moments like that.

Diamonstein Now you teach in an architectural school, head an architectural practice and serve as a frequent consultant and jury member. Do these various identities ever clash?

Polshek Well, they clash sometimes in terms of time. But no, they don't clash.

Diamonstein Do they complement one another, these different hats that you wear?

Polshek It seems to work for me. I have a short attention span but I focus intensely. I read only three or four books a year, which is a terrible thing to say in front of people!

Diamonstein Particularly when you have a wife in publishing.

Polshek That's correct. We have a lot of books around the house, and very literate children, as well. You know, you learn after a while. I mean I really don't waste a minute during the day for anything. I eat on the subway or I correct papers or I do budgets with my machine on the subway. Whatever you can do on the subway I do, like sketch details in a little sketch book. Very simply, I just use the time. And then I was born with an excess of metabolic energy or adrenaline or whatever. So I keep going.

Diamonstein What do you see as your primary interest?

Polshek Oh, I don't know. That's the kind of thing you pay shrinks for.

Diamonstein Well, considering the fact that your undergraduate major was in psychology and that you spent a great deal of time working in clinical situations before you decided to become an architect, I assume that you must have given considerable thought to your own identity, more so than most of us.

Polshek I did not. Less probably. I became interested in architecture by accident.

Diamonstein What was that accident?

Polshek Some friends of my family in Akron, Ohio asked a friend of theirs who had worked at Taliesin to come back and design a house for them. I think it was the first time I had ever seen a rubber plant or an Eames chair or a glass wall that went down to the floor. And I thought it was very revolutionary. Instead of doing the obstreperous things that I was doing in those days with my friends, I used to go up in the attic and build models of weird houses out of shirt cardboard, which I would color. I think my family thought I had lost my mind. I just got interested, and I gave up pre-med.

Diamonstein Well, it was revolutionary, at least then. And more and more thought is being given to that movement. It has been hailed, and now some say it has failed, as an instrument of social salvation. In a recent piece in the *New York Review of Books,* Ada Louise Huxtable said that architecture is now at a genuine crossroads, quite unlike any other time in history. She adds that architecture is backing blindly away from a sociological or environmental context and into the realm of pure art again. I guess architects have always battled over whether their mission was to create art first and serve special needs second. What's your estimate of that debate?

Polshek I don't know quite how to phrase it, because I talk about it so much, and I just don't want to insult anybody. Well, I read Ada Louise's article in the *New York Review of Books,* and I told her and I will tell you that I thought it was, for the most part, a very courageous piece of work. She told me that it was very difficult to write that way in the *New York Times.*

Diamonstein Why do you think the piece was so courageous?

Polshek For one thing she publicly took on Philip Johnson. At the end, I thought, she kind of wound down, you know, in a way that was unfortunate.

Diamonstein Rather than concentrating on individuals or one particular article, I think we should talk about the larger issue, and that is the validity of modernism and/or of the post-modernist movement.

Polshek I think it's a lot of nonsense. The whole argument is kind of inconsequential.

Diamonstein A debate is raging . . .

Polshek I think it's a journalists' debate. It's a debate among people who don't do it, as opposed to a debate among people who do it.

Diamonstein But there are so many architects involved both in writing and discussing. . .

Polshek There are? I don't think so.

Diamonstein Mr. Stern. . . .

Polshek Well, Bob, he's one. Name me two.

Diamonstein Mr. Graves.

Polshek No, Mr. Graves doesn't, actually.

Diamonstein Mr. Moore.

Polshek No, he really doesn't, either.

Diamonstein Mr. Venturi. Mr. Johnson.

Polshek Well, Venturi doesn't any more. Mr. Johnson does.

Diamonstein I really would like to address the issue, and that is where do *you* stand?

Polshek Let's go back to your first question, a more serious one, about architecture for social purposes. There was an article by Paul Goldberger yesterday about a very interesting symposium we had at Columbia, last Saturday. I think that young architects today—students and younger practitioners—express themselves differently and have obviously different concerns. It does not mean that they are necessarily any less concerned. They may be more scared and they don't talk about it so much, but they're no less concerned about the application of their skills to social problems. I think they are more realistic about the limitations of those skills, because, for all the ranting and raving—and I was one of the ranters in the sixties—architecture is, in the end, I believe, an inherently conservative profession. I don't mean conservative politically; I mean conservative in the sense that it depends upon vast amounts of human labor—slaves, or in the absence of slaves, vast amounts of money and machines. It is not like painting or sculpting. You can't go off into a corner and do it. And in that sense architecture is inextricably connected to whatever social, political establishment you happen to be working in. I always fear that last Saturday, for instance, would be a kind of backslapping sort of thing among those wonderful idealistic people who graduated in '70—you know, weren't we wonderful? And it really wasn't that. I think there was a kind of honest expression of the limitations that they found. That's why I think pastiche is a bad word.

Diamonstein How about historical quotation?

Polshek Well, I don't know what that means, exactly. I mean that's writing. But pastiche is a word used in French zoning law to describe something which you are not allowed to do in certain neighborhoods. A historic district may not do pastiche. I think a lot of the stuff that we are doing is pastiche. Venturi or Stern or Charlie Moore are really incredibly skilled architects. But the danger is first that everybody begins to do it without a scholarly background. I mean people that really don't know classical architecture from wigwams. And secondly, there is an ignorance of the fundamental compositional principles and organizational principles that make any building good. Strip the decoration off of Lutyens and you're still going to have a very superior piece of architecture. So there is that danger. Also, it does affect students to a certain degree. There's the Bloomingdale-ism, the *New York Magazine*-ism, that has crept into architecture to a degree. It has gone a little too far.

Diamonstein Is revisionism currently the vogue in academic circles?

Polshek No, I don't think so. We're really trying to teach people very serious things, you know. Then journalists get hold of it, and it's something to write about. It's the same in all fields.

Diamonstein So you're suggesting it's really journalists, rather than architects, who have created this debate?

Polshek Some architects promote it because it's good business. Obviously that happens.

Diamonstein Do they design it?

Polshek Some design it. Some are better than others.

Diamonstein And where has it all gone too far?

Polshek We have moved too far into this art for art's sake business. There is an anecdote I will tell about it, but I can't name any names. So you will have to guess. It will be like a—what do you call it—a roman à clef. There was a competition held in a western city for a building, a tall building. And the budget was, everybody knows, unrealistic for the building, and there were three final entries. One of the entries was way over the budget and two of them were about on the budget. The one that finally won, picked by very famous architects, had a building that was kind of elaborate and polychromed and stucco. Now if you know anything about the earth and seismic questions in this far west city, you don't build a tall building out of stucco. But then it happened that a bunch of reactionary architects in the same city raised hell, and maybe some of them were not so reactionary, but well-meaning. They caused the architect to make changes in the building. What the architect had to do was take all the post-mod off the ism. The polychroming went, and the festoons and the little houses and all the allegories, and all that stuff. What was left was a big, gray box.

Diamonstein So there was a big difference between his beautiful drawings and the final design?

Polshek Time will tell. I haven't seen it yet. Well, the lesson is that architecture which is too painterly, too historicist or too classicizing, that does not seek to solve larger problems of building, of habitation, of urban design, is an architecture that, first of all, hasn't been built, right? I mean you can paint city walls or stucco that's going to collapse in a few years. But if you really believe that the world is going to go on for a bit, which is not an entirely reasonable proposition, but if you do believe that, you are going to want to build buildings that hang in there for a while. So, I think that underneath it all there is an importance in principle, there is an importance in scholarly research. That's also one of the problems of historic preservation, which we could talk about. And that's Charlie Jenck's yo-yo. But the world is more complex than that.

Diamonstein Why has all this happened—in the name of change, progress, creativity, commerce?

Polshek Well, I don't know. I walked into Bloomingdale's today, by accident. It's a nightmare. It is a nightmare of black glass. You can't orient yourself and you can't hang on to the railings. It is environmentally, in every way, an offense to the human body and intellect. I think that the problem perhaps has wider implications than just the marketing of all that chic stuff they sell. I literally ran out through the freight entrance. I would not go back through all of that. And they're doing more of it now, you know—decorators.

Diamonstein Let's go into your own work for a moment first. There are certain recurring aspects to it. For example, biaxial symmetry and a tripartite system of building. Perhaps you can tell us what some of the manifestations of that recurring, in your own words, "unconscious expression" are.

Polshek You are quoting from something that I wrote for a Japanese magazine, called *Space Design*. I did practically a whole issue on my work. They wanted to know my philosophy so at five o'clock one morning, I wrote my philosophy out. I did refer there to recurring formal organizational principles. I do have a tendency to organize things in three parts.

Diamonstein Some illustrations are the university in Old Westbury, the Tiejin Central Research Institute, the Bar Association, Rosemary Hall, the Pool Pavilion, Wesleyan, and others have that tripartite arrangement.

Polshek Well, that, plus a symmetrical organization. For a long time I think, as a child of the Beaux-Arts, I was afraid of asymmetry. But I would frequently organize buildings symmetrically along an X-axis and asymmetrically along a Y-axis. I used to justify it by saying it's organic architecture. It's just like a human being. I mean that's the way we are organized, right? We're basically symmetrical this way and asymmetrical this way. It's a bit of a crutch. I don't think I will ever get away from it. I think it is inherent in how I solve problems. I don't know where it comes from.

Diamonstein What is the major determinant of a building's ultimate form for you?

Polshek Usually the circulation system, vertical and horizontal. That's always the most important thing. For instance, corridors are more important than rooms, frequently. I spend an immense amount of time on the proportions and the lighting and the color of vertical and horizontal circulation. That's how you begin to design a building. Actually, I don't know any other way. Maybe other people do, but I don't.

Diamonstein Do you think that an architect should have an easily describable, neat, definable, recognizable style? How would you describe your style?

Polshek Stern described my style better than anybody's ever done in an issue of *A + U*. It was on forty architects under forty. I was in the original show when I was under forty, and then they did an issue when I was among the forty over forty. As much as we argue, I think Stern is very perceptive. In the issue, I think he said that my work was characterized by a dependence on classical ordering principles, but he also said something to the effect that I always break the very rules that I set up. You know, you go by the recipe and then at the last moment you do something unpredictable. I like to do unpredictable things. I would like to go on the building site and change things right then and there, which would be a very expensive thing to do.

Diamonstein How do your clients feel about that?

Polshek If it's a big enough job it could get all muddled in the change orders. But if it's a small job, sometimes I might end up paying for it myself. Actually we just completed what I think is an absolutely beautiful interior for Consolidated Edison up on 181st Street. It's not even open yet, but it will be in a week or two. They wouldn't pay for some painting at the end, a change I wanted. A couple of people in the office, one of the young architects, Jim Hoffman, went up with his brother-in-law and actually painted the wall. I paid for it. Con Ed wouldn't pay for it. But I wanted it right. Sometimes I have to do things like that.

Diamonstein You have been particularly interested in commissions that relate strongly to an existing context. Your historic preservation work represents one outgrowth of this. In 1968, you did your first historic preservation, the old courthouse and jail that you did together with Mr. Toscanini.

Polshek Right.

Diamonstein You also began the State Bar Association.

Polshek Do you work for the FBI?

Diamonstein No . . . we want to have some orderly system to unfold your work and your views. We were talking about historic preservation, which has been an important part of your practice. Since "recycling" and "adaptive" are words that you don't find particularly appealing, I wish you would give us substitutes.

Polshek The worst now is "retrofitting." That comes from the defense industry.

Diamonstein Well, let's refer to projects such as the Bar Association, the Brotherhood Synagogue, the Villard Houses, and now the Custom House as sympathetic intervention into the historic texture. Tell us what your concerns are and what solutions you have developed for the wide variety of problems that these projects represent. We are all aware of the fact that combining the new and the old is not only a delicate task but sometimes an economically costly one. Why don't we start with the first project of real significance, which was the State Bar Association?

Polshek That was mostly a new building. There were four brownstones on an important park in Albany. In urban design terms, it was a very important corner of the capital complex up there, with Richardson's State Capitol as the centerpiece. Then his Albany Town Hall and a couple of mediocre courthouses formed that corner. At that time, nobody knew about historic preservation. Saving old buildings was something that little old ladies did, you know. My clients wanted a new symbol that would stick out in the park. And the Hudson River Valley Commission raised hell. I knew that there was going to be a big problem. I did look at the street, and I knew that it was the wrong thing. If given a choice to build a building on a barren green hill—I don't like to do that. Rosemary Hall is a good example of that. The master plan that I. M. Pei had counted on was to put the new girls' school up on the top of the hill. I didn't want to do that. I buried it down the hillside and terraced it so the whole thing is kind of gobbled up by the jungle. That may be an ego problem of mine. I would rather not, if I could avoid it, be in the position of having to force myself to be a part of a continuous history of architectural new-form making. I hate doing houses. I've done some houses, but they were either for clients that are so famous you can't publish them or they're underground.

Diamonstein Which house was underground?

Polshek It's a pool house up in Purchase, New York. So with the Bar Association, I saw that coming down the pike, and I said, "Look, let's save the old building, and chop off the back." For one thing, the new building didn't have to be severely compromised, at least so the argument went, by cornice heights and the scale on the street. It could do something that was reasonably free and still scale itself to the back streets and these little Dutch houses. And that's the way it worked out. Then all of a sudden, I was in the preservation business.

Diamonstein It was described as prize-winning and the most civilized kind of architecture that served both the needs of the community and the Bar Association very well. From there, you went on to do a number of other preservation projects.

Polshek And we still do. A third of the work in the office is probably preservation. The Custom House, when it ever happens, is going to make it even more so. Preservation, like post-modernism, is getting a little carried away, in my view. As I said last night to our mutual friend, Kent Barwick, the chairman of the Landmarks Preservation Commission, there could be a backlash of the most reactionary forces in the society. What I mean is a whole bunch of accidental comings-together of people who could create a terrible uprising against the kind of excessive regulation of historic preservation and against the fragile basis of its taste. You know, a bunch of commissioners of some landmarks commission, of whom you are one—it isn't New York City, it's primarily the state—but they get together and they say, "Well, you know, it looks nice from here, put it on the. . . ."

Diamonstein What do you mean, carried away? Jim, I share your concern about designating any kind of property, but that's a rather sweeping charge to make.

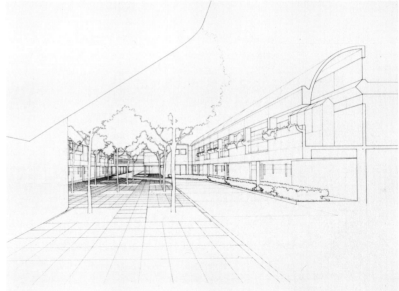

Medical Center, Napa, Calif.,
drawing

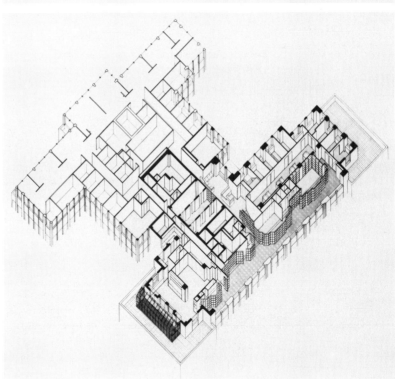

Backer and Spielvogel, Inc.,
New York, N.Y.,
axonometric drawing

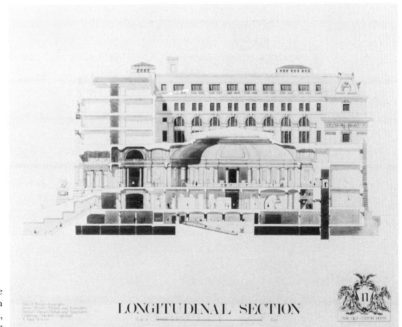

United States Custom House
competition for restoration
with Marcel Breuer Associates,
New York, N.Y., drawing

Laboratory Tower, Central
Research Institute, Teijin
Limited, exterior, Tokyo, Japan
Picture credit: Akio Kawasumi

And I wouldn't like you to be leading that backlash, particularly at this time, when there is more sensitivity and understanding of the need to keep the best of distinguished buildings.

Polshek Don't misunderstand me. If you're not careful it's going to disappear. Institutions, churches, universities, students, architects are going to draw the line. The next thing you know, politicians are going to remove the budget.

Diamonstein Where do you think that line should be drawn?

Polshek I think—and I have experienced it—that the judgmental basis upon which these designations are made is often done really off the top of the head.

Diamonstein Where have you had that kind of experience?

Polshek At Columbia.

Diamonstein With the New York City Landmarks Preservation Commission?

Polshek No. No, not with the New York City organization. With the state, the Department of Preservation. Commissioners walk out of Low Library and they look across at Butler Library and they say, "Oh, what a wonderful vista. We'll save the whole campus."

Diamonstein A little hyperbole.

Polshek Oh, no, no. It's documented in reams of paper. There are reasons to save some things and reasons not to save other things.

Diamonstein Is there any direction, in terms of the education of architects? Are they being taught to build in context, in more sympathetic ways, and to adapt buildings that surely were not considered part of architectural education in the past?

Polshek Well, I don't think the question is necessarily one of the building being sympathetic in terms of appearance. But I think there are very complex questions of scale and proximity, of light and dark, of vistas and visual easements, of texture. They're really not studied enough. It's a very complicated business. There should be modeling of things. I mean literally modeling. How do you see this, and how does it look? I think the budgets of preservation agencies should not be cut, they should be raised.

Diamonstein Do you see preservation as a planning tool ultimately?

Polshek Unfortunately, I think the real risk is if it becomes a political tool. Politicians begin to use preservation issues to further their own aims, for whatever reason.

Diamonstein You run the most important school of historic preservation in the country. So how do you deal with that on an ongoing basis?

Polshek We are struggling with exactly what you can teach people, trying to create a discipline. You know, it's no longer an ethos. It's a discipline. In the end, there are three ways you look at it. There are conservators, who are chemists basically, like Norman Weiss, who knows all about stone pathology, and that kind of stuff. It sounds funny but it's important. Then there are planners, who deal with problems of neighborhood conservation and economic tradeoffs and legislative strictures. And then there are the architects. They have to be excellently trained architects.

Diamonstein You're suggesting that the only arbiters of taste or public determination should be architects?

Polshek No. I do not mean that. What I am saying is that when it comes to physical matters, absolutely, positively. With any kind of landmark preservation commission, the staff is all-critical.

Diamonstein What sort of jobs do you envision for people whom you are training in historic preservation and who are not architects?

Polshek Well, conservators, technical conservators working in various planning agencies, historians, writing legislation, guiding legislation, working for private foundations, raising money to save buildings, publicizing, writing about it. There are a lot of things. In fact they're getting wonderful jobs, and an increasing number of students are getting two degrees, architecture and preservation.

Diamonstein In the past several years you've taken on such diverse projects as the Napa Medical Center, a kind of drive-in medical supermarket. You have done a U.S. Consulate residence in Lyons, France, and the Delafield Estates, which are thirty new one-half-million-dollar houses in Riverdale, New York. Can you describe these projects? The last one is now especially important. You have described the Delafield Estates as controversial. Tell us why.

Polshek It's on a beautiful ten-acre site, with 258 specimen trees. The neighbors are afraid that their country lanes will be widened, and our job is to place these houses in a way which will save as many trees as possible. We are doing that. We also have to site houses in ways which will complement the architecture of Riverdale, and we are studying that. It is a very, very, very difficult project. It has questions of form, questions of style, of botany. It's all there. Politics, and so forth. But it's going ahead in a very nice way.

Diamonstein And the Napa Medical Center?

Polshek That's almost built. I am working with Peter Gluck, who is a younger partner in the office for this project, and for the Delafield Estate also. It's a very interesting, inexpensive building built like an aircraft carrier.

Diamonstein Tripartite?

Polshek No, but biaxial. The circulation in the building is very important. It's like a couple of ships that are parked next to one another with two gangplanks connecting the open decks where people walk. They're under plywood vaults. It's a very interesting building. It would be more interesting if the budget had had another million dollars in it for better workmanship and materials. But conceptually it's very important. And the planners gave it such a hard time. It was unbelievable. They added at least four hundred thousand dollars to the budget by delay. And now they don't like the color of the building, and they would like it changed.

Diamonstein What color is the building?

Polshek It's kind of raspberry, cream and terra cotta. It's a very tough-looking building. And it's a very interesting building, programmatically. Medical buildings are interesting. I could talk about it forever. I like it a lot.

Diamonstein Let's talk about Lyons, France. I know it's a consulate and a residence that you took particular pleasure in designing. As is often unfortunately the case with architects, it will become part of your archives. Tell us the evolution of that project and its current status.

Polshek Well, its current status is dead. The Office of Management and Budget of the Federal Government stopped it because they thought it was going to cost too much money. Too few Americans are working in it. But it was very important to me and to the office, because it formed a kind of continental divide. After all my ranting and raving about free-standing buildings, it's in a very specific situation with a beautiful park on one side. It's as if we could build villas on the edge of Central Park, except the park is even more beautiful than Central Park. There's a big museum facing it, and a big, wonderful boulevard, and a lot of other embassies. It was kind of a watershed, in the sense that it brought together an awful lot of things that had appeared in my work on buildings in the past.

Diamonstein Do you see that as a summary building for you?

Polshek It summarizes some things, but more importantly it started a new direction. More importantly than that, it changed my work with people in the office. Years ago, I used to go away and do my things and come in and say, "Here it is"—you know, like "real architects" are supposed to do. Many still do, I suppose.

Diamonstein I notice on your letterhead that "James Stewart Polshek" now says, "and Partners."

Polshek Yes, there are younger partners.

Diamonstein You referred to the fact that you were involved in a collaborative effort with Peter Gluck. And you are collaborating with Max Bond on the Harlem Mall. How does that all work?

Polshek Well, it works pretty well. It stretches things out a bit. When you're making decisions with somebody in your office they tend to argue a little bit less than somebody who is a joint venturer. But it works quite well, because we see things in a very similar way. I like working with people I like. And I like working with people in the office on design questions.

Diamonstein How close does a busy fellow like you get to the boards? How involved are you in the design process and how much responsibility do you delegate?

Polshek Obviously, there are people who could answer that better. I'm very close to it. I'm always very close to everything in the office. But I delegate more. I have the best office I've ever had in my sixteen, seventeen years of practice. You have to get to know people and you have to get to work together and see how they work. And they have to be able to predict what you're thinking. But I am extremely close to them. One of the reasons is so banal it's silly. The office has moved to one floor. Before, it was on two floors. Going up and down, you just don't tend to get close to people.

Diamonstein With all the work and multiple identities you have, how involved can you get in the design process these days?

Polshek Well, I get very involved. I really like doing interiors. It's an admission that Charlie Gwathmey and I made to one another once. We both like doing interiors. We had to whisper it. Now it's okay to say out loud, I guess.

Diamonstein You've said you have little interest in the single-house commission. Obviously, your early practice didn't require your doing that.

Polshek No, that isn't the reason. I just don't like doing that. It's either one of two ways. Either it's a kind of worship act, where it's, "Oh, my god, you're my artist, do me something." Or it's the reverse. You're a slave, running around like some decorator over at the 939 Building picking out light-switches and fabrics. And I don't really like either of those extremes.

Diamonstein You say that you don't like the personal commission and the single house. At the same time you say you are interested in interior design.

Polshek Well, I think it's architecture. You know what I am interested in? It's the immediate results. You can test things. You can actually try out theories about movement and sight-lines and color and lighting. You can't learn that out of a book. I mean you just have to do it and do it for years.

Diamonstein You find that there is a satisfying laboratory aspect to interior work. . .

Polshek Oh, yes, wonderful. And I thank the Consolidated Edison Company profoundly. They've been a very good client, and we've had four wonderful commissions with them now. Three are interiors, and I think they will all be very interesting. They will give them exactly what they need, and we learned a lot, too.

Diamonstein From what you said earlier about interior design, the place where many people spend most of their lives is this country's most neglected area of design—interior design—particularly offices. Is that what you meant?

Polshek Yes, somewhat the same as preservation. You see, I really believe there are a lot of really appallingly trained people around. In some places, you don't have to have a license. People who are creating places for human beings to live and work in aren't very well trained and don't know how to put things together very well. I'm not talking about decorating now. You may like burgundy or red socks and I may like something else. I'm not talking about that. I'm talking about the forms that create or don't create anxiety, that cause you to move, that cause you to smile, that cause you to cry. I'm talking about the extent to which that behavior is modified by architecture, which is something nobody knows about. So I think interiors are important, and we are doing a few very important interiors now. One, which doubtless you've heard of, are the offices of an advertising agency on Forty-second Street for Backer & Spielvogel, Inc. When that interior is completed, I think, it will also be a kind of watershed. It incorporates a lot of ideas that have come up before, like in the Simon & Schuster offices, but then it's gone considerably beyond to predict, and to try to solve a problem in ways which we haven't done before. It's been a very important learning experience for myself and people in the office who have worked on it. And I think it will be successful for the owners.

Diamonstein What are the problems that you solved as a result of that assignment?

Polshek We haven't solved them yet because it's not completed. On one of the firm's five floors, we took the wonderful facade that faces on Bryant Park and the Public Library. The client wanted to put offices against the facade—you know, those are nice offices; they get sun. We talked them into moving the offices back and creating a public gallery, kind of a deck, very much like the Napa Medical Building. Off of that are all the major public spaces for this firm, its library, its board-room, its exercise-room, its lounges. They're behind a glass screen, a grid of sixteen inch-square glass panes, which are sometimes translucent and sometimes transparent and sometimes mirrors. The activity gets indirect light or view, and everybody takes advantage of this promenade. It's going to be wonderful for their clients and everybody in the entire office can share it. There are certainly going to be a lot of visual effects. The use of mirrors is going to be fairly startling.

Diamonstein When you did the Simon & Schuster office, their charge to you was that they didn't want any ad agency glitter. What did the ad agency want, and what are they getting?

Polshek They didn't want any publishing glitter! They wanted something classic—

actually very much like Simon & Schuster. Those are the kind of clients I get along with. I mean I have a traditional streak in me, when it comes to those things. I don't like glitter, either. They both wanted a rather classical interior, muted and quiet and not flashy—certainly, not Bloomingdale's.

Diamonstein Your various identities cause you to zip back and forth between identities . . . between the academic field, which deals in theory, and businessmen, who deal with another kind of reality, and politicians and builders who focus on yet another reality. How do you think academic architects are treating such issues as economics, energy, and zoning these days?

Polshek What do you mean, academic architects? Am I one?

Diamonstein I would say, yes.

Polshek I'm an academic architect? I mean there are architects and there are academics. I mean you either build or you don't build. That's the difference. Building is very scary. Once you do it, you become somewhat sobered about things. But I think your question is reasonable.

Diamonstein The question was, are they paying as much attention to such issues as economics, energy, zoning, as they once did?

Polshek The answer is, even if you don't want to, you have to.

Diamonstein Why?

Polshek Well, I'll tell you. We're doing a school, a wonderful project I didn't mention to you, which is well along. It's an addition to a middle school in Montclair, New Jersey, called the Glenville Middle School, which preserves the old and adds something new. I think it's going to be very successful. There are school boards and school committees. There are environmentalists. Green Belt people. There are State Department of Education people in Trenton who are into everything, including the sill heights. I mean, there are regulators on top of the regulators. There are budget people. In that sense, there is no way in hell that you can be irresponsible today. There are all these economists and botanists and planners and soil engineers and traffic people, and God knows what else. The trouble is in the midst of all, you can still end up with a very mediocre and awful building which is economically and environmentally responsible.

Diamonstein Well, do we blame the regulators or the architects?

Polshek No, blame the architects.

Diamonstein But how much designing of the building is left to the architect?

Polshek Oh, a lot. It just takes a lot of time, that's all. There are meetings with clients, who used to have to bring two people, you know? Now they'll come with eighteen. I'm not exaggerating. In private organizations, corporations which will go unnamed, they'll bring fifteen people to a meeting. And that takes a lot of time. Everything's regulated to death, and the fact is that it has a very profound effect on the fees that one begins to charge.

Diamonstein How much attention do you feel the public sector is giving nowadays to design; more than before, or less?

Polshek Oh, I think a lot more. Everybody's buying architecture books and design books and things.

Diamonstein How is that manifested?

Polshek Well, people are visually much more sophisticated. Sometimes I wish they weren't. It wasn't so many years ago when we came back from Finland, you know, having thought we'd discovered Marimmeko and carrying baskets and Charlotte Perriand straw chairs. We were just happy to have these rare works of folk art or new designs. Then Ben Thompson came along with Design Research and the whole business became popular, so that everybody has twelve Italian clocks, and all that stuff.

Diamonstein So good design becomes a cliché when too many people own it?

Polshek Well, it doesn't really. For all of the people concerned about the handicapped and the elderly and children, and I don't know what, I am not in any way convinced that we live in a society that is in any way more humane today than it was before all these regulators existed. Have you been to 132nd Street lately?

Diamonstein Are regulators an unnecessary class?

Polshek No, they're not totally unnecessary. It's just that they amaze me. If you talk to anybody in the Department of Health, Education, and Welfare, they will make a direct correlation between the existence of these regulatory agencies and the quality of life. But I'm telling you that it really does not make that great a difference.

Diamonstein But it joins the argument that we talked about earlier, that architecture is more and more for art's sake, while the relationships of architecture to social needs and social purposes is being threatened. It's not only being threatened from within the profession. You're now suggesting that the threat comes from without, as well, because there are so many incursions on the design process.

Polshek Yes, there is no doubt about it. I tell you, today architects have to know how to write and talk, as well as draw. Since whenever the first professional architects existed, I guess, in the fifteenth century, I guess, there's been a kind of combination of con man and visionary. And that part really hasn't changed. But it's increasingly rare that you have a client whom you have direct contact with. We are fortunate to have a few of those left. But everyone wants committees and managers, and so forth, and that's not a happy state of affairs.

Diamonstein I don't know in which category you place your role with the Urban Development Corporation. You've been especially active as the consultant to UDC for the Convention Center site. . . .

Polshek And for Roosevelt Island, too.

Diamonstein How does that work?

Polshek Well, that's an important role. It's somewhat ambiguous, like Columbia. I see my role as first, helping to select and then to protect the architect, and protect the integrity of the design with respect to the construction manager and the public agencies, and all the people who would eat away at the design. And that's worked very well in the case of the projected housing on Roosevelt Island and in the case of the Convention Center. But I'll tell you, it's not something I would like to do every day of the week—the meetings—it's terrible.

Diamonstein Where do the eighteen people come in? What are the constraints that face Mr. Pei and his partners, the architects of the Convention Center?

Polshek Oh, lots. Incredible. A site that is, *de facto,* too small for the program. The program is too big for the budget; the budget is too small for the detailing. And those are a lot of constraints. But they really are the right architects for that commission. And Jim Freed, the design partner on the project, is absolutely the perfect person. He is Mies Van der Rohe-trained, enormously disciplined. And the office has technical capability and artistic sensitivity. That whole Convention Center is going to have four major details in it, repeated endlessly. I'm exaggerating, but especially the joint in that truss, where the glass is held, where it hits that aluminum, is going to be repeated over and over again. It is . . . beautiful.

Diamonstein In the light of all these constraints and limitations, what kind of building should we expect to have?

Polshek It's a great crystal palace. It's a big beautiful barn. Essentially, it's a great big thing that goes from Thirty-fourth to Thirty-ninth Streets, and then it has a bridge. You see, we did a design feasibility study for the building to establish the price, and the study we did is in fact uncannily like the final product in the deposition of the major axis through the building.

Diamonstein Are there ways that we can improve the design process?

Polshek Well, the quality of developer is improving. There are developers who are more enlightened and there are developers who are less enlightened. Like anything else, they are not all bad or good. I think that we're coming together. I really think the New York City Planning Commission, what was the Urban Design Group, the Office of Midtown Planning, and the various planning offices have really excellent people in them, for the first time in any American city that I know well. If there was one legacy of the Lindsay administration that I think was a very good one, it's that. Boston has a good public authority. They both have groups of very responsible young architects and planners. When you do a building for a developer and you come in and you discuss the process with them, they can help you or they can hinder you.

Diamonstein Can you give us some examples of significant developer-built buildings in New York in the last few years?

Polshek Yes, 80 Pine Street, which is also a Freed building. That's the white steel building downtown. That's an excellent building. It looks like it should be in Chicago.

Diamonstein You're saying that the outlook is more promising?

Polshek Yes. There was this recent competition for the development of the East River south of Waterside, where developers and architects teamed up. They all seem like very good teams, and I think no matter who gets the job, they will probably be a hell of a lot better than Stuyvesant Town.

Diamonstein What's the general mood of the architectural community in New York these days? Is it optimistic?

Polshek Very nervous.

Diamonstein Is there a sense that we are moving toward an active period of good innovative work? Why are they so nervous?

Polshek Because there's no oil. You don't know when the lights are going to go off. There's relatively little money. Inflation is insane. There has been consistent talk about recession. So I would say we are all very nervous. I spend an awful lot of time trying to secure commissions that will be recession-proof, so that we can keep the office together in those times. And I hope I am being successful.

Diamonstein I hope so, too. You might learn to love historic preservation again.

Polshek We love it a lot now. I don't want my comments about regulators misconstrued. But as your very own Landmarks Preservation Commission chairman said to me, there is an emerging problem. Probably commissions should sit down, with people from other spheres of life and maybe have some very quiet sessions together, let their hair down and say, where are we at?

Diamonstein I do think that new and fruitful alliances, and certainly exchanges of ideas are very important to both the preservation community and the architecture and development community. What about the art community? Do you think there are a closer set of ties to the architectural community than in the past, or is there more distance?

Polshek Well, I don't know too much about the art community. I know what I like.

Diamonstein What do you like?

Polshek My Japanese client introduced me to a sculptor. Names aren't important. There were two big walls on the end of a longitudinal axis of a major reception building, which was part of my first Japanese building. And the sculptor showed me his things, and I was a little nervous about it. Now that I think back, I was probably rude. I went out to his kiln, and I saw all these pieces from the kiln lying around on the ground—bricks and curved pieces and ribs, and some were black, and terra cotta and ivory. And I thought, that's it. So I said, "Come on, we'll get up on the ladder." And we got up on two very tall ladders and had another guy arranging these things on the ground, and then I'd run down and move pieces. And we both got into it, and we actually made a design. He took it from there and filled it in and then built it. And it's really quite wonderful.

Diamonstein Are there any artists with whom you would like to work now?

Polshek On what?

Diamonstein On any project that you're involved in.

Polshek You know, I love Richard Diebenkorn. But I wouldn't work with him. I wouldn't have the nerve. I would fall down at his feet. I mean how could you talk to a person like that? You're talking about working in a sculptural sense, like with Noguchi, for instance.

Diamonstein Yes.

Polshek Well, if I had an appropriate building I could easily talk to Noguchi. I also love textile art and Japanese folk art. I like any kind of folk art, but I am particularly interested in Japanese folk art. You get clients and you say to them, "You need a tapestry here." And when you tell them that the tapestry is going to cost sixty-five thousand dollars they get very nervous. And so do I, because they could say, "Terrific. We'll buy the tapestry. Now we'll use cheap hardware."

Polshek . . . and the price comes off finish costs. . .

Polshek Well, it will come off of someplace. If you can build it into a public building, that's wonderful.

Diamonstein Well, more and more it will be public buildings. A bill appropriating one-half to one percent of funds for art in architecture will very soon be enacted into law. Now there is only a gentleman's agreement on the part of the GSA. So for better or worse, more collaboration will occur between artists and architects. What's your view of that?

Polshek Well, I was going to ask you a question. You know, the great sculptures that proliferated for a while all over New York City? Do you think that's illuminating to the ordinary person on the street?

Diamonstein I guess I will have to quote Gyorgy Kepes on the collaboration between art and architecture. He has talked about the ephemera dotting the countryside, as knickknacks on a Victorian mantelpiece, rather than sculpture. Obviously there are first-rate artists and first-rate architects who work together from time to time. But because of the amount of money that will be available, if nothing else, and the ideological aspect of art in public places, more concern must be given to it as a collaboration between good architects and artists. It's not just ornamentation—and not *post facto*—but should be done during the design and evolutionary process.

Polshek But then somebody had to build that in early.

Diamonstein Schools of architecture really should be making architects sensitive to that possibility.

Polshek We don't sensitize students. We are lucky to even do a little teaching. To think that you can teach somebody a little bit about architecture in three years—I mean that's really stretching it. I think we do a very good job, and a better job than anybody else, all this ideological nonsense aside. But three years is a very short time, and you simply can't learn all about building codes. People say we should teach computers to architects. Computers!

Diamonstein What do you hope to accomplish?

Polshek Teaching design—teaching people how to synthesize ideas and to communicate on paper to a lot of other people. I mean that's. . .

Diamonstein During the course of our conversation, there has been an almost wistful reference to mediocrity in many professions. What do you think of the current level of architectural education, not only at Columbia but in the country in general?

Polshek It's very worrisome. It's not so terrific. It's getting better in that the pool of people that can teach is increasing. The trouble is that they all want to live in three cities, when in fact, somebody has to go to Auburn and somebody has to go to Kentucky, places that are really out of the way. But at bigger schools I think it's okay. I think there's a lot of things we could do. But there are interesting forces. I find myself somewhat of a conservative in the sense that these accrediting people come to you and they tell you've that you got to teach handrails for the handicapped. You've got to have a course in that. You've got to have a course in—I don't know, quantity surveying, which is a kind of English estimating business. And you've got to have a course in waterproofing and solar energy. By the time you get done, you don't have any time to draw. You simply have to balance these things off. I think that the way we do that is to say that you learn those things later.

Diamonstein And what about the state of American architecture now?

Polshek Oh, boy, I think it's pretty good, actually. The trouble is that the world is not made up only of Stanley Tigerman and Michael Graves and Bob Stern and Venturi and Moore. I mean there are other people, not that they are bad or good, indifferent. We all know they are good, or funny, or whatever. But there really are an awful lot of architects whom people don't know about who are practicing in a lot of the out-of-the-way places.

There are people that just aren't recognized for making important contributions that don't look terrific at the Venice Biennale. Probably these architects have never heard of the Venice Biennale. That's a kind of cult thing, magazine fodder. People know how to manipulate journalists and journalists know how to manipulate architects. I'm sure it's like that in the art world. But the stakes are a little bit higher in architecture.

Diamonstein Why?

Polshek Because somebody publishes some silly building, with a thing here, or whatever. . . .

Diamonstein Is that a pediment that you are drawing in the air?

Polshek I don't know what it is. You know, the AT&T Building is going to be a much better building when it's built than most of us imagine. I think it is probably going to be a very fine building. But I didn't mean that building in particular. You publish something in a magazine, like *Progressive Architecture.* A lot of people read it, and bango, off they go. You go to cities in the Midwest and occasionally you see some weird looking structure that looks like kind of a Richard Meier clone. I've made a lot of jokes tonight because I guess we're supposed to be entertaining. But I think architecture is very serious. It's a very deadly, serious business, and I don't think it's something you play games with. I think that you can't rationalize something for a client by saying it's high art. Your client has every right to say, well, that's ridiculous; you can't have a hole there because you want a hole. You have to have a reason. Now, it can be a formal visual reason. *That* could be a rationalization. But there has to be a rationalization. It can't be that the architect wants to remind people of more meaning. Come on—out in East Tiatuck, Iowa—more meaning? That's not right.

JOHN PORTMAN
JONATHAN BARNETT
RICHARD WEINSTEIN

John C. Portman, Jr.
Born Walhalla, S.C., 1924
U.S. Naval Academy, 1944-45
B.S. Arch. Georgia Institute of Technology, 1950

Richard Weinstein
Born New York, N.Y., 1932
B.A. Brown University, 1953
M.A. Columbia University, 1955
Graduate School of Design, Harvard University, 1958
M. Arch. University of Pennsylvania, 1961

John Barnett
Born Boston, Mass., 1937
B.A. Yale University, 1958
M.A. University of Cambridge, 1960
M. Arch. Yale University, 1963

Diamonstein There are three men whose careers bring together nearly every aspect and reality of urban architecture today—urban planning, urban design, finance, legislation, education, and of course the often exhilarating, often exasperating fine art of architecture. Richard Weinstein, an ex-psychologist and an architect, is now a consultant on urban design. One of the founders of the Urban Design Group during the Lindsay Administration, he went on to serve as director of the Office of Lower Manhattan Development. He was also among the fathers of the Museum of Modern Art condominium plan. He is now vice president of "The City at Forty-second Street," a massive communications, cultural and entertainment complex that has been proposed for Manhattan's West Forties. Jonathan Barnett is equally diverse in his achievements. Formerly director of New York City's Urban Design Group, he is a writer, critic, professor, and consultant to major cities on urban design problems. He is director of the graduate program in urban design at City College of New York, president of the Architectural League, and the author of numerous articles and highly regarded books, including *Urban Design As Public Policy*. Another is entitled, *The Architect As Developer*. It hinges on the work of John Portman, with whom he has written that book. John Portman, one of the nation's best-known architects, is based in Atlanta. He pioneered the notion of the contemporary architect as real-estate developer. His Hyatt Regency Hotel in Atlanta sparked the current trend toward atrium hotels and propelled him into the major league of real-estate developers. His best-known works are Peachtree Center in Atlanta, Embarcadero Center, San Francisco, the Bonaventure Hotel in Los Angeles, and the Renaissance Center in Detroit. His newest hotel is currently planned for Times Square.

    All three of you are concerned with cities, and two of you are more involved with cities than with individual buildings. Perhaps we should begin with urbanism. It is a word we throw around without much of a definition. Can you provide us with one? In fact, Jonathan, I have heard you define urban design as designing a city without designing the buildings. Just what does that mean?

Barnett To answer that question would mean describing my entire life's work. Perhaps, I could begin by outlining the conflict of interest that could exist for an architect designing a building in a city; between what is best for his client and what is best for the city itself. For example, in Pittsburgh, I am a consultant. Developers wish to build on the corner, right next to H. H. Richardson's masterpiece, the Allegheny County Courthouse. We have suggested that the developers shouldn't put their building exactly next to Richardson's building, because of the lack of continuity between the two structures. So here's a conflict, if you like, between what's best for Grant Street and the city and what the owners of the building, at least, think is best for them. One interest involves architecture, the other concerns urban design. So that's a part of the answer to your question.

Diamonstein Is there a difference between urban planning and urban design? Are they separate disciplines?

Weinstein Well, at an intuitive level I think that urban planning does not necessarily begin with aesthetics. aesthetic considerations are secondary to decisions about traffic, and so on. At least it is assumed that aesthetics are separate from economics or moving people out of subways. I think the urban designer would take the reverse position, that aesthetic concerns are continuous with financial, political and engineering concerns. I guess you'd say in contemporary parlance, the urban designer comes from a different place.

Barnett I have a recorded announcement in answer to that question also. Planning is the allocation of resources according to projections of future need. Of course, that's not done by planners, it's done by politicians. But that's what planning is. And urban design is the design of large-scale public spaces or an environment.

Diamonstein There is an urban planning tradition that involves graphs and statistical charts, instead of architecture. I have often wondered how and when those planner's tools combine with design, with art and with physical forms.

Portman Basically I think what we're talking about is people. Traffic is important and so are technical, economical and financial considerations. But the root of what we are talking about is the creation of a new kind of environment that puts people first. We start with people and we end with something that's physical.

Diamonstein You have often used the phrase "planning for people." I have never really been quite sure what you mean by it. How is that different from what other architects do?

Portman Well, I think that we are all creatures of nature. Unlike painting or sculpture, or other forms of art, architecture sits out on the corner and it's exposed to everyone, from all classes, all backgrounds, and all educations. It's not elitist; it's for people. How do we get at that? Basically, we approach it through the innate reactions of people to environmental conditions. The word "innate" is very important, because it eliminates prejudices due to backgrounds, and whatnot. The animal instinct that's within us, that responds to physical environments, is really where we begin. We have to deal with those common denominators. I try to break them down into constants and variables. The constants are those things that people respond to because they are human. The variables are what architects work with, such as sight and orientation and traffic.

The final design, is of course, a happy marriage between these constants and variables. But we mustn't forget that the essential purpose of architecture is to fill a need, functionally and spiritually.

Diamonstein How do you react to that, Richard?

Weinstein It's John's way of saying something anybody who is in the design profession would have to agree with. That view is more or less useful, depending upon the scale you are working on. If you want specific answers to sizes of things, you don't begin where John did. You ask other kinds of questions. If you're ranking values, then I think you do refer to John's concept. He has a personal way of formulating these things. I think all of us confront these issues with language tools. But I would have to agree with what he said.

Diamonstein There are certain recurring themes in the Portman festival: variety, movement, water, nature, people watching people. Perhaps you can expand on these to describe to us your design philosophy.

Portman Design philosophy begins with the individual. And it begins with me. I'm an individual. I'm a creature of nature. I'm a human being. I have experienced things and have recorded the impact of architectural experiences, and I have tried to watch other people when they don't realize that they are being watched, and to record those reactions. Really, my philosophy is to try to understand a human being more. Architects and the history of architecture, going back to the pyramids, the great cathedrals and the Parthenon, are testimonies to political and religious power. But, we haven't yet developed an architecture really concerned with the human being, and not with propaganda.

Some of the great historical monuments were made as propaganda. Julius II wanted to build great monuments because of the illiteracy of the public. It was a way of controlling the masses. When you go back and begin to see the motives behind architecture through history, you soon realize that no one has ever said—why don't we start thinking about people as a mass—all of the people, not just a select group?

Basically, my approach is to try to humanize. In the early sixties I abandoned the so-called international style and started with this approach. I don't believe that architecture can be meaningful if it's flippant. If you are bored with something, and do something else this Monday morning, and next Monday morning you do something else, again, you're being superficial and I don't think your work will stand the test of history. We are dealing with a new society, new problems related to our society and consequently the architect of today has to face those issues. And it goes right back to people again.

Diamonstein Jonathan, you have been covering the career of John Portman for almost fifteen years. What engaged you initially, and what continues to engage you? What's the significance of Mr. Portman's work and business organization for other architects and real-estate developers?

Barnett When I first met John Portman, around 1964, I was an editor of *Architectural Record* magazine. The editor-in-chief had said to me that, because I had been to the Yale School of Architecture and only knew people who went to cocktail parties in New York City, that I ought to make a trip to see what the rest of the country was like. All the editors were given territories, and my territory was the South. I was a reverse traveling salesman; knocking on doors to see whether there were any buildings that we ought to publish. And I knocked on John Portman's door in the Merchandise Mart at a very early stage in his new professional career. The Merchandise Mart was the second building John developed and built. I saw that here was a radically new way of practicing architecture. The traditional way of practicing architecture is to assist in social climbing, because the architect is the person who validates the status of the newly rich person or the newly rich institution by creating their setting. Therefore, the architect becomes a kind of lackey to these social-climbing people or institutions. John, by making himself his own client, short-circuited that whole process.

Diamonstein What does that mean now to architects and developers, in terms of both practice and business organization?

Barnett Well, I think that John Portman is a very radical architect. But he reminds me a little bit of President Carter, because he talks about complicated issues, not in a simplistic way, but a simplified way. By saying that architecture is for people, he is making a very general statement, and avoiding invidious comparisons, because Southerners are much more gentlemanly than people up here in the Northeast. He doesn't say, for example, that Walter Netsch's latest building, as published in *Architectural Record*, is based on a pattern which is entirely geometric; that is, the origin of the building and its whole arrangement is based on an abstract geometric system. So when John says that the person is where he wants to start, he is also saying that an abstract geometric system is where he does not want to start.

In fact, I think that John Portman is practicing a kind of environmental psychology which is very much related to real-estate development. In a department store, let's say, you are subject to environmental psychology the moment you walk in the door. You may have noticed that the refrigerators are not right inside the door. They are on the eighth floor. And you have to walk by gloves and neckties and handbags, and so forth to get to them.

John began his career as a designer of department stores. To start with people and to understand what motivates them and then understand how you can, to put it rather crudely, make money from it, is a very radical new way of looking at architecture.

Diamonstein Jonathan, you have pointed out that there are regional differences in manners. Now we should see if there are regional differences in taste, as well.

One of the reasons that the three of you have come together is because of a project—the proposed Times Square Hotel. It's a testament to the reputation of John Portman that this project has become known, at least in the popular press, as the Portman Hotel, even though I presume that is not its name.

Portman Absolutely not.

Diamonstein Can you tell us something about the design of this building? How did it take its present form, and just what is that form?

Portman When you go in to design a building, you have to take all factors into consideration. We had to consider Times Square as it exists today, not as we envision it ten or fifteen years from now. Consequently, the environment becomes a very important ingredient. It's an unusual location historically, at least for a hotel, in New York City. We had to make sure that we would succeed. It would be much more dangerous to do something less than to do something more. We used the same philosophy in Detroit in the design of Renaissance Center. To have done less would have guaranteed failure. And to a much lesser degree, the whole programming of the New York hotel came from this.

We had to create an environment of such scale and magnitude and of such desirability that during a period of neighborhood transition, it could stand alone. We were very concerned with security because of the fear of crime in the area. How do we get people into the area? The design took all of that into consideration. We had control points. We felt that this would only be a temporary situation, because if this project is implemented, of course it will catalyze many other things. It can change the whole environment of Times Square.

But if you take the dimmest view and say that it won't be a catalyst and Times Square won't change, then you have to design defensively. This becomes a very important ingredient in the design concept. We attempted to do a building that is not skin-deep, which is what Times Square is. Everything there is—it's a shirtfront. We wanted something with real substance to it, that would begin to be a catalyst. And frankly, that's what excited me about coming to New York. It wouldn't be much of a challenge to do a hotel on Fifth Avenue or Park Avenue. We have spent literally years and millions of dollars trying to do this thing. You know, I could have done many other things. But the challenge in Times Square is something that I think we just could not back away from. And so we have persevered and I think we are very, very close. Hopefully, in the next few weeks or months we will have something very positive to say about the implementation.

Diamonstein What will the complex look like? Can you tell us some of the components, and how similar it is to what we have come to expect from Portman hotels?

Portman The only preconceived idea that I have about anything goes back to space. People in space. That's what architecture is all about. All space breaks down into two basic, fundamental areas: public and private space. Cities have been building a lot of private space, increasing density. The city started out with little one- and two-story buildings on the corner, and then they have expanded into four- and five-story buildings, and so on to fifty-story buildings. The public space, the street and sidewalk, stayed the same. All that density keeps piling up on infrastructure that doesn't expand to carry it. Our approach has been to try to open things up and to let buildings breathe, not only internally, but externally.

I worked on the original Regency in Atlanta, many years ago, and this was on the busiest street in the city. We started analyzing the hotel—what is a hotel in the central city? At that time it was a tower. It had a very cramped lobby, with a newsstand over in one corner and a dark bar in another, and a few leather chairs sitting around. You went up in a closed elevator and you got out into a narrow double-loaded corridor, and you went into a room which had a hole in the wall, and a bed and a table and a chair over in the corner. And that was the hotel. What we really wanted to do was to explode all of that, to give the urban scene what the urban scene needed desperately, and that was space. The explosion of a huge space in a volume would create a sense of excitement and serenity at the same time, which is a paradox. Within an urban setting, off the heavily trafficked area, we wanted to create the feeling of a resort, if you will.

Space is really the key. And our cities need space. We need space inside our buildings, we need space outside of our buildings. We need to think in terms of people instead of things. Things have taken over our cities. The streets are mobbed; the sidewalks are cramped. You know, the Seagram Building came along, with a little plaza out there, and a fountain. That was wonderful.

But we haven't gone beyond that. We have to think in terms of external and internal space. And this is what we have tried to do in the New York hotel.

Diamonstein Are the private spaces a departure, too? As I recall, the greatest innovation in Portman hotels is the public spaces—the hotels are rather traditional, and conventional if you will, in the private spaces.

Portman It is a question of economics. There are many more private spaces than there are public spaces. A hotel room is a private space. And a private office, that's private space. When people leave private space, they enter the public arena. And that's where the play begins. Private space is essentially functional. But the public arena goes much beyond that—that's essentially what the hotel is.

Diamonstein Richard, can you describe briefly the evolution of the Times Square area from its heyday as a theater district to its current state? Tell us where it's going, what the options are, what effect this hotel will have on the area in general, and specifically on your project, "The City at Forty-second Street."

Weinstein When seven subway lines were put at Forty-Second Street and Times Square, shortly after the turn of the century, the garment industry moved up from Canal Street. The area's accessibility also made it suitable for the entertainment industry. Out of that grew a symbiosis between the very profitable entrepeneurs in the garment industry and the financing of the Broadway theater, which continues to the present day.

With Prohibition, the Depression and the motion picture, the theaters began to decline. During Prohibition entertainment became private, so that the public aspects of the theater were no longer enjoyed. Then the Depression came, and the movies. Both had a bad effect on the theater. With all those things acting together, the street began to decline, and the legitimate theaters, along Forty-Second Street at least, were converted into movie houses. And then they declined into pornographic uses.

The theaters north of Forty-second Street, because of the inherent financial vitality of the garment district and the cultural vitality of the arts in New York, the theaters north of Forty-second Street survived as an island of civilization in an area that otherwise declined for the very reasons that it originally flourished: primarily accessibility. The transient population through the area is over fifteen million a year. Now, that can support theaters and hotels, or it can support drug traffic and prostitution, particularly child prostitution. The main market for prostitution on Forty-second Street is children between nine and eleven. Today, the same infrastructure which once supported, as Fred Astaire said in *Bandwagon* the carriage-trade on Forty-second Street, has produced a negative social ecology which is reinforced by traffic, accessibility and physical decay. What John perceived, in being willing to adventure with his hotel, was the latent strengths in the area: proximity to the central business district, particularly the communications industry; the entertainment industry; the growing health of the theater; the accessibility of the place. All of these things, if you could just turn them around, could make for an area that was lively, glamorous and extremely suitable for any hotel, especially a Portman hotel. We are trying to do essentially the same thing on a larger scale. We believe that the measures required to turn around Forty-second Street, not Forty-fifth Street, which is where John is—he's surrounded by the healthiest part of the theater district. Forty-second Street is another world, as I discover by talking with the *New York Times,* which lives on Forty-third Street and never ventures onto Forty-second- Street.

They don't have the faintest idea of what happens two hundred feet away from their front door. In order to turn that street around, which is in a far worse situation than the site of the Portman hotel, we feel we have to do something large in scale. So we propose to use Urban Renewal powers, appropriately, probably for the first time, to assemble the land, restore the theaters, build shops and restaurants, and build commercial space to fund the cultural activities of the restored theaters. That would require about six hundred million dollars of investment by the private sector, and about forty million dollars of money not otherwise available to New York from special Federal programs to help acquire the land.

Then all the things that presently support the disease of the street would once again support its health. It would help the garment industry, it would help the theater district, it would help the central business district, and it would provide a relief value for the westward growth, planned I hope, of commercial space, so that the central business district can expand outward, instead of upwards, dumping more and more people on the same size street as John said earlier.

Diamonstein But are you telling us, Richard, that this redevelopment will cater to entertaining executives and the privileged middle class?

Weinstein No.

Diamonstein How do you intend to accommodate all classes and serve a variety of functions?

Weinstein The third, fourth and fifth floors of the two blocks on either side of Forty-second Street, between Seventh and Eighth Avenues, would be a cultural entertainment center available to the general public, not at Broadway prices but at the price of a movie ticket. We hope to get foreign and American corporations to pay for theater, dance, ballet and film—twelve hours of various kinds of entertainment of one kind or another for the price of a movie ticket, four-fifty or five dollars. There will also be ballet and opera. Believe it or not, right on that block, there is a 750-seat chamber opera house, which was built by Oscar Hammerstein for David Belasco in 1906, which has the finest Italian plaster work in the United States. It shows triple-feature pornography today, despite the commentary to the contrary by the owner of the theater in the *New York Times* a couple of days ago. That theater we would hope to operate perhaps for the Big Apple Circus, or for chamber opera or the Bronx Opera, or performances from the Brooklyn Academy of Music, and so on. We would subsidize the tickets out of revenues from the office space that we would build around Times Square. The commercial parts of this project will fund subsidized cultural activities on the block, in exactly the same way that the condominium tower over the Museum of Modern Art is going to pay for a doubling of the museum space underneath. It's the same principle.

Diamonstein You have talked about hundreds of millions of dollars and urban renewal designation, a designation that other entrepreneurial architectural developer types are seeking as well. Will "The City at Forty-second Street" happen? What is your plan's current form? Should it be attacked incrementally? Is it too big?

Weinstein We have concluded, after spending a very great deal of money, with the help of the philanthropic community—we are a not-for-profit organization funded by foundations, and various major corporations—that an incremental approach to the development of this part of Forty-second Street will not work. You know that there is a superb organization called the Forty-second Street Redevelopment Corporation, which has restored a group of theaters between Tenth and Eleventh Avenues. There, the incremental approach, buying one theater, and then another, and fixing it up, works. But the real marketplace for crime, pornography and child prostitution is on the blocks between Seventh and Eighth Avenues, where the real value of the property is abysmally low and where there is nothing in any building above the first floor. Two or three of the buildings actually have no electricity and light. Squatters have just gone into the cold shells of those dead buildings and started doing business there.

With a situation like that, with the highest felony rate, and the center of prostitution and drug sales, you can't change it on a building-by-building basis. You have to develop a critical mass big enough to turn it around, and to do that you need a certain dimension to the project. In order that the project will serve the general public as well as the connoisseur of ballet and opera, you have to have new sources of subsidy if you are not going to raid the sources that Lincoln Center and the Brooklyn Academy use. We are trying to use the commercial space to pay for these cultural projects so that our sister cultural institutions will look upon us as supporters in the struggle for civilization, and not as enemies trying to get at the trough that they barely get enough sustenance from. In this instance we do need to make the big gesture.

There are corporations who are interested and who are trying to work with us on a financially feasible plan. What is difficult is the public's perception, shared by thoughtful people in government. There is negative feeling about large-scale government intervention in the marketplace. There are memories of projects associated with Robert Moses, with large-scale residential relocations, and so on. I hasten to add that nobody lives on these blocks. They are either empty or have commercial uses.

We are encountering a good degree of caution, for fear that the public will perceive this kind of intervention as big government moving in on behalf of private real estate interests. That is not the way we view the project, non-profit. Our point of departure is with the people, with the theaters, and with the uses that we could add to the area that would support its history and its inherent strengths, and there are healthy forces to the north and south. So I don't know how realistic this plan is. It's up to the city government, and then to the public approval process, which will take six months, once we start public hearings, if we get to that point.

Diamonstein Richard talks about symbiosis and John Portman mentioned catalysts. Jonathan, would you say a word about Portman hotels throughout the country and their track record as catalysts? Tell us about them as buildings which have a major effect on what is around them. Which ones do you think have worked best, and how?

Barnett Of course there is an attribution problem. John Portman has done a number of hotels, but nowhere near as many hotels as people think he has done, because there have been so many imitations. So we are talking about the Hyatt Regency and the Peachtree Plaza in Atlanta, the Embarcadero Hotel in San Francisco, the Bonaventure in Los Angeles, and the

Hotel at Renaissance Center in Detroit. And ultimately about Times Square.

It's very hard to look at the Atlanta hotels outside of the context of Peachtree Center. The development of that part of Peachtree Street is really Portman's kingdom. He owns it all. He is lord of it all and it's all his design. To answer your question about catalysts, perhaps the most important, as a catalyst is the Embarcadero Center Hotel in San Francisco, because it is in the financial district, which is not where you would ordinarily expect to see a hotel. One of the requirements of that urban renewal project was that there be a hotel there. And I am not sure how excited John and the other investors were about building a hotel in that location. So that hotel had to be spectacular because otherwise it wouldn't do any business. I was at the AIA convention in 1972, before the hotel opened, but the lobby space was full of people. We discovered that the favorite recreation in downtown San Francisco was to look at the Embarcadero lobby.

Diamonstein There was less than positive reaction on the part of some critics to the Renaissance Center in Detroit, a spectacular complex with four office towers and a seventy-three-story hotel. It was designed to help revitalize Detroit's deteriorating downtown area. There has been a great deal of concern about the Renaissance Center. Some suggest that the sleek, bold design might be a bit too dramatic for that city, and that it is not an integral part of its environment. Some of your hotels are said to be aloof from the cities around them, that they create an alternative urbanism that is not related to the existing city scale. I'm sure that by now that criticism is familiar to you. How do you react?

Portman Well, you know it's one thing to take something out of context. To understand the Renaissance Center, you have to understand the basic situation of Detroit when we started that project. The first time I went, at the request of Mr. Ford, I stayed at the Pontchartrain Hotel. I got out of a taxi, and as I was checking in I was told to not walk on the streets. If I left the hotel, I had to take a taxi to go to a restaurant and when I came out of the restaurant I had to take a taxi back. This was the circumstance in which we found ourselves. We were asked to come up with something that would revitalize Detroit, and to change the attitudes of people outside of Detroit about the city. But even more than that, we were asked to begin to change the attitudes of Detroit people about themselves, which was a very tall order. And we were given a site between the Detroit River, and the Jefferson Boulevard, an eleven-lane freeway, which separated us from the city—a vehicular river, so to speak. So we were cut off from the existing fabric of the city. Whatever we did, we realized we would be an island. It became clear that the most important thing was to create an environment of such size and magnitude that we could overcome the isolation and the fear. So, we had to do two things. Number one, we had to do something so large that it could stand alone. And it had to make people feel safe. So we have been accused of building a fortress in Renaissance Center. In a sense it is a fortress. It has this vehicular moat on one side and the Detroit River on the other side. But we were physically isolated to begin with. We proposed to Mr. Ford that it was absolutely necessary to build four forty-story office buildings, a seventy-plus-story

John C. Portman, Jr.
Renaissance Center, Detroit, Mich.
Picture credit: Harr,
Hedrich-Blessing

John C. Portman, Jr.
Hyatt Regency Hotel Atrium
with Charles Perry Sculpture,
Embarcadero Center,
San Francisco, Calif.
Picture credit: Alexandre Georges

John C. Portman, Jr.
Times Square Hotel, exterior,
New York, N.Y., model

John C. Portman, Jr.
Hyatt Regency Hotel,
Embarcadero
Center, exterior,
San Francisco, Calif.

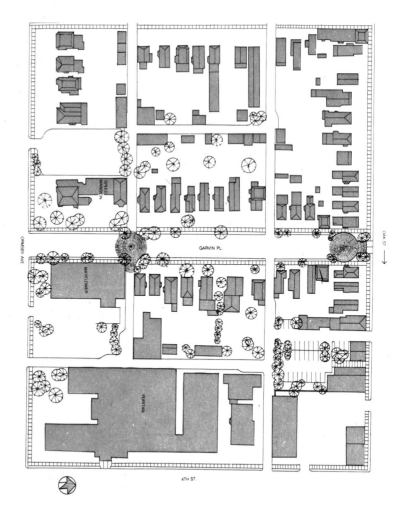

Jonathan Barnett
Louisville Alley Study,
Louisville, Kentucky, drawing
prepared as part of the study
by Jonathan Barnett and the
Louisville Community Design
Center.

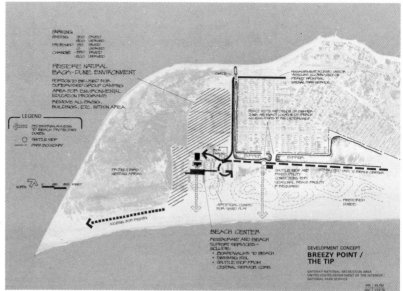

Jonathan Barnett, co-ordinator
(Richard Weinstein,
Environmental Design
Consultant, with the staff of
the National Park Service and
other consultants),
Gateway National Recreation Area,
part of plan, Breezy Point,
New York, N.Y.

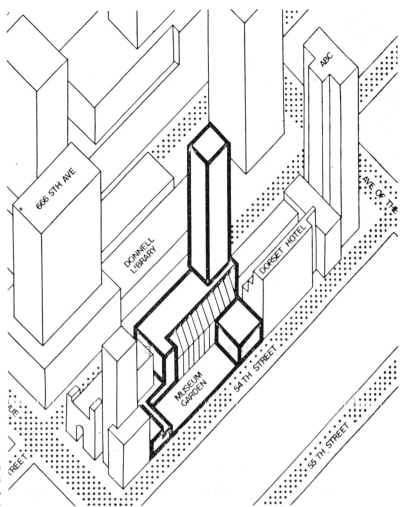

Richard Weinstein
Museum of Modern Art Expansion
Project, urban design concept,
New York, N.Y.

Richard Weinstein
The City at 42nd Street,
New York, N.Y., model
Picture credit: William A. McDonough

hotel, 350,000 feet of retail, and parking for the whole complex, and he had to do it all at once. It was going to cost three hundred and fifty million dollars. This was quite a shock. But after thinking about it he came back and said, "Let's go."

Weinstein I'm ready.

Portman It really happened that way. But I was convinced that to do less would have been an absolute failure. Consequently, we have had critics and architect types who say, it is divorced from the city. It was divorced to start with. It's a fortress and it's turned inward. All that's very, very true. But it all grew out of the local environmental and social conditions. It was right. It has been very, very successful. We are now building Phase II—Rockefeller Center has joined the Ford Motorland Development Company to build Phase II. And we are designing Phase III. There have been articles even here in the *New York Times* and in the Detroit papers that people are now walking the streets of Detroit for the first time since the early sixties. And they attribute this to Renaissance Center. It has created a different atmosphere, a different feeling in the public. The cab drivers, instead of moaning and groaning, now start telling you how great the city is.

I think the critics are criticizing from a very superficial and strictly external point of view, without really understanding the whole evolution and the problems that were being faced. The success of the project has caused five or six other major developments in the city.

Diamonstein The Times Square project—what will its name be?

Portman I don't know. Do you have a suggestion? We're open to suggestions.

Diamonstein I'm sure you will have many from this group.

Portman We would like to name it something that would be special to New York City and not just another name. There have been many names mentioned. The Astor, for one. There was an Astor Hotel there many years ago. But we still are looking for a name.

Diamonstein In describing that project earlier, you said sometimes one has to design defensively. Is that going to be a problem in Times Square? Will the hotel have stark, concrete walls? Will they create a cold presence in the midst of that part of town? Is it really turning one's back on the city to create a separate city within the city?

Portman No, I don't think so at all. In a city with many, many high-rise structures, people are only aware of buildings up to fifteen degrees above the line of sight. Of course, you can look up. But the normal experience really concerns only fifteen degrees above the horizontal.

Our original design of the Times Square Hotel was criticized as too sophisticated for Times Square. It didn't have the character of the city. We have changed the building at the base, for many reasons. One was that we had a submerged theater there and we discovered that we couldn't build it because of all the trains underground and the vibration. There was no way we could isolate it. And so we had to pull the theater out. Consequently, we have redesigned the whole base of the building to give it a more Times Square look.

Diamonstein And what is that look?

Portman Well, I guess you would say that Times Square is light and signs and kinetic activity in the facades. It's a very special kind of thing. We have tried to incorporate that special kinetic quality in the new design of the base.

I think that we are very pleased with it. It's good that the trains were there. I think we have an improvement.

Diamonstein John Portman is lucky enough to have found a way to be his own patron. Jonathan, who represents the public interest in terms of design?

Barnett Well, Richard Weinstein likes to talk about the development process as a three-handed game between the community, the government and the private investor. The community doesn't always feel that it's represented by government. The urban designer could conceivably work for any of these three. So all of these interests are working, we hope together but sometimes in conflict. I like to talk about designing cities without designing buildings. A lot of this comes from what Richard Weinstein and Jack Robertson and I and others, did in the City Planning Department ten or twelve years ago, using the existing zoning controls and the fact that New York City has a very strong real-estate market. One of my favorite tags is that, since the environmental and zoning regulations tend to specify development, if you can get what you ask for, why can't you get what you want? So we learned that if you made some relatively minor adjustments in what was apparently a very boring legal text, you could get some quite spectacular differences on the ground.

Of course every city is different. I work in Pittsburgh where they have a very permissive zoning ordinance, but discretionary review by the city before any building is built. In that context, designing cities without designing buildings means laying down ground rules for developers to follow before they design their buildings as standards for site plan review. However, the design of the transportation system, the design of the park system, highways, streets and public buildings, all of these things contribute to shaping the city. In most instances, decisions about them are made for good reasons, but they are not made from the point of view of city design. The process proceeds perfectly rationally within very narrow confines, but, viewed overall, it's totally without direction. In urban design what we would like to do is design a city. That does not mean making a picture of it the way it might look in twenty years. It means trying to get into the process and shape it as you go along.

Diamonstein It was about ten years ago you wrote and talked about how optimistic you were about the future of cities. And you called for then, and I guess continue to call for, a national planning policy. To what end? Is there still cause for optimism?

Barnett Well, I said I was optimistic by temperament. There are a lot of problems which we have not figured out how to solve. One of them, to put it very simply, is that between twenty and twenty-five percent of the people in this country don't seem to fit into our economic system. Now, this is a pre-inflation estimate. Maybe as fixed-income people lose more and more of their ability to buy things, that percentage goes up. Our system works very well for a large number of people in this country. It doesn't work at all for some. And it's in-between for a growing number of people, who are having a lot of trouble holding their lives together.

As the time that I wrote that book a lot of my friends believed that reforming society completely was the only way to deal with these problems. I think that the Maoists are fewer in number now than they were ten years ago, as Albania remains the only correct country in the entire world, as far as Maoist philosophy is concerned—solving social problems is like starting on a long journey. We are not going to come up with a magic solution, but you might as well start. And that's what I think is being optimistic by temperament. On balance, things are a little bit better for the center city now than they were ten or twelve years ago, and no better for the inner-city residential districts. You are starting to see cracks in the older suburbs that perhaps weren't as visible ten or twelve years ago. So we're about where we were, and the problems are a little different.

Diamonstein Were you nodding in agreement, Richard?

Weinstein In the things that I have said and that both Johns have said, there is a common thread. You have to understand the processes that produce phenomena in cities before you can change them. John begins by talking about people, but he also has, as you can see, a very sharp eye for pre-existing circumstances, like eleven-lane thruways and a position by the Detroit River, which give the context to what you have to do with your building. Just as you talk about a human context, or a physical context, or John talks about a legal context, there is also a real-estate, marketplace context. John takes these forces for granted because he was a developer as well as an architect. Unless you understand those forces, you can't really do anything about cities on a large scale. That is, you can't create the kind of impact of Renaissance Center without understanding how these processes function, both at the individual level and at the collective level of the way cities function. The generation of architects and planners who preceded all of us on this stage disassociated themselves from that body of knowledge and believed that they were making a radical break with the past. It was those people who governed the education of planners and architects in this country for two decades. And to a large degree, the state of the cities as we all found it, resulted from the absenteeism of professionals at the time that decisions were being made, like the mortgage plans promoted by the Federal Government for soldiers coming back after the war—the plans that built the suburbs and the highway system, and all the rest of it, the eleven lanes that John had to deal with. These decisions were made by people with no sense of the context and no professional commitment to becoming involved in it. They regarded that kind of involvement somehow as compromise with the forces that they were revolting against. Now we are in a counterrevolution. We are all Revisionists up here.

Diamonstein Now I am going to serve as your transititonal spacer, taking a leaf from your book. You mentioned perception. Let's extend that thought. It was almost sixty years ago that the Bauhaus first opened. What happened to the collaboration that the Bauhaus envisioned between modern art and modern architecture?

Portman It's alive and well.

Diamonstein Could you tell me where?

Portman Certainly, in most of the projects that we are working on. In Embarcadero Center, for instance—I guess we have two and a half to three million dollars in major commissioned work throughout the complex. We have taken that as a necessary ingredient of the type of environment that we hope to create.

Diamonstein Have the works been specifically commissioned, or are they merely purchased, as is often the case, to fit into a particular place?

Portman In each case, they have been specifically commissioned.

Diamonstein Do you work directly with the artists?

Portman Yes, very much so.

Diamonstein And how comfortable are you with the idea of such a collaboration?

Portman I think I am very comfortable. We have worked with many, many different artists—I find that it's hard for the artists to do something in context.

Diamonstein Do most architects permit them the opportunity?

Portman Oh, yes. I think the architect's role lies in determining scale, material, texture, color, if you will, the kind or direction of form. The architect has thought about the spatial context and he has a feel for form and space and the kind of thing that should happen at a specific point. An artist who is looking at drawings and models, doesn't have that. I have found that artists really do not understand scale. Maybe one of the reasons is that most artists deal in museum-size things whereas in Embarcadero Center, for instance, we have one piece by the Swiss artist, Willy Geitman. It's a group of three pieces. One is eighty-four feet high.

Diamonstein How do you select the artists?

Portman On the basis of the kind of apposition, to the space and to the architecture. The artist who we feel can provide that special quality which we think will be most compatible with the type of setting that is being created. There's much freedom, of course. We don't try to impinge on the artist in any way. All design, whether it's sculpture, or anything else, is really problem-solving. So, we spell out the problems for the artist and the kind of considerations that we want him to take, as he develops his idea. We certainly don't want to inhibit him. But there is a necessary collaboration that must take place.

Diamonstein Some critics have suggested that there is both a psychological and/or a professional barrier between artists and architects that prevents a profound sympathy between those two arts, let alone collaboration. What do you think?

Weinstein I am nostalgic about the historical examples of the fusion between visual arts and architecture—I think of the cathedrals or the mosaics in Byzantine domes. I feel that we don't have anything even remotely approaching that kind of rapport between architecture and sculptural or two-dimensional embellishment. I think that's a consequence of the kind of culture and civilization we live in, and the kind of pressures on us. I think sculpture is an expression of the individual and architecture is an expression of the collective institution of society. Today, there are a variety of ways that the individual can relate to society, rather than a systematic hierarchical way, like the feudal way, where everybody knew exactly where he was on the ladder. That's why you have a ladder of form in a cathedral, in a sense, from the biggest shape to the smallest embellishment. When that breaks down, when we have a pluralistic society and everyone has a different idea of how we ought to be related to the social order, you necessarily get a break between the conceptual arts and the contextual arts, the first being sculpture and painting, the second being architecture. And I think there will always be an uneasy relationship between these two, because I think that's the nature of the times we live in. John has tried heroically to bridge the gap, by cultivating artists who will build eighty-four-foot high pieces. But if you really examine the piece itself and wonder just how good it is as a piece, and whether it's really better as a paperweight than at eighty-four feet high, then the whole thing becomes much more depressing, because I don't feel the quality of what's being done is that commendable. Whether it's eighty-four feet or two feet isn't the issue. It's the relationship underneath that I find lacking. Alas, in my view, that's just a consequence of the times we live in. I don't think much can be done about it.

Diamonstein There are two different views. Jonathan, is the collaboration between artists and architects in this country healthy? Can there be and should there be closer collaboration?

Barnett At least in retrospect, the Renaissance and the Medieval periods look as if there was much closer rapport between artists and architects. If we could go back to those times and actually find out what went on in the decision-making process of designing a tympanum over a doorway, we might find something entirely different. We are used to looking at our own time as an age of individualism, where the collective vision that we think animated, say the Renaissance, doesn't exist any more. And there have been various attempts to bring back that collective vision, certainly what is called sometimes the American Renaissance.

I think of what Richard Norman Shaw said at the end of his life about efforts of that kind, that what he had been dealing with were cut flowers, beautiful but dead. They simulate collaboration but don't represent actual collaboration.

In reaction to that, we have the Bauhaus, which sought true collaboration by reducing everything to a very abstract and minimal area, so as to find a common denominator. If you go down the escalators in the Pan American Building, you will see an integration of art and architecture. That red, white and black series of panels is by Joseph Albers. Walter Gropius was the consulting architect for the building. He and Albers were both from the Bauhaus.

I think that the vision of modernist painting and modern architecture which you see in the Pan Am Building is one that we are now reformulating. We don't know where we are going. I think it's quite interesting and exciting, however. We are not exactly bringing back Colonial Williamsburg. I used to think that was the only avant-garde position that was left. We've learned from Las Vegas, we have appreciated Victorian architecture. Ethan Allan furniture, sort of fake Colonial, would seem to be the next frontier. But I think that we may be getting past that. Architects and artists are both experimenting in a very interesting way. Architects now want to have a richer, fuller building. And artists, many of them, seem to me to want to be architects. They want to design environments instead of objects.

Diamonstein Some artists think architects want to be artists.

Barnett Okay. While there may always be a lot of elbowing back and forth it's potentially a very useful conflict, and something interesting is going to come out of it. I can't say anything startling has come out of it yet. But I think it's promising.

Diamonstein Is architecture an art or a business?

Barnett It is an art. It is a profession. It is a business. It's all these things. That's what makes it both exciting and very difficult. Most people don't want architecture to be an art. So the architect has to sneak the art part by the client, by explaining that it's in fact very economical and very efficient.

Diamonstein In a recent *New York Times* interview, Harry Helmsley said, "I think it is important that you have an architect who realizes you are a commercial developer, as I am. In the final analysis, if the building doesn't make a profit, the architect hasn't served you. I have seen many a monument that is a monument to the architect but a disaster for the developer." How do you all react to that statement?

Barnett I agree with it.

Portman I agree with it.

Barnett There are other categories of building, of course. There is the Ford Foundation. The Ford Foundation gives away money, it doesn't worry about profits.

Diamonstein One last question. Earlier, Richard referred to the Museum of Modern Art Tower. Some observers have asked whether a museum should get involved in a commerical real-estate venture, in the very first place. Is involvement in a money-making real-estate deal consistent—without being esoteric or removed from the realities of contemporary life—with a museum's role, the museum's mission as a disinterested and scholarly observer of culture?

Weinstein I don't know why commercial profits laundered through a foundation and given to a museum are any different from profits directly realized from the museum's control of the development from which the money was coming. I think it's ridiculous in a civilization whose value-oriented goals were achieved through a marketplace arrangement, for the institutions that are anointed to protect those values to divide themselves from the mainsteam of American life, which is the marketplace. If they don't have the nerve and the conviction to be able to make money themselves, then they don't deserve to tell me and my children what values to cherish. The values I cherish the most arise in a country which has survived and made its own civilization on the marketplace, on diversity of choice, on pluralism, on invention, on venture and adventure, too. It all depends how you look at it. If you look at it the way Thomas Jefferson looked at it, he saw the exchange of money and property as the chief purpose and responsibility of the free individual in a democratic society.[1]

Diamonstein What did you have in mind with a Trust for Cultural Resources? Obviously not only one institution, what can it mean for others?

Weinstein When I was in government I observed, as John noted earlier, that sometimes, with the slightest adjustment of a regulatory procedure, enormous amounts of money could be directed in value-oriented directions. We

[1] Gary Wills on Thomas Jefferson, *Inventing America* p. 237: "For him, property was the transferable commerce of those who pledged moral 'fidelity' to each other and have an equal stake in the public good. To commit one's fortunes and sacred honor to the common effort of society is a duty arising from the belief in property as a form of 'Language' meant to promote human intercourse and solidarity."

twiddled with the city's zoning ordinance and built seventeen million dollars' worth of theaters for nothing. By allowing developers to build three or four floors more, we got two 1800-seat theaters and two experimental theaters, the American Place Theater and the Circle in the Square, just by a relatively casual manipulation of the regulatory dials. With the arts desperate for funding, it occured to me that by intervening in marketplace processes like that one, at more and more sophisticated levels, like the Trust for Cultural Resources, we would have sources for money for value-oriented purposes that made the National Endowment, and all the rest put together, look like a pittance. The Museum of Modern Art's benefit over the next thirty years, from that one building project, will be seventy-five million dollars; for a quarter of an acre of air, they were paid seventeen million dollars in cold cash. That will erase their deficit, which was diminishing their endowment by the rate of over a million dollars a year. It's an endowment of thirteen million. They would have been out of business in four or five years. It allows them to build a new museum space and totally renovate their old building, which will double their square footage and give them another auditorium. They don't have to go to the bureaucracy and plead each year on their knees, like poverty-stricken waifs, to get their money. The Mayor of New York cut three million dollars out of the city's arts budget. The Museum of Modern Art's got its own endowment of seventy-five million. It doesn't have to worry about the vagaries of politics or circumstance. It can carry out its mission more effectively because of its decision to build this project. It is competitive in the marketplace, in other words.

Diamonstein Are you nodding in agreement?

Barnett I'm certainly nodding in acknowledgment. That's a very cogent description and a very cogent reply.

Diamonstein Do you want to go any further than acknowledgment?

Barnett Well, I think in a perfect world the government would subsidize the museums. They wouldn't have to go and in effect take in boarders in their air-rights in order to be able to make ends meet. But this isn't a perfect world.

ROBERT A. M. STERN

Robert A.M. Stern
Born New York, N.Y., 1939
B.A. Columbia University, 1960
M. Arch. Yale University, 1965

Diamonstein Robert A. M. Stern is a writer, professor of architecture at Columbia University, and, since 1977, principal in the firm of Robert A. M. Stern Architects. He is perhaps best known for his exquisite town and country houses, and for his scholarly defense of the post-modernist movement. He published his first book, *Forty under Forty: Young Talent in Architecture,* a year after graduating from the Yale Architecture School. He has been a prolific contributor to professional journals and has organized design exhibitions. President of the Architectural League of New York from 1973 through 1977, he is an architect for whom the communication of ideas is a true responsibility, an attitude that is paralleled in his architectural design.

Let's begin with an issue on the mind of so many people, the so-called post-modern movement.

The word "post-modern" first gained widespread circulation in the art world around 1976. Since then, the phrase has been applied indiscriminately to nearly any trend that runs counter to modernism. When was the term first initiated? From what I gather, in architecture it goes back about thirty-five years.

Stern It's very odd, but so far as I can tell, it was first used by an architect, Joseph Hudnut, in an essay in the late forties. Hudnut was talking about how the newly formulated "modernist" architecture had to adjust to post-Second World War conditions. As you probably know, Hudnut, who had been the dean of the Graduate School of Design at Harvard in the late 1930s, brought Gropius there, and so he was very instrumental in introducing high modernism to this country. But ten years later, around 1948, he was beginning to criticize the doctrinaire quality of that movement.

Diamonstein I believe the essay was called "The Post-Modern House." To what was he referring then and to whose work?

Stern No one's work in particular—but more to the machine aesthetic, to the kind of impersonal qualities of the high modernism of that period. Hudnut felt they were inappropriate for the major problems of the post-World War II era as he saw it, which were the reconstruction of towns and the building of housing. There was a tremendous shortage of housing as a result of the War and the Depression before it.

Diamonstein Will you clarify the current usage of the term, and relate it to its orthodox definition?

Stern As you have quite rightly said, it's misused as often as it's used correctly, so, who is to say? But I think it means the thing that happens post—after—modernism. It's not the rejection of modernism, but an attempt to make something after modernism that revivifies architecture and reintroduces a lot of themes that modernists, in their revolutionary fervor, cast aside. It means the reintroduction of historical themes and the rerecognition that architecture is a communicative art, rather than merely an existential situation.

Diamonstein You have defined post-modernism in three aspects. Why don't you describe what you mean when you talk about contextualism, historical allusion and applied ornament?

Stern Well, those are three possibilities, but I don't mean to suggest that they

(This interview was audiotaped, unlike all the others, which were videotaped before an audience.)

are the whole ball of wax. Contextualism suggests that a building's physical and cultural context should be taken into consideration in its design. That is the opposite of the modernist aesthetic, which is object-oriented and takes as its principal expression the internal function of the building and its constructional processes. A contextual architect considers what the building should mean in relationship to the street it's on, in conjunction with what people expect a library, or a house, or whatever, to look like and to be like. The second aspect, allusionism, is a kind of next step. If something is to function in a culturally loaded, symbolic way, it has to make references beyond itself. You know, when you meet a young person on the street, you say, "You look like your father." That's a way of defining that person in relationship to his or her origin. Buildings always have some of that character—yet the ideology of modernism disparages that quality. The third point, ornamentalism, is a strategy for achieving the references implicit in the idea of allusionism. Ornament is not just decor to relieve boredom, as some proponents of modernist architecture claim. It is a kind of system of reference which can have a basis in the literal structure of a building, or with abstract patterns, or with images from nature. It is the way that architects have always taken building beyond its literal function as a container for action to its higher role as architecture.

Diamonstein Is the post-modernist debate real, is it semantic, or is it stylistic?

Stern It includes the latter two, and for that reason it's real.

Diamonstein Some people I have spoken to in the course of these classes feel that it's a conversation they won't even join.

Stern I don't see how anyone can avoid joining the conversation, when it's so very lively. I think that the architecture of the fifties and sixties, so-called late modernism, was very limited and dull—focused as it was on a few very specific references that were usually utilitarian and technological, as opposed to cultural. Younger architects, starting with Venturi, and going forward for twenty years now, have challenged late modernism in many different ways. To say that the challenge isn't there, to say that the issues being raised are not real, is preposterous in my opinion. People who are heavily invested in late modernism see post-modernism as a threat because their view of architecture is so single-minded. If they bring in other meanings, look in other directions, they almost have to repudiate what they have stood for. I hope that we won't have such a narrow architecture again for a very long time, if ever.

Diamonstein Would it be accurate to refer to you as a hard-core post-modernist?

Stern I started to say that I hate the term "post-modernism," because everyone hates labels. I'm not a hard-core anything. I'm just trying to make my architecture, and encourage other people to make their architecture, in a little less single-minded a way than those who immediately preceded my generation. If that makes me a hard-core post-modernist, so be it.

Diamonstein Among the things that you are known for is felicitous phrases. Since you are not pleased by the current usage, perhaps you might invent or devise a new one. How would you refer to this new development in architecture, this new direction?

Stern By the hallmarks I mentioned earlier. I advocate an architecture that is rich, by which I mean formally rich and rich in cultural references, that is not minimal, but that takes on as much as possible. To achieve such an architecture, the architect has to read the cultural context very carefully. Unfortunately, in my opinion, too many influential architects are not well enough versed in the events of their time or in history to do this well. This deficiency in the profession, like so many others goes, back to modernism and its educational methods. Gropius and Le Corbusier and Mies were raised in an academic tradition, rooted in deeply traditional cultural situations. When they themselves proposed models for architectural education, they tended to reject the very thing that they knew best—the killing-of-the-father syndrome. As a result, in my opinion, the generation now riding the crest of prosperity and influence in architecture, the late modernists, are really not so well-equipped to deal with historical and cultural issues. They are antitradition because, in a way, they have no tradition and fear it as an unknown quantity. By tradition, I guess, what I am talking about is the continuity of tradition.

Diamonstein How would you describe this, rather than leave us with post-modernism? I am searching for a new word. . .

Stern If I use another word I'll be even more attacked by my colleagues, hoisted by my own petard is the phrase, I think. Why don't we just call it architecture? Architecture has always been about all of these things—it has always been about tradition. Until the antihistoricism of modernism, architects have always looked to the past for models of behavior, in terms of composition, cultural meanings, symbolic meaning, whatever, and then tried to adapt those models to current situations and move forward.

Diamonstein Do you accept the theory that the modern period started in the fifteenth century?

Stern I absolutely do. Modern historians of the political and cultural as opposed to the art historical variety believe that the modern world began with the Renaissance. You know, that's what historians of architecture thought until the late 1920s. Then, under the impact of the modern movement certain historians like Giedion and Pevsner, caused a kind of flack shall we say, in a certain way, to the modern movement. There's a book by David Watkin called *Morality in Architecture,* which does quite a job of analyzing that phenomenon. Things got confused, and people wanted to make up a story to fit the architecture. I don't think that's what historians should do.

Diamonstein Charles Moore asked why he should have to be post- anything? Why not neo- or pre-? You called Charles Moore and Robert Venturi transitional figures in this whole debate. Are they still pace-setters?

Stern Transitional. They certainly are. But both of them, in terms of their education and their actual age, being more than ten years older than I am, are to some extent my teachers.

Diamonstein Mr. Venturi was your teacher at Yale.

Stern Yes, and Charles Moore was very much my teacher once removed. He came to Yale after I left, but we had many, many conversations before then, because I commissioned an article from him for *Perspecta,* the Yale architectural journal, an issue of which I edited. The article turned out to be one of Moore's best, certainly one of the lynchpins of this whole operation. It's called, "You Have to Pay for the Public Life." Among its many wonderful propositions is the idea that if you want to have a public experience in California, i.e., an urban sort of street experience, you have to go to Disneyland and pay two-fifty, so that you can walk down a street with real people on it.

But how did we get into this?

Diamonstein We were talking about whether Venturi and Moore were still pace-setters.

Stern Well, I think they have drawn back—they are a little nervous about some of the issues being raised by younger architects. One is the issue of authenticity, or accuracy. Now, some people—not myself but, say, Allen Greenberg—feel that the classical language of architecture is the one true viable language for the West. It has rules and a body of experience. One can latch onto that, lock into it, and can do one's buildings very, very straight. Now, in my view, this is a moment—as all moments should be—in which everybody should be able to do what he wants. So of course I think Greenberg should go ahead, yet I wonder whether one can do it quite so straight. I think that in fact architecture since the Renaissance has not done anything straight. I think that the great classical architects, whether Soane or Lutyens or Borromini or McKim, Mead and White combined and distorted things. Not in a willy-nilly way—they didn't get up in the morning and say, let's have a little of this and little of that—but in relationship to the complexities of the modern cultural conditions, these architects undertook a very complex reading of their culture. Because they had very difficult problems to solve, they inevitably synthesized aspects of the classical language with certain vernacular strains to produce work that was at once traditional and innovative. They made far richer buildings than we have been able to imagine in our own time.

Diamonstein Who are the younger figures, and what theories are they refining as they try to make their positions known to both the profession and to a wider public?

Stern Well, Allen Greenberg goes to one extreme, a sort of literal representation of traditional forms. He is doing a house now in Connecticut, which is closely based on Mount Vernon, so far as I can see, only about four times larger than the original.

Diamonstein Did all this start with his Valley Forge Bicentennial flagpole?

Stern I think that was the first public announcement of it. Greenberg, like myself, is a product of modernist education. His time at Yale partly overlapped my own. He also worked for the New Haven Redevelopment Agency, where he got firsthand exposure to the problems that modernism brought to cities. Since then, he's moved to a point for which I don't think his education prepared him. But I think he feels that he is trying to redress a lack in his education through his work. Stanley Tigerman, he's our most playful colleague in this group. Stanley started out being more Mies than Mies, more modernist, more reductionist than anyone, and now has seen the limitations of those ways or so he says. Certainly he's introduced all kinds of references in his work, from high-art painting of the twenties to cubism to the most vulgar symbols of everyday life not to mention human biology. Stanley has a tremendous sense of humor, which only now is expressed in his architecture.

Diamonstein With all due regard for Mr. Tigerman, can you envision using his Hot Dog House, for example, as a reference? Do you envision architecture as sight-gag?

Stern I don't think architecture is a one-liner. But on the other hand, I don't think Stanley's buildings actually are one-liners. I have not been to the Hot Dog House. I have been to the Library for the Blind, which is extremely moving. I had a very moving encounter with a blind person who was using it for the first time, and it was quite wonderful. Stanley sometimes falls—we all fall—into the traps of our own theories and natures. And sometimes he does make buildings that are a bit one-dimensional, in a way, and one-liners. But on the whole, I think . . .

Diamonstein He's obviously a very serious architect. Is there something about the profession or the public's acceptance, however limited that public is, of the profession, that forces some architects to do some publicly outrageous acts, if you will, in order to call attention to their more serious and considered works?

Stern I think it's in the nature of our society. Man bites dog is still big news. Almost all of Stanley's work has been in Chicago, which is full of the ethos of Mies and the serious, heavy-handed Germanism that went with one side of Mies' nature—Stanley had to take the most outrageous counter-position to get even a moment's hearing by the press or public. Of course, one pays a price for it.

Diamonstein So Mr. Greenberg and Mr. Tigerman are among the younger people refining their theories. And there is, of course Michael Graves.

Stern Well, there's Mr. Moore and Mr. Venturi, among the older people. Mr. Graves is a little bit older than I am, and he is a very interesting case because, as you know, he participated in a group that has come to be called the New York Five, which exemplified high modernism revived. I think Michael Graves was really very much interested in that revival. Yet I don't think Graves has done an about-face now, as some people say. I prefer to think that he has developed. He is able to combine the spatial and compositional lessons of cubist architecture of the twenties, with a much, much richer vocabulary, which seems at the moment to come from the late eighteenth and early nineteenth centuries. But I am sure that Graves will explore other themes, and I am happy to see this direction in his work. I think it enriches the argument.

Diamonstein We are talking about a handful of very gifted men, whether or not one agrees with their theories. But is this handful of men, yourself included, having a real impact on the profession?

Stern I don't know. I suspect we are. We are all verbally and artistically articulate. The work we have done, whether it's good or bad in the long-lasting, historical sense, is certainly challenging at the moment. People may want to bury their heads in the sand, but burying the head in the sand is a reaction. We travel a lot. We give lots of lectures. I find people more sympathetic all the time. Students are influenced by us. One of the ironies of the American profession is that you may talk of Skidmore, Owings & Merrill, I. M. Pei, or whatever, but the rank and file, the people who are really evolving designs in those offices beyond the initial conceptual level, are very young. They're already my students. And Graves' students are all over. So there is certainly an influence. It would be nice to have more large-scale work sooner to get more shakedown time for these ideas. We have to wait so long for commissions in architecture the time between the idea and its realization is really quite agonizing.

Diamonstein In today's world, with inflationary pressures being what they are, is it possible to find a client who is interested in responsible, cost-effective service, and interested in design as well? How does a small firm manage to produce large and artistic projects in a businesslike manner without having had the experience? It seems to me that that's the catch-22 of architecture.

Stern It is a problem. The bigger problem is how a smaller imaginative firm makes the transition to the larger-scale work without losing its quality in design? One way is to unite with larger firms that have the technical expertise, but not necessarily the design ideas. That has worked many, many times.

Diamonstein Have you been involved in such a collaboration?

Stern I have been invited to compete or to be considered for things, but it hasn't worked out so far. The person I know who is nearest to achieving that is Michael Graves, with his buildings in Portland and in Fargo.

Diamonstein I think the Portland City Council finally approved the Portland project, just this week. To get back to the younger architects—the third generation, I guess: the two prevailing philosophies have been described as exclusive and inclusive. Would you describe the two approaches?

Stern Exclusive architecture is best typified by the mirror-glass, high-rise, office building, which sits like an independent object in its landscape, and gets its form in relationship to its own program to an *a priori* idea about shape that the architect had. In a way, mirror glass is the perfect material for an exclusive architecture. It doesn't allow you to see into it much of the day. It even repels your visual penetration by mirroring you, so that it excludes you, or perhaps its own character. It has no formal connection with the buildings next door. Lever House is a good early example of exclusive design. Its shape derives from an idea about city streets that was totally contradictory to the Park Avenue of that time. Even though Park Avenue has been redeveloped the building is still idiosyncratic. Inclusive architecture tries not only to fit into the context of the street, to join the conversation between the site and the street, but also to converse with formal ideas across time. We have got to make a public architecture, so that a person coming up to it doesn't say, "Hey, what is this? What's supposed to happen here? Why does it look like a factory when it turns out to be my son's high school?" I think if we can make buildings both richer and more referential, people will have fewer of those problems and architects won't be so alienated from the public.

Diamonstein You have referred to public architecture as self-conscious selectivity, along with the rejection of any single dominating style. In the competition for housing at Brighton Beach, the jury split over the decision to award Venturi and Rauch third prize. The minority group said, "In our view, it offers real benefits"—referring to Venturi and Rauch's design—"for the people who might occupy it, rather than polemic satisfaction to those who consider it." It seems to me that from time to time architecture becomes a private conversation among architects, rather than the public it might serve. Has architecture always been an elitist discourse?

Stern I think architecture, insofar as it is an art, is no more or no less elitist than any other art. Of course, the ideas we are discussing are largely ideas that architects share with each other and other artists and don't generally discuss with their clients. But architecture has become more elitist in this exclusivist phase than ever before. You're quite right. The production aspects of architecture have been allowed to overwhelm any other consideration, so buildings for all different kinds of programs, from the single-family house to the church and the school, all end up looking pretty much alike and pretty much like the available production means. A man working all day in a Vega plant, on the assembly-line, does not want to come home to a house that looks like another form of the Vega that's parked in his yard. That explains the tremendous split between popular taste in architecture—the neo-raised ranch colonial—and what an architect imagines the house will be—let us say Philip Johnson's glass house, although he never imagined it as a model for public consumption. The last architect who understood these things and really could speak positively to the public was Frank Lloyd Wright. The public may have thought that the Guggenheim was funny-looking, but they certainly took to it as a meaningful comment on modernist art and a breathtaking experience in its own right. I think the Guggenheim survives largely because it's a fabulous building. It's become a landmark, independent of the art in the building.

Diamonstein You are very concerned with the heterogeneous nature of modern society, and you once said that "architecture is no longer an architect's image of the world as we wish it to be or as it will be, but as it is."

Stern Take a very simple analogy. In modernism, an architect believed that one style, which was related to production, would take over the entire world. When questioned about the meaning of that style—for example, the difficulty that people in India, as opposed to New York, would have in adjusting to it—the standard reply was people will come to understand it. Well, that's hogwash. We are not in the business of educating and transforming human nature. We are in the business of responding to the human condition. We're not reformers or revolutionaries. I don't think that is cynical at all. I think it's much more cynical to say, screw it; they'll understand eventually what it is.

Diamonstein Is there such a thing as an architectural spirit of the time—or is that simplistic or false?

Stern Oh, the *zeitgeist*. I always used to think that every morning Walter Gropius must have gotten up and had a special hot-line to the *zeitgeist* to see where it was at that day. Let the *zeitgeist* take care of itself. Every morning get up, brush your teeth and go and do your work.

Diamonstein Well, what is the spirit of this time, as you see it?

Stern I don't know. I suppose the nearest thing to a description of it is that everything is in a state of wonderful frustrating flux. All the icons that I was raised on in the art world are being questioned. The Museum of Modern Art is showing things that they would never have shown in the 1950s, when I was an habitué.

Diamonstein Maybe it's the Museum of Post-Modern Art . . .

Stern It's a very confused institution, as it very well needs to be. Well, no, it should use the term "modern" in my sense, going back to the Renaissance. Then they can show the Beaux-Arts . . .

Diamonstein Modern versus contemporary?

Stern That's right. They can show the Beaux-Arts. They can show Daumier. They've always had this problem. As they push back the sources of mid-century modernism, they've got to come to grips with the fact that the modernism they proselytized is a thing of the past and that contemporary art is in many ways an extension of the reality. Representational painting they vilified in the thirties and forties. I think everybody should be allowed to make his own artistic statement—whether it's well done or not is another thing. There are aesthetic standards but no set modes of presentation, or conception. You can't say one mode is bad and another is good.

Diamonstein But when that range is so eclectic within anyone's work, be it visual arts or architecture, doesn't it take on a schizophrenic quality?

Stern Look at Picasso. Do you think he's schizophrenic? He would explore a certain theory or a certain attitude, and then go on to something quite different. And he would often do different things at the same time. He would often turn back to Velasquez and other artists from the past and redo their pictures to make them his own and to refresh his talent. To my knowledge no one has ever called Picasso a schizophrenic. But, I do think you might say that someone like Mondrian was an obsessive—what's the opposite of schizophrenic? Monophrenic? I think we have come to not only value lack of change and lack of contradiction in people's work, but we have often entrapped our artists so that they are forced to crank out the same thing. Look what happened to Larry Poons when he tried to stop doing those dot paintings. The art world did a job on him. Now, Stella, probably being a better artist, a bit more furtive, has been able to make a break.

Diamonstein But not without a backlash as well.

Stern There are people who think he has gone crazy. He hasn't gone crazy—he is producing the most vital, vibrant work I have seen in a long time. But is he schizophrenic? No.

Diamonstein Let's talk about your own work for a moment, which has evolved considerably over the past few years, as you take on more and more assignments and have the opportunity to express your own philosophies. You have designed many very beautiful houses. Should a house be described in terms of the required lifestyle of its occupants or in terms of certain abstract notions of the architect?

Stern Both. A house, more particularly, perhaps, than some generalized condition like an office building, has to really work for the initial occupant. It should respond to that person's style, mindset, all of those things. On the other hand, the house should be a work of architecture, in the sense that it should have general characteristics. Other people should be able to live there without a great deal of adaptation, and the building should have meaning to everyone who sees it or studies it in a photograph, or whatever. Houses are wonderful testing grounds for ideas. The space, the plan, the image, can be really measured against the person you know is going to use the building, as well as against general conditions. Too many buildings in our society are built for no one in particular, or they are commissioned by some governmental agency, which you have to deal with across a desk. The process often produces a terribly alienated kind of architecture.

Diamonstein Whose ideas should come first, the architect's ideas about space or the client's ideas about ways of living? What's the best kind of client, the kind who tells you nothing at all, or the kind who is the starting point for your designs?

Stern In my experience, the best clients are those who have ideas but who know the range of their capabilities. They express their ideas articulately, and criticize the work as it goes on, but don't try to hold the pencil themselves. This is very difficult to do. The person who really only wants a commodity, a building by a fancy architect, can be a very good client. But it's better if that person has some idea about why he wants that particular thing, and how he would like to see it changed. I think the hardest thing many architects face, maybe all architects, is the client who wants that architect's last building. If you're at least slightly restless and explorative, as I fancy I am, you'd like to do your next building—you don't want it to be the same. It's the same with writers—I am sure everybody wanted Margaret Mitchell to write *Gone with the Wind* a second time, so she never wrote anything. I don't want to get into that trap.

Diamonstein Many of your buildings are composites of fragments. You've mixed various elements in what emerges as an unexpected combination of the past, the present and the future. What is your notion of fragments? Is there an underlying structure? Do you have a general theory, or is each project completely new and individual, presenting its own problems and solutions?

Stern The fragment is a problem for many people at the moment, because the word fragment leads you to the word "fragmented." It's too close for comfort. Initially, I drew upon fragments from the past, as in the Lang House, rather than taking a very ordinary building—cheap, accommodative, straightforward—and making it like something else. More and more I want to explore not just fragments, not just little attached emblems, but to try to see if the language that those fragments come from, the actual moment in time, can be brought forward, and made alive once again—and in so doing make the buildings more vital. It's a very strange in-between world. On one hand, I cannot imagine being as literal as Allen Greenberg. On the other hand—to make a comparison with other work—sometimes when I look at Michael Graves' work, I find too many fragments and not enough synthesis. So the things I now have under construction or on the drawing-boards, attempt a synthesis somewhere in-between.

Diamonstein In the sense of historical quotation?

Stern They use more history but in a less quoting way—more full sentences and paragraphs. Where this will lead me I don't know. Each project has been a little different. I am doing a house on the Vineyard, where the new zoning tries—and quite rightly I think—to legislate against that eccentric kind of modernism, the ski-house syndrome of the sixties. Because of the way the code is written, we were given a mandate to produce a low-gabled, hipped-roof kind of architecture. Once I had that mandate, I discovered that the architecture of, say 1910, had a lot of things going for it. One could just continue it. We've made a new design that is clearly of the moment in many, many respects. You would have no problem identifying it. But then you could put a little gauze over your eyes and say, "Hey, wait a minute, maybe it was built in 1910 and the guy had a lot of foresight." I think that that continuity, where the use of the past is neither so literal nor quote-y nor quirky, but suffuses the entire project, is really quite a rich lode to be mined. I am convinced that architects until the

Poolhouse, exterior, southeast
elevation, Greenwich, Conn.
Picture credit: Edmund Stoecklein

Poolhouse, living room, interior,
Greenwich, Conn.
Picture credit: Edmund Stoecklein

Lang Residence, exterior,
Washington, Conn.
Picture credit: Edmund Stoecklein

Lang Residence, interior,
Washington, Conn.
Picture credit: Edmund Stoecklein

extremes of late modernism have always explored that approach in a certain way, and that's where my work is trying to go to now.

Diamonstein You referred to the Lang House in Washington, Connecticut, with its grand country manner based on a Palladian villa. There you used color and applied decoration. Somebody once referred to that—and please understand the spirit in which I use this . . .

Stern I'm ready for the knife. Go ahead.

Diamonstein No, it's not a knife at all. It's an attempt to explain your intention. It may have been none other than the great list-maker, Charles Jencks, who referred to it as modernism in drag.

Stern Peter Eisenman coined that phrase, but I don't think he used it for the Lang House. I thought he used it to describe the work of Hardy Holzman Pfeiffer. The Lang House was very interesting—in terms of my development and beyond. The Langs were highly articulate, very well-educated clients. He is an eminent musicologist, and his wife is very interested in Catholic theology. They had very definite feelings—they wanted what they called a modern house, which means a contemporary house. Big windows, wall ovens, low maintenance materials, all the stuff that makes household life much better today than it was a hundred years ago. On the other hand, Mrs. Lang had a little folder of clippings of things that she liked and would show me saying that "This is really what I would like," and expecting me to say "But you can't have it." And in a certain way she couldn't have what she wanted—farm houses in Europe, fine craftsmanship and so forth. Even if one wanted to make a pastiche of these models, the Langs couldn't afford it. But it seemed to me in our conversations that just to make the house on the site, with the walls and the windows and the plan all working out, really wasn't enough. It didn't satisfy their needs and clearly didn't describe what architecture should be about. Hence, the decorative overlay. Painting the house yellow, made it look like South German Baroque architecture, which was very much on their minds. The ornamental system, which syntactically relates neither to Palladio nor to South German Baroque, comes from a building at Eton School outside London interpreted with the carpenter handbook strategies of the early nineteenth century.

Diamonstein And the curved wall?

Stern The real model for the house is Governor Gore's house in Waltham by Bulfinch. It has a similar condition. The curved wall—I've used it in other houses—allows you to look up and down, as well as across a brilliant view, in this case a long valley. I've used it in houses on the seashore. Another problem I had with modernism is that the glass box, with wall to wall windows, trivializes all views. A framed view is often much more convincing and meaningful than an unframed one. So the curved wall helped frame the view. Once we got into conversation about South German Baroque architecture, then it reminded me of the Chapel at De Wies, perhaps some others. The ornament could contribute to a kind of rhetorical reference to the classical tradition. When I began to look seriously at South German Baroque architecture, I discovered that was present in those models as well—little vernacular buildings that had been decorated to look like classical buildings.

Diamonstein Let's talk about the Greenwich Pool House. There you saw the possibility of architecture as sculpture.

Stern Yes. It was very sculptural. Again, it was the owner who said, "I want something absolutely fanciful, and I want a piece of sculpture." I was asked to make something very sculptural and appropriate to a playhouse. But I also felt that I should adjust that sculptural feeling to the rather reticent main house that was slightly without energy. Hence, certain colors and materials in the pool house are repeated from the main house. But then the new composition is given a great shot of adrenaline, I hope. But of course in all this discussion of fragments and formal references from history, one tends to forget that architecture is still about space-making, the play of light, all those wonderful things that we heard about *ad nauseum* in the fifties, so that one reacts against them now. But they are still very much a part of my definition of architecture. I am not interested in making decorated boxes with no character and no great rooms. Some of my colleagues, I think, are more interested in that than I am. But I am interested in the space-positive architecture, with wonderful framed picturesque views. I am not embarrassed to be picturesque at the right moment, to make your jaw drop so you say "wow." On the other hand, I want those other things to occur that connect you up, as well. In enriching buildings historically, I don't want to impoverish them spatially.

Diamonstein To the works of which architects do you most respond?

Stern Which day of the week?

Diamonstein Today.

Stern Today. Well, I have a continuing love affair with Lutyens at the moment, because his work seems so compositionally orderly and intelligible, and yet so rich. Soane I set as a kind of model. I do so much looking at his buildings and his details. I get sustenance from that spatial richness, which particularly characterizes his own house-museum. Everything in the world is there, each object taken for its own value. Things are put next to each other so that you say, "my God, that doesn't go with that." But of course on another level it does work; just one beautiful object next to another.

Diamonstein So it's the eclecticism of his view that draws you.

Stern The eclecticism of his view, the confidence with which he manipulated a tiny little place, the way he brought in light, the way he modeled tiny rooms after the grandest rooms of antiquity, and the way he emblazoned his architectural beliefs on the facade. He simply said, "The facade is something that many people see even if they never come in my door." This is what I believe in—put it right out front. That is the opposite of mirror-glass architecture, which says, "I believe in nothing—your own reflection, or the reflection of somebody's better building from the 1920s, is the only meaning of that sort of building."

Diamonstein Is Lutyens' influence more pronounced in your interiors?

Stern Oh, no. Right now we're working on a house which is in a troubled state, but I hope it will go forward—which depends very much on what we have learned from Lutyens' late essays in classicism, in the Georgian style. No, the influence is very much on both sides. I think you ask that question because I've done more interiors than exteriors. Those commissions seem to come more easily to me, sitting in the middle of Manhattan Island. I have also had a love affair with Borromini since my recent trip to Rome. Borromini's classicism is so wonderfully personal that it's transformed, yet it's absolutely accessible. I never realized how marvelous Borromini was until I was privileged to be taken around Rome by Portoghesi and by Norberg-Schultz and Thomas Gordon Smith, a young architect with a very good eye. So I am very much in a Borromini phase.

Diamonstein You have also written a great deal . . .

Stern Sometimes, I think *too* much.

Diamonstein And continue to do so. Are you writing a book now on post-modernism?

Stern No. I said I would, but I think I'm not going to; it's ill-timed. I'd rather do the buildings than write about them. I am concentrating on historical things, aside from occasional articles on theory that I am asked to do. Much that is meaningful in architectural history to me I can best express by sharing my feelings about it by writing. I think that may be of use to other people, because it's a little off the main stream interest for architectural historians. It's very interesting that architects in my generation and the previous one have often pointed the way to scholarly research and not the other way around. I find that very comforting.

I have done an issue of *Architectural Design* devoted to the Anglo-American suburb that should come out very shortly. If I can scratch up some funding from a foundation, I'd like to develop that into a full-fledged book. I am also exploring the resort architecture at East Hampton—its evolution and how it changed under the impact of modernism—in order to both document that fascinating history and to clarify how one can work today.

Diamonstein Somehow you also managed to find the time to engage in a rather dazzling troika, that is: to jointly edit the writings of Philip Johnson with Peter Eisenman. How did that come about?

Stern That was an act of friendship, of Peter's and my true affection for Philip. We believe that Philip is the only architect in his generation who really has a marvelous body of written work. Eisenman and I console ourselves with that fact sometimes when we begin to feel overwhelmed by this project. It was our way of making—public those good feelings.

Diamonstein Paul Goldberger has called Philip Johnson's design for the new AT&T Building the first major monument of post-modernism. How would you describe it?

Stern I think it does represent the tendencies that we have been discussing in a very explicit way, and I think it's a very important building. Whether it's a success or not remains to be judged when it is finished. More than any other building that I can think of in recent times, it depends on its context, its position in the landscape, for its success. How it will look from the Queensborough Bridge, how the top will look from other vantage points in the city, how the tower will define Madison Avenue—those things cannot be foretold from a model or any renderer's perspective. Johnson was on the fence. He says he is not a post-modernist, and I think that's true—he is a modernist architect. But he is very eclectic, with a very keen eye, and he has latched on to many ideas that others who are younger have developed. To learn from one's younger colleagues is rather remarkable, I think—I admire that. To keep an open mind is very, very rare in our society.

Diamonstein Your own mind has been engaged by the Anglo-American suburb for quite some time now. As I recall, you have indicated that the precedent for the American suburb is really the nineteenth century English model. You go on to point out that for the past thirty years architects and planners have emphasized the commercial revitalization of the inner city. Several years ago, you suggested an alternative approach to revitalizing those areas that you refer to as "the middle city." That's the land between the inner city and the suburbs. Instead of continuing high-rise, high-density development, by moving the inner city outwards, you suggested using the suburban development model and moving the suburbs inward. You suggested that one-, two-, or three-family houses on individual lots would be as technologically and economically viable as high-rises. Do you still hold to that approach?

Stern I am more convinced of it than ever. First of all, on historical grounds, the suburb is a fascinating architectural and planning model, which has been largely ignored by modernist architects and theorists, who use the tower and the park as the most desirable model for redevelopment. Even though the modernist architects of the twenties and thirties worshipped the car, they never seemed to want to use it like Americans to give them complete mobility. Le Corbusier envisioned great highways carrying people from one major city to another. But he didn't quite come to terms with the fact that the car provides personal transportation that allows each person to live anywhere. In that sense, the car has been a completely liberating and confusing device. Frank Lloyd Wright did understand. Wright more than anyone else is the father of the current kind of spread suburb. But there is another suburban model which is not as spread out, not auto-dependent, one which can work in the middle-city. It's the model that in New York we see in Forest Hills Gardens, or even Sunnyside. We had ignored those places in our theoretical analysis of the growth of cities so that architects don't pay attention to them. But I think it is a very viable model sociologically. We know the tower in the park doesn't work for families, particularly families with not much discretionary cash. The tower traps people in their apartments far away from their children, who are playing outside. I don't want to rehash that argument. We have to make a social decision in this country as to whether we want to build cities on the suburban model, because the suburb has always been reserved for the white middle class. Are we going to allow Federal subsidies to build inner city suburbs at a very low cost, as one you can do in the South Bronx, where the land is worth nothing, the utilities are already in place? It's more a matter of whether Congress and the people of the United States will permit the suburb, which preserves the middle class, to be used more democratically for those at the lower end of the economic spectrum. In this sense, mine is a fairly revolutionary proposal. I am encouraged by two things. The middle class, to some extent, is abandoning the suburbs, if we can believe certain reports, and it's regentrifying the city. It's not really abandoning its home base, but it's diversifying it. Perhaps along with that development will also come the possibility of opening up the suburbs and the suburban ideal to the lower spectrum, for whom it really works the best.

For the person without much means, having a house and a lot and being able to grow a little something, letting the children play there, tinkering with the house and expanding it according to need, identifying very firmly with a piece of property and a place on the street—that might really go a long way toward reintegrating that income group into the urban development process. So far, everything we've built for the extremely poor in our cities has been unsuccessful. We have used the model of the tower—the model of high-density, highly technological, affluent living. It has not really worked.

Diamonstein You did a project for the 1980 Venice Biennale, entitled, "The Subway Suburb . . . ".

Stern That project was originally proposed for the Biennale in 1976. It's the father, or the earlier version of the middle city project. In the Subway Suburb, I took a site in Brownsville, the East New York section of Brooklyn, a site that had been largely abandoned and burned out and with only a few trees, a network of streets and utilities, and an elevated portion of the IRT subway. On one side of that elevated subway line is a lot of fifties high-rise housing, and the high-density, low-rise housing project that the Institute for Architecture and Urban Studies did, is of something I am critical of. I think its intentions are good, but by not going the full distance of saying "These people don't want to live in row houses—they really want to live in the suburb," it ends up a halfway house, like a kind of barracks. I imagined redeveloping this site according to a suburban model, which I labeled "Subway Suburb." In other words, you don't have to build at the edge of the developed city, way out in Hauppague, or some remote place in New Jersey, but you can build that kind of housing for the lower middle-class, and even less advantaged, very much closer to the city on all this empty land that sits there.

Diamonstein You also have an idea for low-density suburban housing for the elderly, St. Joseph's Village.

Stern That was a competition I entered to try to explore this further. I didn't win. I am rather miffed. But it was to try to make a place for retired people. My project wasn't based on the model of the ski resort, which is what passes for high-style, low-rise housing these days. What won the competition is something that looked like housing in Stratton, Vermont. My plan was based on the fact that many of the people who were expected to live in this development, out on Long Island, were not coming from inner-city apartment houses but from suburban houses, and were simply moving to another stage in their lives. I grouped the apartments into units of four, which were designed to look like individual houses. Then I grouped the houses in an orderly site plan, based on the planning principles established for the University of Virginia by Jefferson. This allowed the cars to penetrate into the site relatively close to the various dwelling units, but then created open, car-free green areas down the center. I reinterpreted traditional elements of domestic architecture with ordinary materials including asphalt shingles, a common material. I used decorative elements to make the fourplexes look more like traditional houses.

Diamonstein You were awarded first place in another national competition for one thousand housing units on Roosevelt Island. Can you tell us about the project, its design and your expectations for it?

Stern Well, my expectations for it are very dim. I don't think it will be realized. It was one of the designs I feel best about of the things I have done. A thousand units of housing on 9.1 acres is incredibly dense. What I think I succeeded in doing was breaking the model—here, subconsciously—of the development of Roosevelt Island, which I do not accept. As it now stands, the high buildings on Roosevelt Island step down towards the water; as though the Island were a Mediterranean landscape, with bougainvillea on everybody's terrace, while, in fact, the terraces are inaccessible. It is very neutral in its forms and rather boring on the main street. I tried to make a very much more lively main street, by contrasting the scales and the heights of the buildings, and putting the towers at the river's edge, where more people would be willing to sacrifice the convenience of walkup, or low-density living, for the views of Manhattan. I developed an eccentric profile for those towers, so that most people would face down the river to the main view. I tried to make Roosevelt Island not a dense version of Forest Hills, but a slightly less dense version of Manhattan. I don't think people move to Roosevelt Island to be closer to Queens. I think they want the life of Manhattan with its forms and vitality, only at a slightly lower pace and a lot lower rent. I guess the jury agreed that it was plausible and outside the model, yet appropriate to the site.

Diamonstein Then why are your expectations so limited? Is your plan another victim of the brutal state of the economy?

Stern The previous economy. The competition was announced in '75. Midway, it was called to a halt, then started up again, but already with a statement from the sponsors, the UDC, that they couldn't guarantee building the winner because they were in financial trouble. I completed my scheme because I thought it was worth completing, and I had already invested a lot of energy in it. Then the UDC went bust. Now they have been reborn and have tried to start up development on the site again, with different architects. Gwathmey Siegel's been given the job. But even their scheme—which I have not seen—is apparently not going to be built.

Diamonstein That seems to me a hazard of architecture since time immemorial. What happens to a prize-winning scheme? Do aspects of it get absorbed in later projects that are a more summary project of your work? Do you see another, or future, use for this scheme of yours?

Stern Well, to begin with, the exercise of doing it is good. You know, it's like a practice session before a football game. I am trying to be positive about it, since I was madder than hell and I wish it had been built, and think it would have been a great contribution. Sure, you learn from it, and you hope other people do, too. One hopes it sets a more favorable climate for one's ideas. Certainly at the time the scheme was designed, José Luis Sert's conception of what mass housing was about seemed to define the extent of possibilities for housing in this country.

Diamonstein And it went to Roosevelt Island.

Stern And now Roosevelt Island looks like a suburb of Cambridge, Massachusetts.

Diamonstein Where it came from . . .

Stern Maybe my scheme and other schemes, and what was said about them helped make people reexamine the housing models. But, the question remains—should we build a thousand units of housing at a time in any one place?

Diamonstein And your view?

Stern Probably not. Too much at one time causes too much social disruption in a place. You can't make a community. A party of ten is wonderful. A party of a thousand is not a party; it's just a throng of people.

Diamonstein But isn't part of the problem with Roosevelt Island the fact that it lacks critical mass, that there aren't enough units there now?

Stern Yeah, that's a problem with starting new things. Instead of trying to build the whole site at once, maybe they should build smaller increments to build up the critical mass. We always seem to have to go at it gangbuster style. Certainly, it's easier in a new, totally isolated place like Roosevelt, where you get a kind of pioneering spirit among the community. But these large projects inserted into existing city neighborhoods really have not worked.

Diamonstein Let's talk about another project of yours, your plan for the Venice Biennale of 1980. What were your intentions there?

Stern They're not quite mine. I do not plead guilty . . .

Diamonstein Partial guilt?

Stern I did cook up the title, "The Presence of the Past," and I was asked to contribute ideas along the theme of post-modernism. As you know, I feel that talking about that is like talking about the *zeitgeist*. But I do think a theme that unites architects at the moment is the notion of the presence of the past in their work and thinking. The idea that twenty architects would be invited to contribute facades, that for a mock street will line a nave-like space in a basilica building in the Arsenale, was not my idea but the director, Paolo Portughesi's. I am doing one of the facades. There are seven other Americans, and the rest are Europeans. It should be, if it comes off at all well, quite a remarkable opportunity to see what architecture is about in our time, equivalent, in a way, to those housing fairs in the twenties, like the Weisenhof Exhibition in Stuttgart, which Mies organized, where ten or fifteen architects each did a building. Here each architect is being asked to do a cardboard and plywood facade, representing his own ideas about the presence of the past, and his own use of traditional elements in architecture. These facades are imagined as a kind of advertisement for the architects' own ideas, in the same way as the facade of Sir John Soane's house-museum was an advertisement for his concerns. So it might be quite an exciting place. It might also be a catastrophe.

Diamonstein You have said that our great hope really lies with younger persons and students. Since you spend so much time teaching, tell us what specific evidence you have to support that view.

Stern I find that students are much more open to exploration. Just by exploring the traditional methods of composition and forms of architecture, just by doing limbering-up exercises, I think they enhance their capacity to design buildings. Student work is much richer and more diverse than it used to be. When I went to architecture school, students seemed only to deal with buildings in the plan, because the plan was, of course, the aspect of the building that was related to function. Then they would do a framing and that was it. Now students are much more concerned with how buildings look. I have this odd view of architecture, as I really believe that it is a visual art. Some of my colleagues think it's literature, and some of them think it's engineering. But I think that if it's at all worth doing, it's visual. Students now are much more concerned with how their things look and why and how to manipulate their appearance. It's very encouraging.

Diamonstein What are the major preoccupations of the future architects you're training?

Stern Certainly the social motivations of the sixties are no longer with us to anything like the degree they once were when architects completely, or almost completely, repudiated the plastic aspects of the art in favor of a position that viewed art and design as a kind of a social engineering.

On the other hand, I would not take the negative view that we have lost all social concern in the schools. I think the kinds of problems the students are asked to address, and the way they go about tackling them, are very responsible. They do seem to have—and I would applaud it— much more concern for the development of craft. This is to the good—if you develop craft, skill and insight, you can better take on social issues. I think more than in the late sixties architects realize that architecture does not cause social change, but can thwart social change if used wrongly or can help social change really take root, if used sensitively. That's a big shift back to a more normative state in architecture. There's been a lot of writing about schools. In particular, there was a panel this spring at Columbia that undertook to discuss the period after the bust of 1968. Among the panelists, there was a certain nostalgia for revolution, for the old values. I think that nostalgia is fair. There certainly was great passion then. For me, in the period of the late sixties, fluctuation occurred between my own education and the beginning of my teaching career. But I think that a whole generation of students emerged from the universities of the late sixties unable to deal with architecture with a full deck of skills— they're a hampered generation. On the other hand, I think they have not been able to deal with social issues because architecture is not the place to begin to deal with social issues. Become a lawyer or go to Congress. Work for your congressman.

Diamonstein But you can't separate architecture from the most pressing social and especially urban problems.

Stern No. But the architect's job is not to analyze the social problem, but to analyze the ways that buildings can meet the social problem. The architect must also have enough intelligence to say that sometimes a building can't answer the problem. You have to know a lot about buildings to know that buildings can't solve certain problems. There was a period in this country where, if there was any urban ill, we tore down a neighborhood and we put new buildings up, as though they would solve the problems.

Diamonstein You're suggesting that the best architect not only needs to know how to build a building but needs to understand the time in which he lives. If that is the case, what is the best way to educate an architect?

Stern I believe that architects should commence their professional education after they have completed what in our system is a basic four-year B.A.

liberal-arts education, in which they are introduced on the highest possible university level to the history and theory of art and architecture, to literature, to history, to economics, and to all the things that define education. Then they are able to function on a truly professional level equal to that of doctors and lawyers. Too many of our architects were introduced to the practical aspects of architecture right out of high school. Our high school system—I don't want to go into that—is a shambles. As a result, these architects immediately become tradespeople. They are not able to make design decisions with broad sensitivity.

Diamonstein Is that any more or less true now than in the past?

Stern I think in the 1890s and 1900s—a great moment in American architecture—most architects got well-educated and then went either to American architecture schools or the Beaux-Arts. The twenties and thirties I don't know enough about. I suspect it was rather too much like the present. Harvard, where Gropius molded a great generation of architects such as Philip Johnson, Ed Barnes, Ulrich Franzen, and so forth, was a graduate school. So all of those people can speak very knowledgeably about many, many subjects outside of architecture, and more importantly, can relate architecture to those subjects.

Diamonstein What is the state of American architecture now?

Stern Healthy and getting better every day. It's very alive. There's a lot of discussion. There is more work, at least in the last couple of years, than there was five years ago, when it was really hangdog, and the discussion had the desperate quality of filling up free time. But it's amazing that the discussion has managed to sustain itself, despite the fact that there is much more work in the offices. I am always optimistic—there's no other choice. But American architecture is by far the most interesting architecture in the world. I mean this—despite my permanent romance with Italian rationalism—there is much to learn from Aldo Rossi and other Europeans. But in the sense of a large number of highly committed, talented, energetic people in one place, and one cultural milieu, we in the United States are pretty much "where it's at" at this moment. It's not like the art scene which shifted to New York because the money shifted to New York, although that may be part of the reason why we have a lively architectural scene. But I also think it's because we have a lot of good talent around.

Diamonstein New York now seems to be indisputably the art capitol of the country and the world. Would you say that is true for it being the architectural capitol, as well?

Stern It still is in terms of the sheer number of architects practicing here. It was much more so before the recession of the mid-seventies. Now, there is more interesting work being produced around the country by regional architects. I think there is healthy inquiry in California, which I used to associate with avocados and other things. Of course, the return to the coast of someone like Charles Moore helps. Chicago has become much more interesting again. The American South is not interesting. Houston, Texas is booming but not interesting. The most interesting buildings I know of in Houston, Texas, of any size are designed by Philip Johnson and other New York architects. But Los Angeles, Chicago, New York define what I consider the major centers at the moment.

Diamonstein You're saying that Los Angeles is really a center now because an East Coast architect is there.

Stern Well, no, Charles Moore is really a West Coast architect. He returned to California about five years ago and seems to be saying "this is where I am going to be." Moore began his career in San Francisco, then went to New Haven, and has now returned to Los Angeles. I think that's significant, because Los Angeles is much more open and vital than San Francisco— though there is interesting work in San Francisco, as well.

Diamonstein You have said that you view architecture as an art form. Do you see the ties as being any closer between the architecture and art communities than in the past?

Stern Well, direct ties, in the sense of conversations back and forth, are very few and very far between in my experience. The relationship between certain tendencies in painting and sculpture, say the move toward representational art, very definitely parallels the relationships we have been discussing in architecture. On the other hand, a youngish sculptor like Richard Serra seems to me very much involved with late modernism in architecture, and very much out of date in terms of his rather obsessive concern with the existential aspects of a work of art, and, really knowing what the thing is when you see it on the site. To me, Serra's work is just shape-making. They're marvelous, powerful shapes, but that seems to me part of that late modernist strain. So there are and there are not connections back and forth. I think the relationship between painting and architecture was oversold in the twenties, and later in the late forties when Hitchcock wrote a book called *Painting Toward Architecture,* which, I think, led architects to make buildings too much like paintings. A painting is concerned with the representation of three dimensions on a two-dimensional surface. Architecture is totally different; it deals with three dimensions on its own terms—being able to walk in and through.

Diamonstein How do you see the state of collaboration between artists and architects?

Stern In terms of the real world, it's almost nonexistent. The things we see plopped around the city, the lobby art, all scales inside and out, I have very little tolerance for. Robert Graham and I are working on a collaborative project with the Architectural League. I think there is the potential once again for a viable association between artists and architects, because representational art is shared by both, and that creates the possibility that we will make something that someone else will understand. Architecture now is more inclusive and therefore can involve other modes of perception—painting, sculpture, and so forth. There's a sense that architecture doesn't do it all alone. Maybe the League show will trigger more collaboration. But certainly the level of relationship between, say, the baseball bat by Oldenburg and the building behind it, must intensify—that's not collaboration; that's ridiculous. I think that that generation of artists doesn't understand public scale in buildings. They just take small maquettes and blow them up.

Diamonstein You are saying that the artist doesn't understand the public scale. Does the architect see the need to collaborate with the artist?

Stern It depends on the situation. The Gordon Bunshaft kind of architect needs the Noguchi counterpoint. If you have a building that looks like a gigantic box, you need something that is standing on its corner, to somehow modify its scale. Other architects in the past needed the same thing—Palladio needed the interior murals—I can't remember at the moment who painted them. The idea is to open up those boxlike rooms to bring nature and space into the conception. I think that Graves tends to work as both artist and architect, and he too uses murals to open up his space. I could imagine collaborating with artists. I am most interested in providing the setting and the support system, if you will, for figural sculpture, which I am very interested in.

Diamonstein How successful can a work of architecture be that is designed to accommodate a work of art?

Stern Well, it depends on the conversation and the collaboration, doesn't it? If you make a building with panels between pilasters, and you say these panels will be appropriate for a sculptural program—there are plenty of buildings around like that—and then you call up Richard Serra, that would be hopeless. If you called up Bob Graham, or maybe twenty other artists, just to discuss what the art should represent, you'd have a story that is not embarrassing. We can make elephants that look like elephants, as opposed to elephants that look like dirigibles or abstract patterns. The whole game has changed towards the notion that art can represent things in the world, as opposed to being a representation of the world.

Diamonstein How lasting should a collaboration be between an artist and an architect?

Stern Some went on for years—McKim and St. Gaudens, for example. And others have one magic moment. I can't think of an example, but I'm sure there is one.

Diamonstein What do you think we can do to improve this situation? Do you share my optimism, without being excessive, in our hopes for the Architectural League exhibition? Will it be, if not role-model, perhaps spur or gadfly, to both the art and architectural communities pointing the way to a more fruitful alliance?

Stern I share the optimism, but I think it requires saying some difficult things that will sit very harshly not only with the artists and the architects involved, but with the art establishment. There is a lot of money going into plopping Nevelsons all over the place, and if I see one more ridiculous sculpture heaved onto the Mall on Central Park and then just taken away—that contributes nothing. A public place is not a gallery or living-room. I don't think that contributes to a sense of a public architecture or a public collaboration in the arts.

Diamonstein Do you think that however well-intended, our view of public art has been misguided, that often wall murals have served more as masks for failed social systems than as expressions of art?

Stern Absolutely.

Diamonstein Well, how should we be going about it, particularly when the possession of the rare or singular is less in favor ideologically than it has been in the past?

Stern Well, some artists are incapable of it. Certain artists, like Tony Smith, make the same scale thing to put on your table as they put on a public square. It has to do with the representational element, you see. An object is just an object at any size. A representation of a thing's object-ness, but also its human scale, its building scale, its nature scale, can't all be brought together. It has to change when it's for a big object. I think the heart of the matter—and I think you were right on to it—is that we just can't paint murals on the ends of buildings or plop sculptures onto the Mall. This collaboration exists basically in the public realm, and it should be site-specific, building-specific. When Richard Haas paints a mural, it succeeds because it is building-specific. He did something in the South Street Seaport area—you can see it there—which relates to the Brooklyn Bridge, as well as the building he is painting on. He takes that building—I think he occupies space in it—and paints the missing facade to complete the composition. When you look at it you have a wonderful perception about the world that you never quite had before. Brice Marden, or all those other non-figural, non-representational artists, paint things on the edges of buildings that could just as well be slides of their works blown up to colossal scale. This public work is not successful.

Diamonstein Do you have a project that is a secret dream in that active, fertile mind of yours, some specific building and some specific locations?

Stern No, I really don't think that way. I mean every opportunity is a chance to fulfill the secret dream. It's corny, but I like to be able to do all different kinds of work. I don't want to be confined to any one thing.

Diamonstein How would you characterize your work? How would you like best to be remembered? Quite a question to ask a forty-year-old man!

Stern Oh, I don't know—don't ask me questions like that. . . . Saturated with a love for architecture, its old forms and its possibilities for the future. How's that?